THE SILENCE OF WAR

THE
SILENCE
OF WAR

An Old Marine in a Young Marine's War

Terrance Patrick McGowan

BERKLEY CALIBER, NEW YORK

Any views or opinions expressed in this book are those of the author, not of the FBI.

BERKLEY
CALIBER

An imprint of Penguin Random House LLC
375 Hudson Street, New York, New York 10014

This book is an original publication of Penguin Random House LLC.

Library of Congress Cataloging-in-Publication Data
Names: McGowan, Terrance Patrick, author.
Title: The silence of war: an old Marine in a young Marine's war/Terrance Patrick McGowan.
Other titles: Old Marine in a young Marine's war
Description: New York : Berkley Caliber, [2016] | "Forward Operating Base Delaram."
Identifiers: LCCN 2016016219 (print) | LCCN 2016017536 (ebook) | ISBN 9781101988183 | ISBN 9781101988206 (ebook)
Subjects: LCSH: McGowan, Terrance Patrick. | Afghan War, 2001—Personal narratives, American. | Marines—United States—Biography. | Government contractors—United States—Biography. | United States. Marine Corps. Marine Regiment, 7th. Battalion, 2nd—Biography. | Afghan War, 2001—Campaigns—Afghanistan—Farāah (Province) | Baby boom Generation—United States—Biography. | Middle-aged men—United States—Biography. | United States. Federal Bureau of Investigation—Officials and employees—Biography. | Iraq War, 2003–2011—Personal narratives, American
Classification: LCC DS371.413.M37 2016 (print) | LCC DS371.413 (ebook) | DDC 958.104/742 [B]—dc23
LC record available at https://lccn.loc.gov/2016016219

First edition: August 2016

PRINTED IN THE UNITED STATES OF AMERICA

10 9 8 7 6 5 4 3 2 1

Jacket design by Daniel Rembert.
Jacket photographs of U.S. Marine Corps by Lance Cpl. Brian D. Jones.

Penguin
Random
House

Contents

Foreword by Bill O'Reilly

Marine captain Terrance McGowan is a unique individual. A warrior in a country that is relatively safe, McGowan sought out adventure in places such as Iraq and Afghanistan in his late fifties. Maybe unique isn't the correct word. Perhaps crazy?

Most human beings have no idea about what really happens in a war zone. McGowan does, and his storytelling ability brings remote conflict into sharp focus for the reader. He puts you on the scene whether it's a Taliban assault or a heartbreaking injury to a U.S. serviceperson overseas.

It was the fall of 1967 when I initially met Terry McGowan. He and I were freshmen at Marist College in Poughkeepsie, New York. The sons of working-class Irish parents, McGowan and I had something in common. But it soon became clear that I was the more conventional guy. McGowan consistently sought adventure. And if he couldn't find any—he went to sleep. Boy, could that guy sleep!

The Silence of War is a personal book. Written from the vantage point of a former Marine, FBI agent, and local police officer, it offers life lessons that most of us have never had. McGowan is a "no spin" guy. He tells the truth about what he saw up close in dangerous areas.

It goes without saying that most Americans will never be tested in places such as Iraq and Afghanistan. But good citizens, who want to make educated decisions about policy and who want to vote responsibly, should understand the world we all inhabit. It also goes without saying that it took a man of courage to write *The Silence of War*.

Reading Terry McGowan's book will help make all of us better citizens. I thank him for writing it.

Bill O'Reilly
New York City
October 2015

Preamble

I started sending emails to people back home in the States when I was still in Afghanistan. I was trying to tell them what it was like—while we were all living it—in real time. I got replies such as "You made me cry," "I felt like I was there," and "You should write a book." Well, I decided to do just that.

In the midst of a bleak northeastern winter I sent my first draft to a fellow Marine whom I consider to be my "kid brother"—Zach Wolfe. Zach lost his best friend over there. His name was Andrew "Whit" Whitacre. They were "brothers from a different mother." Whit was killed in action on June 19, 2008. I don't need to look the date up. Whit was my friend too.

I had written about Whit's death, of course, but I had barely touched on it. I care about Zach and I was trying to spare him the pain of reading about and reliving that terrible day. I now realize that was a mistake. People need to know the price they're asking our fine young men to pay when they are sent off to war—the silent price.

Zach's response to me after reading the draft was emotionally commanding. He told me he had only made it halfway through before he started to cry. His very young daughter—seeing her daddy's distress—climbed up onto his lap and said, "That's okay, Daddy. You can have my teddy bear."

Zach told me I had to write the book. He wanted his family to know what he had been through. I knew Zach could never find the words. He knew it too.

When he and his wife had their next child, a boy, they named him Cooper Whitacre Wolfe. Whit had meant that much to Zach. He still does. Whit lives on in Zach's heart. And though the pain dims it is never fully extinguished.

The littlest Wolfe will have to grow up a bit before he learns about the "Uncle" Andrew he will never know. It will be at least a few years before he realizes why he has the middle name that he does. Possibly his dad will never be able to choke out the words that will enable him to understand. Possibly he will have to read this book someday—and in the process learn more about his dad as well.

Zach is blessed with a wonderful wife. I have no doubt that she understands him as well as anyone can. She will understand him even better after reading this book. So will the rest of Zach's family. That's why he wanted it written. That's why I had to write it. Zach's deepest scars can't be seen.

William Manchester in *Goodbye, Darkness* wrote a passage about the battle for Okinawa that stayed with me over the years since I first read the book. He wrote of how much he hated the war and wanted it to be over so he could go home. And how, when he was safe in an aid station being treated for wounds received in battle, he had to get out of the battlefield hospital and get back to his squad. They were more important to him than anything, including his own safety. By that time he wasn't fighting for his country, or world peace, or Mom or apple pie. He was fighting for the guys in his squad.

When Alex "Little Red" Allman was evacuated to the battalion aid station after being blown into a concussion by a couple of rocket-propelled grenades, all he could think about was getting back to the platoon. Life at battalion was good. Air-conditioned sleeping tents, great chow—and access to the Internet. Yet he chafed for what seemed to him to be an eternity until he could finally get back to his buddies.

Sergeant Joe France and Lance Corporal Mike Michalak were pulled off the line permanently—after being blown to hell for the third time by an IED—an improvised explosive device. They were really lousy houseguests. They screamed bloody murder that they wanted to get back with their guys. Despite the fact that they made a real pain of themselves, the powers that be never allowed it. One more IED and they might have been permanently brain-damaged. They knew it, but didn't care. They missed their guys.

I got good and sick, presumably from eating the local food. I had to be evacuated two echelons to the rear to be treated. I couldn't wait to get back. I had the terrible—no, horrible—feeling that something would happen to my guys while I was gone.

That's how it really is. There's a line at the end of the movie *Jarhead* that goes, "All wars are different. And all wars are the same." It's true.

The term "brotherhood" isn't understood properly—deeply enough—by those who have never experienced it. And those who have just can't find the words to explain it. One of the quick "tests" of an individual's wartime experiences—to see if he was real or making it up—is whether he's even willing to talk about them. Typically, someone who's been to war will not—cannot—talk to anyone other than someone else who has been through the same living hell. It's the silence of war.

This book is about all Marines, not just in Golf Company or even the 2nd Battalion, 7th Marines. It's about all the Marines who shared in the brotherhood of war—in Afghanistan, and Iraq, and Vietnam, and Korea, and all the other wars that are all so different and yet somehow all the same.

I had to write this book. I had to be the voice for so many who cannot talk about what they went through. There are a lot of "Whits" and "Zachs" in America's wars.

This book had to be written for all of them.

THE SILENCE OF WAR

Prologue

We were out on the tip of the proverbial spear in the barren, scorching-hot western Afghanistan desert. It was August 20, 2008, and I was with a Marine platoon at Forward Operating Base (FOB) Golestan.

It was my birthday. I had just turned fifty-nine years old.

I had been recruited by a low-key organization comprised of former West Point officers. They had formed what they termed "an elite group of combat investigators." The mission: to embed with the military and investigate the insurgency. To qualify one had to have been an experienced law enforcement officer who had been involved in complex investigations; routine patrol work wasn't enough.

The investigators brought skill sets to the table that the military lacked: an ability to read the "human terrain"—acquired after decades of training, street experience, and working tough investigations. The group was spread thinly throughout Army and Marine units in Iraq and Afghanistan.

I qualified. I was a retired FBI agent as well as a former Marine officer. I kept pushing forward until I came to rest at Golestan. It was the end of the line.

I was lucky. I was billeted with Bravo Squad inside a mud building that passed for home. It was noticeably cooler inside the hut—probably no more than 130 degrees—than it was under the olive drab canvas tenting that housed most of the platoon. I lay on a cot in a pool of my own sweat surrounded by bottles of water inside old socks, which had been carefully hung on nails hammered into the dirt walls. The socks were doused with water until dripping wet, and this cooled the bottles by evaporation. Lukewarm was as good as we could get. Still, it was better than drinking hot water.

Looking out the glassless window—an irregular, somewhat rectangular hole in the wall—I could see cases of Meals, Ready-to-Eat (MREs) stacked against the outer bulwark of our defenses—about four feet away. It wasn't a real FOB; there hadn't been time to build one. The platoon had taken over a couple of run-down buildings partially surrounded by an adobe outer wall and strengthened it as best as could be done with sandbags and razor wire. I stared at the thatch-and-mud roof of the "room" I was in, ignoring the occasional clump of dirt that would drop from the "ceiling" and dreamed of home, my M16 resting against my cot.

———

I had volunteered to go to Afghanistan with one of the first long-term Marine battalions deployed to that war-torn country since the initial invasion after 9/11. We were designated Task Force 2/7. Other Marine units followed in the next few years, ultimately putting thousands of Marines in the country, but 2nd Battalion, 7th Marines (2/7) was one of only two Marine battalions operating in Afghanistan at that time. The Army had been operating for years in eastern Afghanistan, and the Brits, the Canadians, and a hodgepodge of other nationalities had been active in the south, but 2/7 broke ground in the western desert.

The Taliban attacked us during the night of July 2. Their purpose was to annihilate one of the newly arrived Marine units. They wanted to show their stuff right off the bat and demonstrate to the Marines who the tougher fighters were. Since there were only fifty-six Marines at Golestan and we were far from reinforcements, we must have looked vulnerable.

I *felt* vulnerable. The adobe FOB reminded me of the Alamo.

They began the fight at one o'clock in the morning, and didn't break it off until the sky began to lighten. I was asleep when the first rocket-propelled grenades slammed into our walls. I manned a bunker on an elevated portion of the west wall with two young Marines, and for three hours, traded fire with the enemy.

Then, when the sky began to lighten, I could dimly make out the outline of the Stars and Stripes. I got goose bumps as I thought, *"O say can you see by the dawn's early light what so proudly we hailed at the twilight's last gleaming?"*

The flag was still there. And "The Star-Spangled Banner" would never be the same for me.

I began to write to folks on the "home front" about that experience. I tried to put into words what it was like. Waking up to the sound of grenades and rifle and machine-gun fire, manning my post barefoot with no shirt on, then seeing the outline of our flag, dimly at first, finally in blazing color—as it waved defiantly in the superheated breeze.

I was a guy who, at my age, should have been at home chasing a little white ball around, not fighting Taliban on the other side of the world. But there's a saying so ubiquitous among Marines that it almost seems trite. I say *almost* because it is so literally true. *"Once a Marine, always a Marine."* I had earned the title "Marine," and like all Marines who had acquired it, I became part of an anomaly from a bygone era: a warrior caste.

Though technically I was a civilian, in my soul I was still a Marine. I will always be a Marine until the day I die.

1

The Long Road to War

I could say it all started when the World Trade Center was attacked. In a way, it did. I had retired after more than twenty years in law enforcement and was in law school. I had been an active-duty Marine during the mid-seventies. On 9/11 I was fifty years old. I decided to do my part and rejoin the Marine Reserve. The officer on the other end of the phone nearly choked on his coffee when he heard my age. I got a polite rejection,

"Don't call us, we'll call you . . . but only if aliens from outer space invade Los Angeles."

Really, though, it began long before that.

Marines who were trapped at the Chosin Reservoir during the Korean War by the Chinese Army became known as the "Frozen Chosen." When the Chinese attacked, the division was surrounded and outnumbered about ten to one, as the bitter North Korean winter set in. In spite of it all, the Marines fought their way through to the sea. My uncle Bill was a "Frozen Chosen" Marine and my hero. Although he never talked about what went on in Korea, the family did. And it was plain to see that Uncle Bill was proud to be a Marine.

After graduating from college, I became a cop. I pinned on a badge, strapped on a gun, and went out to work the 9:00 p.m. to 5:00 a.m. shift on Christmas night 1971. I was a police officer for about three and a half years before I finally joined the Marine Corps. I was in my midtwenties and pretty happy being a patrolman. But something was missing from my life. I had always intended to join the service; I just never quite got around to it. I decided I had better do it if I was ever going to, or I'd be too old.

Once that decision was made, it was pretty straightforward as to which branch of service it was going to be. Uncle Bill was still my hero. Since I had a college degree in my pocket, I could apply to Officer Candidate School (OCS), which I did. I was twenty-six.

In retrospect, being a cop was great training for a future officer of Marines. By the time I got to the Fleet Marine Force, I was already used to taking charge in an emergency, coming up with a plan, issuing orders, and being obeyed. I also had no qualms whatsoever about telling someone older than I was what to do. I'd been doing it for years. Most importantly, perhaps, I had learned to suppress emotion. Fear is an emotion. Like Commander Spock on *Star Trek*, I had developed the ability to think logically regardless of what was going on around me. The ability to think clearly in a crisis is a survival mechanism, I think. It's a useful trait for a leader to have.

Active duty began on September 29, 1975. With a growing sense of foreboding, I drove past the downsized memorial of the flag-raising on Iwo Jima that stands just outside the main gate at Marine Corps Base (MCB) Quantico. At that point, I wasn't so sure I had made the right decision. I didn't have butterflies in my stomach, I had bats. I drove down street after street of venerable old redbrick buildings that looked like they had been around since the Second World War. As I drove I noticed Marines standing around talking, all of whom looked quite at home.

It was anything but home-like to me. There was nothing normal about the place in my civilian eyes.

Although I had begun a physical training regimen months before, when I took a pre-OCS inventory physical fitness test (PFT) not only did I fail it, but I also threw up. Right there in front of God and everybody. A tall, lanky, African-American first lieutenant, wearing government-issue black frame glasses, in studied tones of understatement uttered the obvious:

"You'll have to do better than that."

Well, I finally passed the PFT—and didn't throw up—so I thought I was ready for what lay ahead. I couldn't have been more wrong. I was worn-out before the warm-up, called the "Marine Corps Daily Seven," was finished. And physical training (PT) was only just beginning.

"O Lord, kill me and be done with it," I implored my Creator. He replied, "Negative, candidate. You'll not get off *that* easily." I didn't yet know that God was a Marine.

To my immense surprise, my body began to respond. If God wasn't gonna kill me, my lizard brain reasoned, I had better get this brain carrier in shape.

Before I graduated from OCS I realized that I had never discovered what my real limits were. The drill instructors always demanded more, and I was always able to deliver. Painfully, suffering more than I thought I could stand, I found that I could always run a little longer, march a little farther, ignore the hunger, the thirst, the heat or cold, the exhaustion, for just a little while longer, and continue on.

The lesson stayed with me throughout my life.

The OCS experience was pure hell. Although we began with fifty-four in the platoon, only thirty-eight were commissioned. We literally counted the days—every day—until we would be free of it. Near the end, we counted the hours. I suffered like I had never suffered before in my life. But there was an undeniable, palpable change inside me. I had become a different human being. I became a Marine. I never looked for the easy way out of anything for the rest of my life.

On January 6, 1976, after Christmas leave, it was back to Quantico for training at The Basic School (TBS). TBS was six months long back then, and it was there that officers learned everything the Marine Corps felt they should know about the business of being an officer. OCS had been "basic" training. TBS was "advanced." It was also the "infantry officer's course" at that time. There was no separate infantry training for officers with the infantry military occupational specialty (MOS), as there is today. Everybody, even those destined for flight training, went through it. Every Marine officer was expected to be an infantry officer first.

TBS was its own little world carved out of the sprawling Virginia woods. It was winter when we arrived, and the trees were bare. The skies were usually gray—it was cold and it was damp. In short, it was as gloomy as I felt. Before we left TBS, it would be summer—a hot, humid, tick-infested Virginia summer.

I was assigned to a room. Each room contained two freshly minted second lieutenants, with two individual gray beds, two gray desks, two gray chairs, and a closet to be shared. That was it for furniture. The floor was gray linoleum, and the walls were the same sickly light green color as had adorned the barracks at OCS. The quarters were barren. Two rooms connected to a "bathroom," known as a "head" in the Naval Service. Four lieutenants shared it. The head contained two sinks, one toilet, and one shower. As with everything in the Marine Corps, cooperation was essential. We didn't have to like each other, but we did have to get along. That's an imperative in the Corps. Married guys had it easier. They got to live somewhere over the horizon with their wives.

Much later, in Afghanistan, living on top of each other with nothing remotely resembling privacy under environmental conditions that would've cracked the pope, the wisdom of Marine Corps training in this regard became apparent.

We soon realized that TBS was only a marginal improvement over OCS. We were yelled at by captains instead of by sergeants, and it didn't take us long to figure out that being a student-officer wasn't quite like being a "real" officer. We coined the term "third lieutenant" to describe our new status. We were a step above "candidates" but not quite real second lieutenants.

Tactical training had commenced during OCS, but it was basic stuff. TBS was different. Everything was much more "high speed." We were expected to know what to do under any and all circumstances. And that's the way we were trained.

TBS was challenging and difficult. The Cold War was on and we were preparing to face the Soviet juggernaut. The Soviet Union at that time outnumbered the United States two to one in men, two to one in tactical aircraft, five to one in tanks, and ten to one in artillery pieces. To make matters worse, their artillery outranged ours. In an attempt to even the odds, we trained hard.

Physical endurance was integrated into everything we did. On one occasion we were faced with one of those freak Virginia days where it was winter one minute and hot and humid the next. I began the day wearing my field jacket with liner, but I had stuffed it into my pack before long. We had spent the entire day conducting tactical exercises deep in the thick Virginia woods and were pretty much done in. We were also about a pint low on blood thanks to the ticks. All the same, we had a fifteen-mile forced march back to the barracks ahead of us.

Unfortunately somebody dropped the ball on a vital substance called "water," because there was none. Major "Cowboy Roy" led the company off at a conditioning hike's inhuman pace nonetheless. We were pretty well exhausted and dehydrated when we started; with each passing mile things got worse. Although I had learned by then to carry four canteens instead of the issued two, I was out. I could feel the heat radiating off my face, and my hair felt hot. Marines began to drop like flies from heat exhaustion. I badly wanted to join them, prostrate on the red dirt road. I kept telling myself to keep going, but not to worry for surely I'd pass out soon and there was no dishonor in that.

Somehow I made it back while still conscious, although I was a tad disappointed to have remained so as I recall. Cowboy Roy was a most unhappy camper. He gazed out upon his badly depleted company and with steam coming out of his ears, addressed us as "real Marines"—as opposed to those nonhackers who got heatstroke, I supposed. After some more pep talk, he stormed off. I don't remember a word he said. I was completely out of gas.

But I had learned a lesson I never forgot. Keep going—no matter what.

As had been the case at OCS, the squad became a tightly knit group. One Saturday night, we all went to an Irish pub in Washington, D.C. There we sang Marine Corps songs that dated back to World War II—*"Well, we sent for the army to come to Tulagi, but General MacArthur said no, there wasn't a reason, this isn't the season, besides there is no USO"*—and there we met a survivor of the Tarawa campaign. For those who may not know, Tarawa was one of the islands Marines had to take by storm in the Pacific. The Japanese commanding officer had bragged that Tarawa couldn't be taken by a million men in a hundred years. The 2nd Marine Division took it in seventy-two hours. However, they paid a terrible price in blood.

The elderly gentleman introduced himself almost shyly. When he told us he had been on Tarawa, everybody just moved over and pulled up an extra chair. When he said his good-byes at the end of the night he had tears in his eyes. He said that we had made him feel like he was part of a squad again and we had sung the same songs that his old squad had. I got the impression that few of them, if any, had made it off Tarawa. That chance meeting had a profound effect on me.

For most of us our only duty to Corps and country consisted of standing sentinel ready to stop the Russian hordes—who never came. Some of us had already been to war, and some of us went later. Nothing like Tarawa, of course, but we—all of us—were, *are* bound by that intangible *something*. We are Marines. He was part of us and we were part of him—although in truth we felt unworthy to stand in his shadow.

I was on active duty for thirteen months—in training—before I got orders to the 1st Marine Division at Camp Pendleton, California. It was my uncle Bill's old division. I checked in early in January 1977.

My first commanding officer was a "mustang"—that is, an officer who had been an enlisted Marine prior to becoming an officer. "Mustangs" were held in high regard by everyone, as they still are. He was a captain—soon to be a major—and I couldn't have asked for a better "on the job" teacher. When I checked in, Mustang asked me what post I wanted. I replied, "Platoon commander, sir."

He replied, "No. It's way too soon, maybe in six months or so."

After being dismissed, I wandered out to where the PFT was being administered. There are three components to the Marine PFT: pull-ups, a three-mile run, and maximum sit-ups in two minutes. We were forced to rely on the honor system when it came to the sit-up count, since half the entire unit held a man's ankles while the other half did the sit-ups, and then they switched. It was impossible to count everybody's sit-ups.

As a cop, I had learned to recognize the "felony look." It's an indescribable expression of guilt that crosses someone's face when they see a cop. It means they either did something wrong, or were about to. As I looked down the long line of Marines about to begin the sit-up phase of the PFT, there it was. I spotted two Marines and the "felony look." Just a quick glance and I knew. These two would lie. So I averted my gaze and, in my peripheral vision, counted every single sit-up.

When I went down the line, recording the number of sit-ups, one of the two said, "Eighty, sir."

I replied, "Eighty? That's very good." (It was the maximum.)

I looked at the other, who had been holding the first Marine's ankles, and said, "Wow, did he really do eighty?"

"Yes, sir," he replied.

"Then why did I count fifty-four?" I said. "Go tell the first sergeant you're on report." That meant they went before Mustang for punishment; lying to an officer is a violation of military regulations.

I hadn't been in the unit an hour yet and I had already run two guys up. They looked at me like I was the Antichrist. They had to be thinking, "Who the hell *is* this guy?"

I got the job of platoon commander that day.

I discovered that being a good leader was sometimes inversely proportional to one's popularity with those being led. I wasn't running for office; the Marine Corps is not a democracy. The platoon would have been outstanding wartime Marines. In peacetime, they were a bit rough around the edges.

Decades later, in Afghanistan, I would tell Marines that they were better than we had been. We had been good at what we were supposed to do—fight a war against the Soviet Union—but they were just plain all-around better than we were. Marines, in 1977–78, would have fought as hard as their fathers and grandfathers before them did. The Marine Corps would have stopped the Soviet Army in its tracks, regardless of the cost, and died where it stood before the Communist behemoth if necessary. But the Marine Corps I served with in Afghanistan in 2008 was qualitatively better.

We continued to prepare for war—World War III, against the Soviet Union.

We dug in on the reverse slope of the highest ground around. That way artillery would have to shoot at a very high angle to get us, making it much more difficult for them. It had the added benefit of forcing their artillery to move closer—so we could shoot back. Furthermore, Soviet tanks would have to show us their bellies as they came over the hill. The belly of a tank, like the belly of a turtle, was the best place to strike. We trained hard, and we trained to win despite the odds against us.

The "official word" was that Marines would be deployed to Norway and the Far East if war with the Soviet Union came. We would protect the strategic flanks of NATO (North Atlantic Treaty Organization). None of us believed it. We all believed we'd be thrown straight against an unstoppable Soviet blitzkrieg in the center of Europe, and we would stop it.

However, the U.S. Marine Corps is a part of the Department of the Navy. Our mission is to project formidable American naval power ashore, whether fighting the Soviets or anybody else. Therefore, we never lost sight of the amphibious nature of the Corps, and much of our training commenced from the sea. In those days two-thirds of the assault force hit the beaches from landing craft. One third went over the side and climbed down nets, just as had been done during World War II. One third came out of the well deck (an opening) in the back of the ship on amphibious tractors, while the remaining third embarked from helicopters and landed behind the beachhead, thereby isolating it.

The movies don't show but a small bit of the time and effort it takes to get an amphibious assault going. Moviegoers would be bored to tears watching it in real time. In the movies it all seems to just happen—and quickly. But it takes time—lots of time. So for those of us who were the first in line, whether in amphibious landing craft, or flying off in choppers, it meant literally hours of circling the fleet before we all straightened out and hit the beach together. During one such assault, I was in my chopper for two hours before going in.

Once ashore, we had the pleasure of busting our butts climbing ever higher into the mountains, hour after hour, day after day. I learned how to carry a heavy load on a never-ending climb. It was there that I developed the frame of mind that if I couldn't eat it, drink it, or shoot it, I wasn't carrying it.

I kept that mind-set in Afghanistan in 2008. I eventually stowed the heavy "bullet-stopping" ceramic plates that came with my tactical-issue vest. They weighed too much. I also discarded everything else I considered unnecessary that had any weight to it. I did, however, carry from eleven to thirteen full rifle magazines, instead of the issue seven. Ammo and water were two things I could never have enough of.

One day, Mustang called me into his office. It seemed our battalion commander liked to have an ex-cop on his staff. He liked "hip pocket" informal investigations, and he liked the way ex-cops could quickly get to the heart of the matter. He had heard about me—I didn't dare ask in what capacity—and if I wanted it, the job was mine. I loved the idea.

I found myself with more collateral duties than I could count. I was privy to staff meetings. I got to see how a battalion was run and was expected to help find solutions to various problems as they arose. Impressively, I was given "by direction" authority. That meant, within set parameters, I would generate orders in the battalion commander's name. I was lifted out of the "mud and tall grass" and got to see a bigger picture. Working on a battalion staff was a great experience.

It enabled me to be of greater assistance to 2nd Battalion, 7th Marines (2/7) in preparing for Afghanistan.

———

In July 1977, the battalion was part of the 5th Marine Amphibious Brigade, which took part in a joint services exercise conducted at Marine Corps Base Twenty-nine Palms. The base was not so affectionately known as "Twenty-nine Stumps" or simply "The Stumps." It was Operation Braveshield XVI, and this was a test of America's ability to fight a war in the desert. The Army, Navy, Air Force, and Marine Corps were all part of Braveshield XVI.

Inasmuch as "The Stumps" is in the middle of the Mojave Desert, where it gets a tad warm in July, it was the perfect place for a desert operation. It was also the perfect place to learn how to survive in "hell without the flames." Knowing that none of my family or friends back home could conceive of the heat we experienced, I recommended with tongue in cheek that they set their ovens to 150 degrees and crawl inside for a couple of hours. Fortunately, no one took my suggestion.

Unlike many forward bases today, there was *no* air-conditioning *anywhere* in the field, and *no* refrigeration of any kind. We learned to cool our water by evaporation using Lister bags made of canvas. Hang one on the mirror of a jeep or truck before taking off and it's the closest thing to cool water you'd get. We also learned not to touch the metal of a truck or jeep with bare skin or we'd raise a blister immediately.

I learned a great many little "tricks" about desert living that stayed with me through the intervening years and helped make life more tolerable in Afghanistan. Like stuffing plastic water bottles inside soaked socks and hanging them to dry—a modern-day Lister bag.

Four Marines died during Operation Braveshield XVI, July, peacetime, 1977: Two infantry Marines had been on a forced march and their hearts were really pumping. When a halt was called they slumped wearily to the ground. Rattlesnakes got them both—at different times and places. One was bitten on the face, the other on the neck. They were both dead before they could be gotten to a hospital. Rattlesnakes at The Stumps are huge.

Two truck drivers drove off cliffs at night. We didn't have night-vision goggles back then, and as noted earlier, to train for Soviet artillery, everything was off-road, on the reverse slope of steep terrain. The vehicles drove at night with only very small "slit" lights—just like in World War II. Two of our trucks went over; both drivers died. Americans don't always die from bullets. And they die in peacetime as well as in war.

I considered staying in the Marine Corps and making it my career. I had been promoted to first lieutenant and life wasn't too bad. But I was nearing thirty years old and I already had a lot invested in law enforcement, so I decided to get out. My last active duty date was January 15, 1979. I was twenty-nine years old.

I had left police work to join the Marines. Fortunately, my boss had been a Marine during World War II. He welcomed me back. I had been granted military leave, which meant that my job was waiting for me when I returned. Marines tend to take care of each other like that. But *something* was different. Not the job, me.

I didn't realize how much I had changed until I got back home. I found that I had difficulty talking to civilians, even old friends, but no problem talking to anyone who had ever been in uniform—any uniform; they didn't have to have been Marines. I've often reflected on this phenomenon. Transitioning from peacetime to civilian life was problematic for me, and took about a year.

It's no wonder so many of today's servicepeople are suffering from post-traumatic stress disorder as they return to civilian life from a war environment. It's not just the war. It's an adjustment from a military to a civilian *way of life*. It was difficult for me to adjust to being what I was very happy being prior to joining the Marines: an ordinary patrolman. After six months, I left the job to attend graduate school.

A part of me also missed the Corps, so I joined the Reserves. I became the executive officer and acting commanding officer of a rifle company in the 1st Battalion, 25th Marines, 4th Marine Division. We were Alpha Company and we were headquartered at Albany, N.Y. There I was promoted to captain on the first of November 1980.

The way the 4th Marine Division was run when I joined, and the way it is run today, are radically different. Today's Reserve component gets called up for extended periods of active duty in a war zone. Today's 4th Marine Division by necessity needs to be war-ready. I did not perceive the same sense of urgency in the division when I was in it. It should be noted that the division was spread across the entire country. I never saw anything of it outside my own battalion.

The Reserve component of my day was meant for World War III. Our purpose was to enable the Corps to expand rapidly in the event of a major war with the Soviet Union. If war broke out, we believed that the "deck would have been shuffled." Active duty Marines from the 1st, 2nd, and 3rd Marine Divisions would have been transferred into the 4th Marine Division, while Marines from the 4th Marine Division would have been transferred as replacements to those divisions. It's how the Corps expanded during World War II, and it's a sound way to ensure an even spread of trained and experienced Marines throughout the divisions.

Since we only met one weekend a month and two weeks in summer, training for war was a formidable undertaking. To make up for the lack of training time, we went to the field as often as we possibly could, using public land in upstate New York. The intense cold of winter did not deter us. We slept around fires at night to keep from freezing to death.

But I confess that I never considered the company to be war-ready. After two years in the Reserves, I was hired by the Federal Bureau of Investigation as a special agent, and I resigned my commission. Law enforcement resumed as my primary mission in life.

Nine years later, however, in August 1990, when Saddam Hussein invaded Kuwait, I rejoined the Marine Reserves. An old high school pal, Jack McMahon, had done his active duty time and remained in the Reserves, rising to the rank of lieutenant colonel. I joined his unit at the Naval War College in Newport, Rhode Island.

Naturally, I was hoping I'd be deployed. I felt like a football player who had practiced constantly but never got to play in a single game. I also felt anxious because the Reserve unit from Albany, redesignated Fox Company, 2nd Battalion, 25th Marines, was called up. Even though after nine years there was no one left that I had served with, I was worried about them.

Worrying about young Marines came all too easily for me. I cared about them—deeply. I still do. Known as the First Gulf War, the conflict was over quickly. To my dismay, the United States won without my help. I never left the States. I stayed active in the Reserves for two more years, keeping high-ranking officers well supplied with coffee. As a mere Marine captain I was one of the lowest-ranking individuals around the War College.

However, minor irritations were more than compensated for whenever I checked into the visiting officers' quarters in civilian clothes. The sailor who checked me in only asked for my rank, not branch of service. When I said—truthfully—"captain," he assumed I was a Navy captain, the equivalent in rank of a Marine full colonel. I got *great* quarters overlooking the bay at Newport. After two years, my time in the Marine Corps ended. That was in August 1992. The Corps didn't get around to actually discharging me until February 1, 1997.

It was my third honorable discharge.

Once I finished twenty years in the law enforcement world, I retired and went to law school. I was fifty years old—what they called a "non-traditional student." It was a nice way to say "old guy." It was while I was in law school that the World Trade Center was attacked and I tried unsuccessfully to get back into the Reserves.

I went to see one of my law professors who had been a Marine sometime during the 1950s. Since he was internationally known in legal circles, I told him of my plight and asked if he had any "connections." Apparently not, as he (surely in his seventies) had already tried to get back in. He was so serious when he told me about it that I had to smile. He just couldn't understand why they wouldn't take him back.

2

Iraq

I finished law school, but watching "kids" I knew grow up and get shipped off to Iraq started to get to me—especially when they didn't come back. Despite what it said on my birth certificate, I felt I was still young and fit for duty. Deep in my heart, I was still a Marine. I searched for a way to get into the global war on terror. I began to take "high-speed, intense" civilian training courses. After blowing the dust off my brain, the tactics and rifle skills I had learned in the Marine Corps came right back to me.

The days of "cowboy contractors" were over, and getting into the war turned out to be easier said than done. However, around the summer of 2006, a friend gave my résumé to a retired Marine officer who handled Defense Department work in Iraq. That led to my becoming part of a team that included two retired British army colonels. Until this time, I regarded working with the U.S. Army as exotic; being employed with high-ranking British officers was positively daunting.

I apprenticed under "Colonel Thompson" (his nom de guerre)—a gentleman who, from his extensive knowledge of alluring places, enthralled me with tales worthy of Rudyard Kipling. He had immense experience in the Middle East, the Near East, the Balkans, and Northern Ireland.

On one occasion he had been shot in the lung by a sniper in Bosnia. He would have drowned in his own blood had his medic not been able to think—and act—quickly. The man slid a knife between the colonel's ribs and drained the fluid out.

It slowly dawned on me just how small my world had been. I could go literally anywhere in the United States and fit in, but my world was limited to our fifty states. Working with the colonel was like brainstorming with my own personal university professor—a private tutor who made it his business to try to teach me about the rest of the planet. I began to feel that although I was safe in the womb of America, the time had come for me to be birthed into the cold, glaring light of "the world," where a sharp slap of bitter reality was waiting.

I began to get nervous about what the future held for me. I didn't have the confidence that I could handle any exigency I might have to face. During my twenty-year law enforcement career, as time went on I became more and more expert in the vagaries of the profession. As a result, my self-confidence grew. By retirement, I felt I could handle anything.

———

But now I heard myself saying, more than once, "Baghdad ain't Brooklyn." Nervousness morphed into fear. I felt it in the pit of my stomach. I had trouble sleeping. It was fear of the unknown. Fear of the war on terror that loomed just over the horizon. It didn't help that I had practically begged to be a part of it. There was no turning back. Whatever lay ahead, I had to face it squarely.

In the spring of 2007, endless hours spent at planning meetings at various locations in the United States were abruptly terminated. I was ordered to meet with Colonel Thompson in London. It was time.

I flew to the United Kingdom and met with the colonel at the airport that evening. We flew together into Kuwait via British Airways. There we checked into the most luxurious hotel I had ever seen. It even had shining brass fixtures in the marble-and-glass bathroom. The room was opulent. TV wasn't very interesting, since I didn't speak more than a few words of Arabic, but I *was* getting my first taste of the world outside of America.

The world of war included.

My room overlooked a cemetery left over from the Iraqi invasion of Kuwait. It was the most unkempt, mournful cemetery I have ever seen. There was no semblance of order, no neat rows, no grass, flowers, nothing but sand and helter-skelter headstones of some type or other. Most graves had no markers of any kind. Many were sunken in. The heavily tinted windows added a sense of gloom that was palpable. I gazed upon it from a room that was luxurious. The view from the window was ghoulish. It was also incongruent—sandwiched as it was between the hotel and—off in the distance—a modern, gleaming, flourishing city.

Being painfully aware that I was leaving my safety zone behind me, I went for walks alone in Kuwait City. Out past the security guards and car bomb barriers I went. As I left the hotel, I would say *salaam* (literally "peace" in Arabic) to the impeccably dressed and perfectly mannered doorman who stood beside the metal detector at the hotel's entranceway. I ventured into a city where the Arab world met the Western world, but on its own terms. Everywhere were men in traditional Arab clothing—flowing, gleaming white robes—reminiscent of the movie *Lawrence of Arabia*. They walked past Western business establishments such as Pizza Hut, which beckoned the hungry with both English and Arabic writing.

As part of my preparations for the global war on terror, I had begun to study Arabic. I made a little progress, and I practiced with the people I met in shops or at the hotel. Their demeanor expressed either approval or slight annoyance with my fumbling attempts to communicate, but everyone responded—correcting my Arabic as necessary. I persisted. A little later, in Iraq, this fledgling knowledge would come in handy.

It was there, in Kuwait City, that I experienced my first sand cloud.

It wasn't a sand*storm*, as there was no wind to speak of. The sand just sort of enveloped the city like a fog. Even the light-sensitive streetlights came on. It grew dark in midday. The airborne sand was very fine, very gritty and very eerie. It hurt my eyes and I tried in vain to squint it away.

I became ever more aware that I was alone in a foreign country, where even the weather was alien to me. I was on my way to Iraq, and I grew concerned that there might be people around me who could tell I was an American and where I was bound. I grew concerned that they might have liked to have captured me. Being alone was disconcerting, but most importantly, in my eyes, I was unarmed.

This wasn't Kansas, Toto.

Being off the tourist track, I would take notice of anyone and everyone around me, watching for signs that I was being followed. Since I had done surveillance work during my law enforcement days, I had an idea what to look for.

I won't lie—I was more than a little nervous—most likely for nothing; I don't think I was being followed. All the same, I changed direction, doubled back, and crossed streets repeatedly. I went away from, then toward, my destination numerous times, ever watchful in all directions, until I got back to the safety of the hotel.

Kuwait City was a curious mixture of extraordinary wealth and abject poverty, which could be taken in with virtually the same glance. There seemed to be no middle class, just fabulously wealthy and dirt-poor. The dirt-poor, I would later discover, were the laborers who were brought into the country to do all the work. The native-born Kuwaitis were so oil-rich they didn't have to lift a finger, and they didn't. Kuwait is a sheikdom. The government is feudal. The royal sheik and his family run the country. They have an advisory national assembly, but it's just for show. To keep their people happy, they spread the oil wealth around. They didn't share any of that wealth with their laborers; that was obvious from the slum-like conditions I observed.

After a couple of days, Colonel Thompson and I linked up with the other retired British army colonel, previously alluded to, and an American Marine major—an intelligence officer. Our activities in Iraq were to be conducted in Al Anbar Province, in the western part of the country, which was the area of operations for the Marine Corps. I bid farewell to the luxurious hotel, and we entered a holding area known as Ali al Salem.

Ali al Salem was a military base run by the U.S. Army that ferried civilians and military personnel to and from Iraq. There we drew gear, body armor, helmets, and so on from the Army—I took more than a little kidding from Marine buddies who saw pictures of me wearing Army equipment—and we were assigned tents while we waited for transportation to Iraq.

Although a far cry from the hotel I had just left, Ali al Salem wasn't an unpleasant place. We had a decent chow hall, showers, and a free Laundromat. There were fast-food restaurants, a small post exchange (store), gourmet coffee, and Internet—all of which seemed highly out of place. We were surrounded by tall concrete walls crowned with razor wire and protected by guard towers at regular intervals. It was life inside a protected fishbowl.

Finally, after numerous delays, we were flown out of Kuwait aboard a C-130. A C-130 is a four-engine propeller-driven aircraft that can carry cargo or troops. In our case it carried both. When used as a troop carrier, there is literally not enough room in one seat for one person when wearing protective gear. We were all more or less layered over one another. Once strapped in—securely—I felt lucky to be able to wiggle my toes. It was not for the claustrophobic and it was *not* British Airways.

But for me, the worst part about flying on a C-130 is *no lavatory*. I learned to *hate* C-130s. If you had to go, you just sat there and tried to take your mind off things. Long flights on a helicopter weren't any easier. I hadn't yet learned to deliberately dehydrate myself before flying—that knowledge would come later. There were interminable flights wherein I literally *prayed* for a refueling stop! Since aviation fuel can be a serious fire hazard, everybody had to get off the aircraft and move a safe distance away when refueling. As the aircraft filled its tank, I emptied mine. One of the simple pleasures of life; the absence of discomfort is comfort.

All flights into and out of Iraq took place at night. The enemy occasionally shot down aircraft, and darkness made it more difficult for them. Also, since heat-seeking handheld surface-to-air (SAM) missiles were used, pilots would perform all kinds of aerial gymnastics at takeoff and just prior to landing. I swear there were times I thought we were flying upside down. I discovered that the pilots wanted to disperse the heat from the engines in hopes of confusing a heat-seeking SAM. I was glad I wasn't prone to airsickness.

When the time came to leave the C-130, at an airfield in "God knows where, it's pitch-dark" Iraq, we were ushered to a plywood shack by military personnel. The barren interior of the structure was ablaze in fluorescent light. We, and others, just sat and waited. "Hurry up and wait" is more than a cute saying in the movies. It's the reality of life with the military. Being tired, I tried to pass the time by sleeping, but I was too excited and nervous.

I was finally in Iraq. It was April 2007. I was fifty-seven years old.

The next leg of the trip was in a large helicopter. Everyone, bound for various places, had their final destination written on their hands in Magic Marker. That way nobody accidentally boarded the wrong helicopter in the inky blackness. Military personnel checked each hand just prior to boarding the copter. Once again the takeoff and landing would have put a barnstorming crop dusting pilot to shame.

I relearned what I had learned many years before on active duty—if there was one thing you could count on, it was getting dripped on by hydraulic fluid when being transported by helicopter. In fact, it's been said that if you're *not* getting dripped on, that's a bad sign; it means the chopper is out of fluid.

We arrived at our first destination—the Marine base at Camp Fallujah—sometime in the middle of the night. The chopper flew off and there we sat on our gear, completely alone, in pitch dark, miles from anywhere—in Iraq. I silently prayed the others in my group knew what was going on and where we were because I was definitely as lost as a little country boy in the big city.

The major was furious. The flush on his face was obvious even in the dark. Evidently he had made all the right prior arrangements and we were supposed to be met by ground transport. I got the impression he was professionally embarrassed, since the British colonels were with us.

Finally ground transport arrived and we were driven to a large tent surrounded by thick six-foot-high concrete barriers. This served as protection from the mortars or rockets that the insurgents fired into the base randomly—and regularly. The tent was—rather ostentatiously, I thought—known as the "transient quarters." A big tent didn't seem much like "quarters" to me, but there were bunk beds and most of them even had real mattresses on them. I found one and crashed. I had been trying to seem nonchalant in front of the others, but I was physically and emotionally wrung out. It was my first night in Iraq.

After a few hours of sleep I awoke to the cheerful sound of Colonel Thompson's voice. He said, "Good morning, Terry. How does it feel to have slept through your first incoming rocket attack?" He continued— sounding downright chipper, I thought—"Even more impressive, you slept through the outgoing counterbattery fire." He was referring to the 155mm howitzers—think *big* boom—the Marines had used to return fire. I really *had* been exhausted. I do believe the good colonel knew only too well how far in over my head I was and he delighted in watching me take my first faltering steps after being "reborn." I still thank God for the colonel's thoughtful, caring tutelage. It was invaluable.

We wore civilian clothes while inside the wire at Camp Fallujah. I wore cargo pocket khaki pants and a khaki-colored shirt *and* my tricolored woodland camouflage Marine cover (hat). Since that particular cover had long since gone out of date as a uniform item in the Marine Corps, it was not inappropriate for a "civilian" to wear it. It was particularly useful as a conversation starter, since it identified me as a former Marine. It felt good to be with Marines again.

While there, at Camp Fallujah, the "it's a small world" phenomenon kicked in as I walked down a street and a former law school buddy, now a Marine captain, jogged toward me from the opposite direction. We both asked at the same time, "What are *you* doing here!?" We had been friends back at law school. Being so far from home, it was really great to meet someone *from* home. As an old friend, I was relaxed with him. I never did feel completely relaxed with the group I was traveling with. They were *way* above my level, I felt.

At Camp Fallujah we were finally issued pistols. Frankly, I would have much preferred a rifle, but at least a pistol was something. I had spent twenty years in law enforcement, often doing dangerous things, but I was never unarmed. The prospect of being weaponless in Iraq did not sit well with me. I probably overstepped the bounds of propriety in making my feelings known about it. In retrospect, I should have trusted that no one would have sent us forward unprotected. But in my life's work up to that point, there was all too often only myself and my personal "persuader" between me and harm. I had come to value self-reliance above all else. And in Iraq that meant being armed.

Always a proponent of the "you can never have too much ammo" theory, I hit my Marine buddy up for more. I didn't want to seem like a hot dog in front of the group I was with, but neither did I want to be in a position where I *wished* I had more. I borrowed as much ammo as I could get from him and kept that fact between us. In addition to pistols, we were issued tan flight suits, which were worn by all Marines at that time because they were made of fire-retardant material. No one was allowed outside the wire without one. Improvised explosive devices (IEDs) were ever-present dangers, and they often caused horrible burns. The flight suits were meant to alleviate that particular threat.

Before we left the relative safety of Camp Fallujah, I had another encounter with incoming indirect fire. This time I was awake. I was sitting at a computer in a large recreation room filled to overflowing with Marines when a rocket exploded nearby. The building was surrounded on all four sides with high, thick concrete as protection from just such an occurrence, but this round landed so close that our computers rattled. Had the projectile hit the roof, the casualty count would have made national news. I would have been one of them. The young Marine sitting to my immediate left shot a nervous glance in my direction. It had made me anxious also, but Marine leadership training is impervious to time. I put on a brave face and calmly said, "Well, they missed." The Marine smiled and went back to his email.

Our next stop was a Marine position in downtown, bullet-riddled Fallujah proper. To get there we went in a vehicle convoy. As we left Camp Fallujah I keenly felt the IED threat. Every bridge, every culvert, every pile of junk by the side of the road was a potential IED site. I will candidly admit I was anxious. I also freely admit I felt the same way every time we convoyed anywhere. I never did get used to it.

The city of Fallujah had been the scene of some of the toughest fighting in the Iraq war. In 2004, Marines had fought house to house, block by block, to clear the city of insurgents. The scars of that battle were apparent everywhere. I doubt I saw a single building that wasn't riddled with bullet holes or partially blown away by something more forceful.

We arrived at a place commanded by a Marine major. All the windows had been sandbagged to protect the occupants from sniper fire. As if to drive the point home, the windows in the head (bathroom) had bullet holes in them. Shrapnel from an incoming mortar round had pretty much torn up the courtyard outside. The signs of war were everywhere evident in the defenses that had been set up. Marines in full gear were on guard around the clock.

The major offered to show me the city as seen at night from the roof.

I took him up on his offer. That this was no mere sightseeing tour became real when he first put on his body armor and helmet. What was called a "helmet" in my day is called today by the bullet-stopping stuff it's made of: Kevlar. I followed suit. He crouched as low as he could to get behind the sandbagged bunker on the roof, and I mimicked him. I was starting to learn—albeit slowly. Snipers were still a real threat. The major pointed out various parts of the city for their battle history and tactical significance. I don't know whether he added that last part out of deference to my Marine officer past, or whether it hadn't occurred to him that not everyone would be able to follow what he had to say; I understood.

At the Marine intelligence officer's insistence, we all had drawn gas masks while at Ali al Salem. The major explained why. He pointed out the place where a suicide truck loaded with deadly chlorine gas had gone off at the entrance to our position. The major believed his Marines were the intended target, but the suicide driver couldn't negotiate the obstacles placed at the access point. Therefore he chose to detonate himself prematurely. No one was hurt, except the driver, of course. Chlorine gas was used extensively in World War I; it was deadly. Anywhere we went while in Fallujah, we carried gas masks. I thought I had seen the last of those ungainly creations during the Cold War. I never dreamed I might actually need one, and I was glad we had trained to don them so often that even decades later, I could slip mine on in an instant.

Meanwhile, Colonel Thompson was not at all happy with me. He explained later that he felt I had placed the major at risk by accepting that officer's gentlemanly offer to show me the sights from the roof. The colonel believed that I should have declined. Given the donning of armor and Kevlar, and crouching against possible sniper fire, I saw his point—in retrospect. At the time, I was desperately seeking the experience of war that I had prepared for years prior. I felt it was necessary to experience danger. There was something ineffable and possibly insane about that feeling.

I didn't even try to make myself understood. The teacher had reprimanded the student, and I flushed with embarrassment. I was still a neophyte. Looking back now, I think he did understand, and the teaching point was: *unnecessary* risks are to be avoided. I still had a lot to learn. The next morning—early—I awoke to the sound of an IED going off at a not-too-distant location. At least I didn't sleep through *that* explosion.

We went on foot to another site where our mission required us to be. We walked as if we were a squad on patrol, in staggered formation on either side of an alleyway. Still feeling ashamed after Colonel Thompson's warranted reprimand the night before, I took slight comfort that at least I remembered enough of my active duty training to get my part of the patrol right.

It was an eerie feeling walking past bullet-riddled buildings in an urban sniper's paradise. I tried to keep a sharp eye open for any sign of them, but there were so many potential hiding places, I knew we were really trusting to luck. No amount of skill could keep us safe. We walked through open raw sewage containing human excrement and didn't bat an eye.

It was life on patrol in Fallujah.

We arrived at the office of a local Iraqi functionary. He had things to tell us about the insurgency in Fallujah. I noticed that our interpreter translated three different Arabic words into the English word "terrorist." After the meeting I dug deeper into the meaning of those words with the interpreter. He was referring to three *different* groups. A better translation would have been "organized crime"—whose members would attack Americans for a bounty paid by Sunni nationalists and al-Qaeda itself.

The distinction was stunning news in my eyes. If an investigation in, say, New York City was pursuing three different drug gangs but thought it was tracking only one, that investigation would surely falter. I spoke up. The group ignored me. I was beginning to wonder why I had been included on this mission. I was beginning to think that my résumé, particularly the part about being a lawyer, was the reason. I wondered if I was window dressing. The thought did not make me happy.

Naturally, while there I made friends with the Marines. One evening they invited me into their barracks room, where music blared loudly and I was offered access to a computer with an Internet connection. I so thoroughly enjoyed myself that I had no idea that a Marine lieutenant colonel, who was responsible for our safety, was anxiously looking for me. And, owing to the music, I didn't hear him calling my name. It even crossed his mind that I might have wandered outside. This caused him no little anxiety.

The lieutenant colonel let me know that he disapproved of his not knowing where I had been. The look on Colonel Thompson's face conveyed unmistakable agreement. Once again I felt thoroughly shamed. I wasn't used to being kept on a short leash. Nor was I used to having my judgment questioned. In fact, I preferred working alone. I had taken care of myself in tough situations for twenty years, and I was not unmindful of my ignorance of Iraq—or how dangerous wandering around outside the wire could be. This mission was not turning out to be a self-esteem booster for me. Nor was I enhancing my reputation in the group's eyes.

We did what we had come to do at Fallujah, and convoyed back to the major base, Camp Fallujah. En route we narrowly missed being targeted by an IED. A convoy that left twenty minutes before us was hit. I have no idea regarding casualties. It probably should have been us. We would have left twenty minutes sooner, but one of the young Marines had forgotten the time of departure and was late. Given the VIP nature of the "cargo" on that convoy, his squad leader was extremely embarrassed and verbally dressed him down in front of everybody. Still, that Marine's error might have saved some of our lives.

Luck, or Divine Providence, plays a large role what happens in a war zone.

Back at Camp Fallujah, we engaged in never-ending rounds of brainstorming meetings with high-ranking Marine officers. I said almost nothing. My self-esteem had taken a real beating by this point, and rightly or wrongly, I felt I had nothing to offer. Perhaps I was correct in remaining silent. The others in the group had real-war fighting experience, while I had not.

Once the meetings were completed at Camp Fallujah we made another night flight, this time to the huge American base at Al Asad. At Al Asad the living was good. We were each assigned to our own personal trailer-like rooms. The rooms were called "cans" by those who were permanently billeted there. Since they were very small and made entirely of metal, I could see why they were so named. It was the first time since we left the hotel in Kuwait City that I had any privacy, and I realized how much I had missed it.

Each "can" had individual thermostats, which was a great pleasure to me. I found the air-conditioning everywhere else to be near freezing and, especially at night, I was uncomfortably cold. It struck me as slightly bizarre that I needed to sleep inside a sleeping bag and wear a jacket at all times indoors, when the temperature outside was so extremely hot. Also at Al Asad, we were conveniently located near showers and personal washing machines with dryers. I was getting tired of crusty socks. Being a total tenderfoot, I brought too much of what I didn't need, and not enough of what I did.

But I learned hard lessons, which set me up for success later in Afghanistan.

The base was colossal. I actually had to wait for a bus to get to the post exchange, which reminded me of a large department store back in the States. I eagerly searched for socks and underwear, which I needed badly. I could find nothing between extra small and triple extra large; no "human" sizes were left on the shelves. So I bought presents for my brother's kids instead—mostly T-shirts and ball caps that said "Property of the USMC, Al Asad Iraq." Al Asad seemed like a minivacation to me. I was learning to appreciate the "little things" in life that we take for granted in the States, such as privacy, thermostats, washing machines—and clean socks and underwear.

All too soon, it was time to leave and move forward once more. When we pushed out from Al Asad we went by convoy to a battalion FOB at a place in the Euphrates River valley. I was enthralled to actually see the Euphrates River, which I had been hearing about since grade school. I thought it was badly overrated as "the birthplace of civilization." The rest of the world must have been a real mess when "civilization" got around to being born. On one side of the road—where the river flowed—the area was green. It wasn't an impressively large strip of green, but it was green at least. On the other side of the road was the ever-present brown windblown desert.

The FOB was the battalion command post for the 2nd Battalion, 1st Marines (2/1). I was billeted in the "guest quarters," which was a wooden bed—I mean *wooden* bed; there was no mattress, just wood. One eighth of an inch of plywood separated my "bed" from the operations center. It was a bedlam of activity day and night. The noise didn't matter—I used my rock-hard body armor as a pillow and slept like a baby. Between the energy-sucking heat and too few hours of sleep, I was continuously exhausted.

On one of our trips outside the FOB I met my first sheik. He was an honest-to-God Arab nobleman, a hereditary leader of his tribe. He wore flowing robes right out of *Lawrence of Arabia*, and he gave me a warm embrace and kissed me on both cheeks. I'm sure I flushed at that, but in the Arab culture, he, a man of noble birth, was paying me a very great compliment.

As dangerous as the country was, it was also enchanting. I was experiencing things I could only have watched on the silver screen at home. I engaged an Iraqi policeman in a conversation about our homes and families. He spoke very little English, and I spoke very little Arabic, but with a great deal of gesturing, we actually understood each other. He communicated to me his hope that one day I would be able to come back to Iraq with my family, but without a gun. I conveyed to him that I wished for the same thing and hoped our families could pose for typical tourist pictures together. It was a fascinating exchange. I was slowly becoming a citizen of a larger world than the one I had grown up in.

We left that FOB and convoyed to another. It was a small Army outpost, and the commander, a lieutenant colonel, obviously had not been informed that we were coming. With professional civility, but with strained punctuation, he asked just who we were and what we were doing showing up at his command in the middle of the night. Lieutenant colonels do not, as a rule, like surprises. This one sure didn't. Somebody had dropped the ball, and our Marine lieutenant colonel was professionally embarrassed. Although his face showed no emotion, his cheeks turned red. I had the distinct feeling that somebody was going to pay for this omission.

The next day we were escorted to a war-torn city by a Marine captain and a composite Army/Marine Corps escort. The city was beginning to show signs of returning to life after years of strife. People were everywhere going about their business, shopping, talking, or walking. The women were conservatively but very colorfully dressed. As is the practice in Arab countries, they were covered from head to foot, but veils were not omnipresent, as they are in some places. Children played without apparent fear in the streets. Rubble was still in abundance everywhere. The war had taken its toll on the city.

The men stopped what they were doing and sullenly stared at us as we passed. They did not seem disposed to be friendly to Americans. Their countenances had a chilling effect on me. I remembered the news showing the blackened corpses of American civilians hanging from a bridge with cheering, jeering Iraqis, just like these men dancing with joy at the carnage. I could feel their hatred emanating from their eyes like heat from a sunlamp. I was damn glad I at least had a pistol. I was also glad for the extra ammunition I had borrowed. I wished I had a rifle as well.

We had come to see a certain Iraqi Army officer who made his headquarters in an abandoned public building. The outside façade was crumbling in places, and the usual raw sewage seeped up from the ground below. Inside, the building was all but devoid of furnishings. His office, however, was as professionally appointed as one could expect in a country that had been torn by conflict for so many years.

The officer, identified here only by the nom de guerre of "Colonel Ahmed," comported himself with grace and dignity. He wore a uniform of the camouflage pattern of the Iraqi Army and sported a small pistol in a covered holster on his belt. He greeted us as if we were invited guests, although we had arrived unannounced. After tea, Colonel Thompson eased into the ostensible reason for our visit. The real reason can never be revealed.

As was becoming my habit, I said nothing.

Perhaps my silence, along with my gray hair, drew Colonel Ahmed's attention. He struck me as a man who was trying to read what was behind my eyes—the *hidden* reason for our visit. During undercover assignments in my law enforcement days, I had learned not to allow my eyes to divulge anything. I projected to Colonel Ahmed that I was a person of no interest. Nevertheless, he continued to stare at me until we left.

When we first arrived, our Marine captain escort—whom I will call "Captain Jones"—casually commented that Colonel Ahmed had said that he could stop the insurrection in his area within twenty-four hours without firing a shot. Moreover, he had done so. I asked the captain if he understood what that meant; the captain didn't. I explained that only the commanding officer could do it so quickly—by *ordering* a cease-fire—and therefore Ahmed was the guy in charge of the local insurgency. A Marine officer from the intelligence specialty, Lieutenant Colonel Smith, overheard our conversation and looked at me strangely.

After returning to the States, I wrote an after-action report and emailed it to Lieutenant Colonel "Smith":

The commander, "Brigadier General Ahmed," is an enigma. Appointed a colonel by the Ministry of the Interior [MOI], "General" Ahmed promoted himself. General Ahmed promised that he could stop the insurgency in [his area] without firing a shot and did so.

Opinion: If this is in fact the case, Ahmed is the leader of the local nationalist insurgency movement.

We were informed by Captain Jones that Ahmed spoke perfect English but pretended not to. This was confirmed by observation. Ahmed laughed at jokes spoken in English prior to their translation and answered questions put to him in English also prior to their translation. At one point he made eye contact with me and spoke in Arabic. I had the distinct impression that he was looking for some sign that I understood Arabic.

Initially translation was conducted by a Sudanese national who did not speak fluent English. At some point into the conversation, an Arab-American from Detroit arrived. His demeanor was different from all interpreters encountered before or since. He took liberties in Ahmed's presence, including positioning himself behind the general, smoking without asking permission, laughing, and making comments in English, all within the context of overly relaxed body English. Ahmed displayed no observable displeasure with the interpreter.

Cautionary note: Although the differences in the interpreter's demeanor might be due to his Detroit upbringing vis-à-vis the other interpreters encountered in Al Anbar, we must consider the possibility that something is not quite right and the interpreter is overly familiar with Ahmed for reasons as yet unknown.

Although he said nothing about Colonel Ahmed for the remainder of our time together, Lieutenant Colonel Smith began to tell me that I should consider becoming a law enforcement professional (LEP). LEPs were not ordinary police. They were a group of "combat investigators" who had been recruited by a company comprised of former West Point officers. LEPs were considered to be an elite team who brought to the table what the military lacked: an indefinable *"something"*—"police intuition" plus years of real-world street investigative experience.

At Camp Fallujah, Colonel Thompson and I had met three LEPs: two retired drug enforcement agents and one retired FBI agent. The retired DEA agents were working hand in hand with Iraqi police detectives, helping the latter to prepare their cases against insurgents who were about to be tried in an Iraqi court. The retired FBI agent was assisting the Marine chief legal officer in getting the civilian courts up and running in Al Anbar Province for the first time since the collapse of Saddam's regime.

I learned from them that LEPs were sprinkled throughout the Marine and Army units in Iraq, doing whatever they could to assist. Their mission was not etched in stone—they possessed the initiative to seek out various ways to be "value added." Thus LEPs were involved in a wide variety of tasks dependent upon the supported military unit's unique needs. Lieutenant Colonel Smith's urging was of particular interest to me because the only time I felt adequate during this entire mission was when engaged in conversation with the LEPs. I knew I could be competent in that job. I understood them and felt that they understood me. It had been a pleasant emotional change.

Next we drove through a place called Kubaisa. We had no business being there. We had no business to conduct there. Young Captain Jones, in charge of our escort, thought we might like to see the sights. He got lost.

We ended up driving through narrow, winding alleyways, all teeming with people. At places the passage was so narrow we could not have opened the hatches (doors) on our vehicles. I felt particularly uneasy. Each vehicle had a turret on top, which opened into the cabin below. One Molotov cocktail (a bottle filled with gasoline with a lit rag stuffed into it), thrown from the rooftops above, could have burned us alive.

Moreover, we were not endearing ourselves to the locals. Our long radio antennae were tearing down clotheslines along with makeshift electric and telephone wires. We were a real nuisance. We were dead-ended in a maze twice. That meant we had to slowly, painstakingly, inch by inch, turn around in the cramped alleyways. Worse, it meant we had to go back the way we had come. If any insurgents were waiting for us, there would be hell to pay.

One turn around took so long that we passengers got out of the vehicles and spread out. Kids began throwing rocks at us. It was tense. I had a flash of inspiration—I took out my camera and gestured toward them, as if I were going to take their picture. It worked. The dropped their rocks and began to gather to pose for pictures.

In broken English one of them said, "Meester, meester, take my peekture!"

At the same time, I kept a discreet eye on their fathers, who were watching from nearby doorways. If the fathers called the kids inside, I'd figure something bad was about to happen. As long as the kids were allowed to stay, I reasoned, we were "probably" safe. And as long as I had a camera in my hands, the kids quit throwing rocks. I was later castigated for this by some members of my party. They seemed to think I failed to appreciate the gravity of the situation and was taking pictures like a lunatic tourist. Nothing could have been further from the truth. It was the street cop in me, acting creatively in a tough situation.

In addition, there was an alleyway running perpendicular to the one we were in, and no one was covering it. I kept going down that alley to peer around the corner building across a large expanse of open ground to see if anyone was coming. It would have been the perfect place to attack us. An attacking force could have cut our column in two and forced us to fire into each other by being between the two halves of our convoy. It would have created an absurd friendly-fire scenario. Marine officer training hadn't been wasted. It's how I would have attacked us. It didn't happen. We weren't attacked. It was still nerve-racking.

And either I didn't make myself understood, or my critics didn't understand what I had done. It was a perfect example of the synthesis of military training—tactical appreciation of our position—merged with the creativity of a street cop. I took heat for my actions. The whole camera bit made me look ridiculous to the others. I was rapidly becoming a persona non grata on this mission.

But if I had to do it all over again, I would do the same thing. I remain convinced that it was the right thing to do at that time and place. We finally extricated ourselves and got the hell out of Kubaisa without incident. I believe that day was the most harrowing for me in Iraq. We were critically vulnerable to attack, and I knew it only too well. Fortunately for what remained of my self-esteem, Lieutenant Colonel Smith continued to encourage me to become an LEP.

Finally we returned to Camp Fallujah for a round of windup meetings with the usual high-ranking Marine officers. This time, I wasn't invited to attend. I had been officially relegated to irrelevant status. It was the coup de grâce to what was left of my morale. I do believe that Colonel Thompson was pained by this turn of events. He hadn't seen the terminus approaching and thus had been unable to let me down easy.

We left Iraq the way we had come in—via helicopter in the dead of night. By that time I had learned to deliberately dehydrate myself so the long flights were not so internally unpleasant. Finally we got a ride on a C-17. A C-17 is a huge aircraft, big enough to transport an M1 Abrams tank. It also had a lavatory. It thus endeared itself to me immediately. We flew in daylight and at such a high altitude that I could look out the window and see both the Tigris and Euphrates Rivers at the same time, with the cradle of civilization in between. It was an extraordinary sight, particularly when I realized that I had actually been on the ground on the banks of the Euphrates River in the not-too-distant past. Whatever else the trip had been, it had opened my eyes to the world of Colonel Thompson.

Ultimately we wound up back at the Ali al Salem holding area, where an Army brigade had only just arrived and was marking time, waiting to deploy to Iraq. Although in actuality only a comparatively short period had been spent in Iraq, I felt as if I had aged years. I suppose deep down I had. The trip, although bruising to my ego, had increased my sophistication immensely.

I sat in the laundry room watching fresh-faced young soldiers who were so new to the Army that their gym shorts and T-shirts hadn't yet had time to fade in the unforgiving sun. They really struck me as schoolboys away at summer camp. They teased each other and joked around as if they hadn't a care in the world. I had the sad feeling that these "kids" didn't know what they were in for. I felt a compelling desire to tell them *something* that might help them, but the words didn't come. I sensed a vast gulf between us. It was a crevasse that couldn't be breached. They would have to experience Iraq for themselves.

At the time, the Army deployed for fifteen months. What I couldn't have known then was that before those innocent "kids" returned to Ali al Salem, as hardened veterans, I would be in Afghanistan.

3

An End and a New Beginning

We turned in our gear and reentered the civilian world. The group split up, everyone making their own way back to London or the States. Colonel Thompson and I spent one more luxurious night in the plush hotel that had housed us on our way into the country, then flew together back to the United Kingdom on British Airways. We flew business class, which was indistinguishable to me from first class.

The colonel and I drank gin and tonics—it seemed appropriate, since the drink was so British. The colonel pleasantly quipped that I should "take my antimalarial medicine." I believe that the Brits during the heady days of empire had used gin and tonic as such. I took his advice, and sure enough I didn't get malaria.

Colonel Thompson went home for a few days, and I spent the time in a lofty Holiday Inn near the heart of London. The hotel was circular, and every room overlooked Greater London. The view was spectacular. Unlike the stereotype of English weather as cold and rainy, the sun shone brilliantly and the air was pleasantly cool without being cold. Spring was in the air, and I could smell moisture. I believe that is what struck me as the most pleasant sensation: the smell of moisture. It was quite a contrast from Iraq and Kuwait.

Everyone I met was polite and friendly. I made friends with all comers, from taxi drivers to grocery-shopping housewives. Being an English-speaking country, it was familiar enough to be pleasant and yet it was foreign and therefore exciting. I played the role of tourist and visited the usual places: Parliament, the Royal Palace, Big Ben, and so on. I even took in a first-rate play in London's primary theater district. I hadn't seen a play since I was a young man. It was marvelous.

Most importantly, I didn't have to be concerned about my safety. There would be no IEDs going off. There were no sullen stares from people who would have liked to have seen my burned remains hanging upside down from a bridge.

It was a wonderful interlude before the ax fell.

I was gently and politely terminated. I should have seen it coming, but I didn't. I had been window dressing after all. The mission was being funded by the U.S. Department of Defense, and an American face—other than an active-duty Marine—was required. My résumé made me the perfect choice to secure the necessary funding. This explained why no one had seemed to be interested in what I had to offer. I had served my purpose.

I was crushed.

I was too old to serve in uniform—by far—so it seemed that I was at the end of the line. It was a line that had begun with officer candidate school in 1975. I returned home filled with frustration. I had been learning quickly. I knew I had more to contribute. Perhaps with a different assignment I could be of service. It depressed me greatly to think I had just had my last chance.

———

Then one day, completely out of the blue, I received an email from Lieutenant Colonel Smith, the intelligence officer who had looked at me strangely in Colonel Ahmed's office and to whom I had emailed my after-action report. The email tersely informed me that they had just arrested Colonel Ahmed.

There really was no reason why he should have taken the trouble to notify me. I had never received an email from that officer before, and have never heard from him since. But he helped to rebuild my battered self-esteem.

At last I realized why he had encouraged me to become an LEP. Apparently I did have something to offer to the war effort, just not as a part of the particular team I was on. I thought about the LEPs I had met in Iraq and realized I had missed a golden opportunity to do something I was actually qualified to do: I hadn't gotten any contact information.

Fortunately, there was Colonel Thompson. He had.

My mentor had, indeed, been looking out for me. He saw my potential as a law enforcement professional and had obtained personal contact information from one of the LEPs we met at Camp Fallujah. Then he emailed it to me when I had been home long enough to recover from the wounds inflicted on my psyche.

There is nothing like the personal touch to get things rolling, and since the LEP contact and I had met in Iraq, there was a certain boost in the application process. It was detailed and time-consuming all the same. The folks who ran the program were picky. They wanted to be sure I met their qualifications. I had the pleasure of speaking with two gentlemen who had been FBI agents as I had, and our mutual recollections of insider-only locations and jokes made the procedure easier. There are some things that only an insider could possibly know.

In December 2007, while I was visiting friends in chilly Utah, a call came. It was a retired Army colonel—a combat veteran from the Vietnam War. He was the man who made the *final* decision. I sat on a cold bedroom floor, nervousness exacerbated by the temperature. He had a training slot coming up very shortly, so he was going to interview me on the phone. I knew that the hardest part of the evaluation would be to convince him that I was worth accepting without sounding pompous. I prefaced my verbal remarks by acknowledging that challenge. He said nothing. I felt uneasy.

I knew he could hear tension in my voice, so I admitted my anxiousness right up front and told him that this assignment was important to me. He asked why, and I told him the truth. Our country was at war. It was the beginning of what might prove to be the defining type of warfare of the twenty-first century, a war of terror and counterterrorism, and I wanted to be a part of it. I had never served my country during war, and I wanted the chance now.

Moreover, I believed I had unique qualifications to help shape the war to come. I was a walking synthesis of military and law enforcement experience. The colonel was decisive. He said, "You're hired." I then volunteered to be assigned to a Marine unit, and the colonel agreed. Unlike the Iraq venture, where it was a come-as-you-are party, *this* outfit had a very informative, comprehensive training curriculum prepared. Conducted at a sprawling upscale location in northern Virginia, it left no doubt in my mind as to what was expected of me. It also reinforced my conviction that I was well suited for the LEP position.

I believe that everyone I met who was associated with the group was a retired high-ranking Army officer and graduate of West Point. I was introduced to more generals than I had ever met in my life. I affectionately referred to them collectively as the "check signers." They were the very epitome of professionalism. Although the days were long and there were no weekends off, I thoroughly enjoyed their schooling; it was well thought out and properly presented. The weeks seemed to fly by. When the training was concluded, I got orders back to the 1st Marine Division. It was just a bit more than thirty years since I was last assigned to the division, and I was elated. It wasn't over for me after all!

The Marine Corps had its own LEP training plan, which was conducted at Camp Pendleton. While there, I reveled in walks down memory lane, marveling at the things that had changed during the intervening decades, and the things that hadn't. Oceanside, the town just outside the base, was a much more entertaining place to hang out in than it had been when I was on active duty. There were many shops that sold things that would be useful overseas.

I bought what I knew I could use and ignored what was useless—which comprised the majority of the stuff I had lugged around all over Iraq. I had learned a lot more in that country than I had realized at the time.

I returned to my old regimental area. It was strange and wonderful to see the very same barracks that my Marines had inhabited lo those many years ago; they had been new then. It was also extraordinary to see the latest construction—an Olympic-size swimming pool. Southern California gets hot in the summer, and many times, finishing a run, I would have loved a quick dip. Unfortunately, the pool didn't exist in my day.

There is a mountain surrounding the regimental area which we used to call "Sheep Shit Mountain." Its name was derived from the aftereffects of sheep flocks brought there to graze by picturesque Basque sheepherders. It was a steep up-and-down mountainous trek, and I used to love to run it. Way back when—in my midtwenties—I would run it twice. or only once if I was wearing a heavy flak jacket. Each leg was two and a half miles. Now, at age fifty-eight, I just had to try it again. I did it, but one leg was enough—without the flak jacket. It was more difficult than I remembered in 1978.

Gravity had to be the reason. Somebody had turned it up.

There was also a brand-new obstacle course. It had to be new. The wood hadn't yet had time to become worn smooth by the bodies of countless Marines passing over it. Splinters were problematic. The obstacle course, known to Marines as the "O" course, is standardized throughout the Corps. I always loved it. Well, not always. At officer candidate school I dreaded it, but once I was in shape, I learned to love it. I think some kind of physical fitness "Stockholm syndrome" kicked in. Anyway, I just had to try it again. Once more, I found I could still do it, but the obstacles seemed higher, the air seemed to be thinner, and gravity was even higher still. In short, I wasn't twentysomething anymore. I was fifty-eight.

Not surprisingly, I didn't see a soul I recognized. There was an air of sadness embedded in that realization. It was the same place I had called home for two years, yet it wasn't at all. In my mind I could still see the faces of the young Marines who had been my comrades in arms long, long ago, and I missed them. I won't go back there again.

In the meantime, I heard that a Marine battalion just had its deployment orders changed. They had been slated to go to Iraq, but now they were going to Afghanistan. They would be the first Marines to go back into that country since the initial invasion after 9/11. I could see that the war in Iraq was sputtering out and I believed the Marines would be pulling out soon. I reasoned that the commandant of the Marine Corps would not want his Marines sitting around, doing nothing, with a war going on somewhere else. I assumed he would side-straddle-hop them from Iraq to Afghanistan. Therefore, Afghanistan—or "the 'Stan," as it came to be known—was going to be the place to be.

I volunteered to go with that battalion, and my orders were changed from Iraq to the 'Stan. I was sent to my old stomping grounds at Marine Corps Base Twenty-nine Palms. I hadn't seen the Stumps since 1978, but I was going back—thirty years later. It was home to the 2nd Battalion, 7th Marines (2/7)—my new outfit.

I arrived at the town of Twenty-nine Palms at about 9:00 p.m. I intended to check in with the battalion the following morning. However, it's almost neurotic how indelibly the Marine Corps has made its mark on me. For example, when I wear a civilian suit I still place my tie clasp carefully between the third and fourth button on my shirt, I still check my "gig line"—the vertical alignment of my shirt with my trousers, I still "blouse" my shirt—and I still remember BAMCIS.

BAMCIS is one of those acronyms the Marine Corps loves. It helps green lieutenants remember things when their brains are shut down from fatigue. It stands for Begin planning, Arrange for reconnaissance, Make reconnaissance, Complete the order, Issue the order, and Supervise. I am still hyperfocused on the downright *necessity* of conducting a reconnaissance.

So after obtaining a room at the Twenty-nine Palms Holiday Inn, my home for the next month and a half, I decided to conduct a reconnaissance of 2/7's Headquarters Building. I got there about 10:00 p.m. My goal that evening was to pinpoint exactly where I was going to check in the following morning—nothing more.

To my astonishment, Marines were still working—not usually the case at that hour. I had expected to find only a noncommissioned officer (NCO) on duty. With the clarity of hindsight, I shouldn't have been surprised; the battalion had a lot to do and only a short time to do it. Until very recently 2/7 had been preparing for Iraq. Half the battalion and all the staff officers had deployed there before. Afghanistan, on the other hand, was a great unknown.

I met the key battalion staff officers immediately—they were all still working. And they began briefing me—immediately. It was typically Marine Corps. Walk in the door and get to work. They liked the fact that I had been a Marine officer; I could understand what they were up against.

We stood before a very large, detailed map of that part of Afghanistan that would be our battalion area of operations (AO). Since a reinforced battalion consists of about a thousand Marines, the size of the AO was intimidating. It was an area larger than the state of Vermont. I couldn't see how one battalion could adequately cover Vermont. In addition, I naturally assumed that we were going to be deployed in the customary Marine fashion, with attached artillery, air, and logistical assets.

Looking at that huge topographical depiction of mountains, valleys, rivers, and ridgelines with the eye of an experienced officer, I saw serious problems. I pointed out that even if we broke the artillery down to two gun sections, there was no way we could cover all the anticipated forward operating bases (FOBs). I also wondered aloud how tactical aircraft could cover our entire AO from the existing air bases and how long it would take air to arrive on station.

The staff officers looked at each other with knowing half smiles. There would be *no* artillery and *no* air support. I think they appreciated the fact that I was stunned. This was not the long-established Marine Corps way of doing business. Additionally, I think my questions and suggestions pleased them. They had already asked themselves the same questions and had already considered the same remedies. I stayed around until after midnight, although I hadn't even officially checked in yet. The staff was still working when I left.

———

The next day—February 8, 2008—I returned at 8:00 a.m. I formally checked with the executive officer—the second in command. Tall, broad-shouldered, and with a shaved head, Major Lee Helton looked like a walking recruiting poster for OCS. Although his countenance was fierce, I found him to be a warm, friendly guy. Soon after, I attended a staff meeting led by the battalion commander, Lieutenant Colonel Richard Hall.

Colonel Hall stood about six feet tall and was built like an Abrams tank. His shaved head and piercing eyes created the image of a professional warrior who would have been equally at ease conquering a kingdom as he was leading a battalion. His intellect impressed me immediately. My law enforcement intuition began to tingle. I wondered if *he* was hand-picked for Afghanistan and his battalion just came along with him for the ride.

I very much liked the fact that I was back with the Marine Corps. And unlike my time in Iraq, I was an embedded part of it, not just traveling along, not just being escorted. I was a bona fide member of the battalion, albeit technically a civilian. I say technically because in my heart, I was, and still am, a Marine. It didn't take long before most members of the battalion accepted me as such.

Shortly after the meeting, the colonel stuck out his hand and introduced himself. I knew right then that I was going to like the man on a personal level. Gone was the piercing stare, replaced by a gentle, good-natured smile. He told me that he had heard all about me from his staff and that I had made a good first impression. After our introduction, he invited me to his office for an in-depth talk. I recall that I kept looking at the floor self-consciously. It was a sign of the deep respect I instantly felt toward him that I did so because I'm not shy by nature. Generally, I'm forward and aggressive.

He informed me of the battalion's mission and asked my opinion. I gave it to him straight. I had picked up on many problems we faced during the discourse with the staff officers the night before. Some of my concerns were born of military training. Others came from law enforcement investigative logic. It all sat well with him. I think he had already reached the same conclusions.

Over the better part of the following year, I was always pleasantly surprised when I would point something out to the colonel, only to discover that he had previously seen the object of my concern and had already taken steps to deal with it.

The essence of our mission was to train the Afghan National Police (ANP). I was instantly and strongly opposed to the idea. I felt that the only reason they were still alive is that they either were Taliban supporters or had made some kind of accommodation with them. Otherwise, I reasoned, the enemy would have killed them long before, since they represented the government the Taliban was trying to overthrow.

I didn't trust the ANP one bit. I told the colonel, with a bit of dry humor, that if he ordered me to train them I would do so, but the training would be:

"This is a bar of soap. Don't eat it. Put it down. We'll talk more about it later." I didn't want to teach them anything they could turn around and use against us.

Many battalion commanders are brusque and businesslike. They have no time or patience for humor. Not so with Colonel Hall. Our personal relationship began well and continuously improved over time. My initial perception of him never changed. I worked for him for almost a year, in the States and in the 'Stan. I still admire and respect him. If he summoned me right now, I would drop everything straight-away and march with him to any corner of the globe.

Of course, I made it clear that I would help train the ANP if so ordered. As a Marine officer it had been inculcated into me that my job as a subordinate was to make my superior right by my actions, even if I believed he was wrong. That was as much a part of my personality as BAMCIS. For his part, I will never forget something he said repeatedly: "Never let me fall in love with my plan."

What he meant was, if I saw something about his plan that I had reservations about, I was not only *allowed* to challenge it, I was *expected* to. That's not typical of a Marine battalion commander.

But then Richard Hall was anything but typical; 2/7 was in good hands.

Shortly after the meeting, I met another LEP, a retired San Diego cop named Frank Canson. Frank was a good street cop; I could tell that just from talking to him. Some things can't be faked. Frank's sense of humor was superlative. Comedy is an absolute essential when times get hard, and sharing tough times with Frank was almost pleasant as a result. I thoroughly enjoyed his company. Frank had never been in the military, so he had a lot of learning to do before we headed to Afghanistan. He had never been around an M16, for example, even though that was going to be his personal self-defense weapon. But it was impossible not to like Frank, and everybody helped him out.

For his part, it was obvious from the outset that Frank genuinely cared about the young Marines. He wanted to impart to them what he could to help them stay alive—his "street awareness." Almost immediately, Frank and I began to coteach classes. We put our heads together and decided what the guys needed to be familiar with, and how we would present it to them. It was a daunting challenge. It takes cops years to learn the things we wanted them to know, but we had only a few short weeks.

When one of us was talking, if the other had a point to make, the transition was seamless. It's rare that two people can develop that kind of rapport, but Frank and I did. His wit was invaluable when teaching. There is nothing that can make a class interesting like a good laugh. I also use humor when teaching. So I don't think too many of the Marines were bored when Frank and I were standing in front of them.

His fatherly fondness for the young Marines impressed me so much that I used to say that he was everybody's uncle. I even introduced him to groups of Marines as "Uncle Frank." Before long, that became his battalion nickname.

Frank and I drew gear just like any other Marine. We got what they got. When I drew a cornucopia of equipment from the supply section, I exclaimed, "I hope I get issued a lance corporal to carry all this stuff!"

I stated, not from exaggeration, that what I drew as an individual was more than what was distributed to my entire platoon when I was on active duty. I couldn't carry it all to my car—I had to drag it. The Marine Corps has never been so well equipped—possibly in its entire history. When I joined, the Corps had a saying about itself, "We have done so much, with so little, for such a long time, that we can do anything, with nothing, *forever!*"

I left at least half of the issued gear securely locked in my car at Twenty-nine Palms; it never went to Afghanistan with me. Another 25 percent stayed in the rear in the 'Stan. Not knowing what I was getting into, I had lugged too much junk around with me in Iraq. But I had relearned the lesson I had originally grasped when I was on active duty: travel light. If I couldn't eat it, drink it, or shoot it, I didn't want to carry it.

The only exceptions to that rule were two comfort items I had been introduced to by Colonel Thompson. I brought a light, warm, highly collapsible moderate-weather British army sleeping bag. The bag was easily secured to the outside of my field pack. During cooler weather I had an equally warm, equally collapsible British army jacket that was also effortlessly secured to the outside of my pack. They came in handy from time to time in Afghanistan.

As had been the case in Iraq, I often needed them to stay warm while inside due to excessive air-conditioning, although too much air-conditioning was never a problem once we left the rear.

Frank and I went to the field with the battalion during March. Being out in the desert for training wasn't a new experience for me, although I hadn't been there in three decades. Being out in the desert during winter was.

Gone was hell without the flames. In its place was bone-chilling cold. I was amazed. That was a side of Twenty-nine Palms that I had never experienced before. Dingy leaden skies hung overhead where the flaming orb of the sun ought to have been. The wind, which blew super-heated air in the summer months, must have originated in the Arctic. It blew hard and incessantly and seemed to pass right through me, carrying with it the debris of the desert: sand. In the summer I was sunburned, in the winter I was windburned. Either way exposed skin turned red. I'm still not sure which season I prefer. I suppose both are equally bad. The desert is as inhospitable in winter as in summer; only the temperature changes.

Fortunately, Marines get issued much better gear than they did in my day. The old-style field jacket, even with the liner, was a very poor cold-weather jacket. The under and outer clothing Marines have now are vast improvements. Most importantly, the winterweight sleeping bags—along with an insulated inflatable sleeping pad—actually keep a man warm at night. The pad kept the wintry ground from working its way up to one's body inside the sleeping bag. We didn't have anything remotely like that when I was on active duty. I trembled through too many nights back then. I still shivered from the cold pretty much all day long, but at least I could look forward to being warm at night.

I already knew that cold weather can dehydrate a man just as hot weather can. The difference is that one doesn't necessarily feel thirsty. In my case, when I began to get a headache, I knew I was dehydrated. I heated water with a chemical mix that came with our rations, and then mixed it with cocoa powder. I drank tepid cocoa until the headache subsided; I couldn't get the cocoa any warmer than lukewarm.

MREs (meals ready to eat), disparaged by the Marines, were first-rate cuisine compared to the "C rats" (C rations) that Marines of my era were issued. The MREs were much more palatable and contained enough calories to help a man's body stay warm and keep him going mile after mile, day after day. As was the case when I was on active duty, I ate them cold. Except when making cocoa, I never bothered to heat either type.

During some of the tactical training I got to watch brand-new second lieutenant platoon commanders maneuvering their platoons. I had to stop myself from stepping in and offering advice. I was not a captain anymore; I was a civilian. They had their own captains who did the teaching. It was difficult for me. I had already learned many a hard lesson during my time in the Marine Corps and knew what to do. But I remained silent. That would have been stepping outside my lane. Besides, they didn't need my help.

Even so, there was the occasional company executive officer who enjoyed a discussion on tactics. I brought the Cold War template to the present-day table. There wasn't a significant difference of opinion. Terrain drives tactics, then and now. And we all agreed that the new enlisted Marines had to become *much* more aware of their surroundings. Clues as to the whereabouts of IEDs were deliberately planted in the training environment. They were all too often missed by inexperienced Marines.

During lulls in the tactical training, the platoons would be rotated, one at a time, to an area where Frank and I were waiting. We realized that it took street cops years to become really proficient at instantly reading what I came to call the human terrain. To make the point I would ask each assembled platoon if it would be possible for the Marine Corps to teach a bright young cop how to be a Marine in a one-hour lecture. It was a rhetorical question, and their animated replies in the negative were expected. I told our Marine students that the challenge was no less difficult for Frank and me. We were expected to almost instantly impart knowledge that realistically took years to acquire.

But "Uncle Frank" and I were apprehensive because the young Marines' lives depended in part upon our being able to do so. It was a deadly serious responsibility, and we felt it keenly. We put our heads together in bull sessions every day, seeking ways to improve our delivery so as to hasten the process. We did our very best. I hope they knew that.

Having been a Marine was a real help. I understood Marines. I knew how to talk to them. I passed the word that I was a former Marine because I knew that carried weight; they would be more likely to listen to what I had to say. After one class a Marine told me that they already knew I was a former Marine before I told them, "Because when we bust on civilians they get pissed. You just laughed and busted right back." "Busting chops" is an art form in the Marine Corps.

I appreciated the fact that the guys sitting on the ground around us were bone tired. I had been in their boots. They were training in numbing cold, day after day, with little sleep. Class time was a wonderful opportunity to take a nap. Most wore sunglasses, and their body armor propped them up. They could be snoozed out in a minute and nobody would know. I couldn't blame them. One of the civilian instructors who spoke before Frank and I did would have put me to sleep if I hadn't been standing up.

Their platoon sergeants and squad leaders were constantly yelling out names and telling Marines to "Stand up!" because it was obvious to them that the Marines in question had fallen asleep. Frank and I noticed too, but we decided on a nonpunitive approach—we kept their interest.

Frank was a natural-born comedian. He kept their attention with his incomparable sense of humor; nobody wanted to sleep through his punch lines.

As for me, I made a game out of class. Since the whole point was to raise their awareness of the human terrain, I would pick out somebody I knew nothing about and tell the platoon something about him. Something I could only have deduced through observation. Then I would ask the platoon to tell me how I knew. Everybody woke up. Many participated. For example, referring to one platoon commander, I asked his platoon, "How do I know that Lieutenant McKendree is from Texas?"

They all looked at him. He looked surprised. They were all dressed alike, in field uniforms. There was no cowboy hat on the lieutenant's head, no spurs on his boots.

I turned to the lieutenant and said, "You *are* from Texas, aren't you?"

He replied, "Yes, sir."

I then asked, "Did you tell me that?"

"No, sir," he answered.

"Did anyone tell me that Lieutenant McKendree is from Texas?"

Marines looked at one another, but no one said a word; they hadn't.

So, I said, somebody tell me how I can tell just by looking at the lieutenant that he's from Texas. It got their attention. Everybody was trying to come up with an answer. There were a lot of creative guesses, some of them humorous (good thing the lieutenant had a sense of humor), but nobody hit on it.

Finally I told them, I noticed the ring he was wearing. It was from Texas A&M University. I admitted there was a possibility that he was from another state and had simply gone to A&M, but I reasoned the probability was that the overwhelming majority of A&M grads were from Texas. Therefore I deduced he was from Texas. They got the point: deliberately *notice* and *think*.

As Frank and I became ever more creative, we began naming the different teaching methods. I called that teaching technique the "rabbit in a hat trick." For the most part there is something about everybody that enables a trained observer to deduce at least a little bit about the person. An obvious example is a wedding ring. Its presence most probably—though not necessarily—means the person is married. In pretty much every platoon there was someone who, by observation, gave me some information about themselves. One platoon, however, had me stumped. Frank was talking to them and I stood in the rear and gazed about. All I saw sitting about me was a sea of uniformity. I realized I was going to draw a blank.

So I cheated.

Marines these days wear name tapes on their uniforms. So I pointed to a sergeant who was dutifully watching over his squad for any nodding heads and, reading his name tape, asked a Marine who had been assigned to assist Frank and me where Sergeant Washington was from. Interestingly enough, it was Washington State. So when I asked the platoon, "How do I know that Sergeant Washington is from Washington State?" I got the same puzzled expressions I had gotten from Lieutenant McKendree's platoon.

One Marine guessed, "Because of his name tape?" That caused a ripple of laughter. I asked him if he thought I was from "McGowan State" . . . more laughter. I kept them thinking and guessing until I had made my point: deliberately *notice* and *think*. They were awake and interested. The game had accomplished its purpose, so I confessed. Sergeant Washington was amused, and since from that time on I would recognize him, we never failed to say hello when we passed each other.

Sergeant Michael Washington was the first Marine killed in action (KIA) in Afghanistan whom I knew personally. When I got the word, I walked into a large equipment container, where I buried my face in my hands and silently cried.

When I wasn't in the field, I busied myself learning all I could about Afghanistan. I had gone into Iraq largely ignorant of the country and its people. Except for learning a little Arabic, I was mentally unprepared. I determined that this time I would do better. I was trying to learn Pashto—the language of the Afghans in the part of the country where we would be operating. I was also studying anything and everything else I could about the country.

I worked at an office reserved for Frank and me at the battalion command building. It was a small room with one battleship gray desk and two similarly painted tables. It had three chairs and a wall locker. And that was pretty much it. The Marine Corps still painted all the walls a sickly green color. It was completely familiar.

Since I was a continent away from home, living at the Holiday Inn, I went to work every day. It was a seven-day workweek. One Sunday, our intelligence officer, Captain Van Osborne, showed up with his father, Bill Osborne. My door was open, and Captain Osborne introduced us. He had work to do, so he left for his office immediately thereafter. Bill sat in one of our three chairs and struck up a conversation. It turned out that he had been a Marine captain and that we were pretty much contemporaries. We chatted amicably about the Marine Corps as it had been when we were on active duty.

Something, though, struck me as familiar about him. We finally figured out that we had seen each other at Civil War reenactments back east. I used to be a reenactor and he still was. That was the beginning of a most fortuitous friendship. Bill wanted to help. He volunteered to sift through scores of articles in newspapers and on the Internet that related to Afghanistan and email me the pertinent ones. His tireless assistance and intelligent editing of material enabled me to wrap my mind around the country and its people; his aid was invaluable, particularly when I was in the field and away from sources of information.

Bill's willingness to help did not end there. Later, in Afghanistan, he—and other fine Americans like him—went above and beyond the call of civic duty.

4

Mojave Viper

Eventually predeployment training evolves into something known as Operation Mojave Viper. Mojave Viper is a carefully orchestrated battalion-size training exercise that includes *everything* a battalion going to war should be proficient at—from tactical questioning of people in a war zone to live fire on the move. But it was more than simply training; it had a built-in evaluation process with permanent personnel as well. They are known as "coyotes."

Frank and I were split up. We were each assigned to a different rifle company. I was assigned to G Company, known by the military phonetic for G as Golf Company. One day, I found a new way to be value added. Two Marines from each platoon in each company were the designated intelligence gatherers. They were known by the acronym CLIC Marines. CLIC stands for company-level intelligence cell. I watched two of them question a role-playing coyote. The role player was depicting himself as an Afghan civilian with information—*if* the CLIC Marines could ask the right questions.

I stood slightly off to the side, watching and listening. After all, this was my forte. Dark-haired Lance Corporal Kyle Howell, about six feet, four inches tall, lean and muscular, did most of the talking. His partner, Lance Corporal Zach Wolfe, exactly six feet in height, had blond hair and was lean and tough-looking—even for a Marine. Both had previously deployed to Iraq, where Zach had been slightly wounded and received the Purple Heart. The small scar the wound had left on his face enhanced the look of a battle-hardened warrior. They had both been in firefights, and both had been awarded the Combat Action Ribbon. They had been together a long time and were natural partners.

After only a cursory exchange, Howell turned to Wolfe and said, "Well, that's all I've got. You got anything?" To which Wolfe replied, "Nope."

The Marine captain in me could be restrained no longer. Like a pit bull watching a mailman impetuously stride up the walkway to the mailbox, the "captain" slipped his leash and attacked. I pointed at both of them and said with unquestioned authority, *"You—here—now!"*

I continued. "That guy wants to give you everything, including a ten-digit grid coordinate to Osama bin Laden's cave! Get back in there and . . ." Counting on my fingers, I rattled off a list of questions for them to ask. When they were done the "coyote" told them they had done a great job. If only questioning people was that easy, I thought. Silently I sighed.

I called them over to a pile of rocks big enough to sit on and that was out of earshot of everybody else. Dusk had arrived, and night falls quickly in the desert. It didn't matter. There was no time to waste. We were on an accelerated push to Afghanistan. I gave it to them straight. I said, "I don't have time for 'nice-nice.' You guys sucked. Now let's work on improvement. It begins *now.*"

I took on the role of "Afghan civilian" and told them to ask me questions. When both of them drew a blank, I'd reverse roles. One of them became the "Afghan" and I asked the questions. I could always break up the impasse and get them talking. Then we'd switch back. Back and forth it went. I had just discovered a previously unthought-of niche for myself.

Whenever we had spare time, throughout Viper I'd get them together and work on their tactical questioning skills. I included other Golf Company CLIC Marines from other platoons. Throughout the role-playing there was instruction: I explained human nature and what motivates people to talk. I offered tried-and-true advice on both how to tweak the memories of cooperative individuals who thought they couldn't remember anything else, and how to crack uncooperative people who didn't want to talk.

I knew I was making progress when, late one night, Howell ran over to where I was trying to sleep. He was all excited. He said, "This shit really works! I just got Zach to admit he was in love with [she shall remain nameless]!" I smiled to myself and thought, "Well, that's not exactly *how* I intended him to use the skill sets I was teaching, but at least he's getting it." Then I drifted off to sleep.

I saw a need. I did what a self-motivated LEP was supposed to do—whatever it took to enhance the battalion's mission. There was no such thing as CLIC Marines in my day. I didn't even know they existed. So I had to imagine what they would be up against in Afghanistan. I drew on the Iraq experience only to discover that in Afghanistan, things would be much different. Looking back, a good deal of what I taught was not useful in the 'Stan. For example, I trained them in evidence collection, by the numbers, and a host of other details that are important to intelligence gathering and prepping for a trial. None of it was of any use in Afghanistan. All of it would have been extremely useful in the Iraq I had come to know.

Sometimes I was pleasantly surprised at how creative they could be. Having explained the concepts underlying fingerprints, Lance Corporal Matt Arguello asked me if it were possible to raise fingerprints using only fine desert dust. I admitted I didn't know, so we tried it. The results weren't too impressive, but his thinking "outside the box" was.

When Frank and I met up again I told him what I was doing and he jumped right on the bandwagon with the CLIC Marines in the unit he was assigned to—Fox Company. For the remainder of our time in the States, Frank and I were usually not in the same place at the same time. But in the 'Stan we would work together again, at least for a time.

Meanwhile, I relished being back in the Corps. One day a Marine was going to receive the Silver Star for heroism in Iraq. The Silver Star is the nation's third-highest military honor. The entire battalion would be drawn up in parade formation—reason enough to come out of the field. Marine Corps regulations state that any honorably discharged Marine who served during wartime may be known by the highest rank achieved during the war, and may also wear the uniform on special occasions—with the caveat that the former Marine had to be within weight and haircut standards. I had been a captain in the Reserves during the First Gulf War, and I wanted to go to the ceremony in uniform.

The battalion staff captains were highly enthusiastic. Captain Osborne gave me the exact location of the regulation that allowed it. The battalion executive officer (XO), Major Helton, had misgivings. Thanks to Captain Osborne I could point him straight to the pertinent regulation. The XO and the sergeant major put their heads together and finally decided that it was allowed.

One of the captains, who was about to be promoted to major, gave me a pair of his captain's bars. I donned the desert "diggie" camouflage field uniform that Marines wear these days and pinned on the bars. Major Helton "volunteered" to accompany me to the ceremony. I realized that was his eminently tactful way of saying, "*Okay, you can go, but don't leave my side.*" I smiled inwardly and complied without complaint.

"My" CLIC Marines were ecstatic when they saw me. They gave me good-natured grief about the way my sleeves were rolled up. They called it "the gunny roll." The sleeves weren't neat enough to suit them. All the same, it was a real motivator for them to see me in uniform—as it was for me to be there in uniform.

Colonel Hall saw me and came over, smiling. I snapped to attention and saluted—for the first time in many years. He returned the salute. It felt good. He quipped something to the effect that I looked better than some of his officers. Inwardly, I beamed. I was back.

We returned to the field and continued with Mojave Viper. One of the most difficult of the training activities is named for its range number: "Range 400." It is a company-size, live-fire, "shoot and move" assault in full gear. Machine guns fire live rounds overhead and Marines fire live rounds from advanced positions while responding to orders from their squad, platoon, and company leaders.

Body armor, rifles, full magazines, water—the weight added up. And it involved running up and down hills—rocky, irregular, tough desert terrain; it takes a lot of cardiovascular fitness. I asked the Golf Company commander (CO) if I could participate. Before he answered one way or the other, I explained that we both needed to know if I had the physical stamina to do this stuff. If not, then now was the time to find out so I wouldn't be a burden on Marines where we were going.

I saw the company gunny in my peripheral vision. He was beaming. I heard him mutter a phrase I would often hear him say, "Now, *that's* what I'm talking about!"

The company commander agreed, and I was sent to 1st Platoon, which was commanded by Second Lieutenant Benjamin Brewster. Lieutenant Brewster stood about six feet tall and was athletically built. His comportment was reminiscent of military officers of a bygone era. That is, he was unfailingly polite under all circumstances. It took a very long time before we became comrades enough for him to cease calling me "Sir" or "Mr. McGowan."

Lieutenant Brewster explicitly told me not to fire my weapon, since I had not yet had an opportunity to sight it in. I was fine with that. At fifty-eight, I was testing my fitness level, not my expertise with the rifle. I just wanted to see if I still had the stamina to move under combat conditions.

The leader of Alpha Squad, to which I was attached, glanced

furtively as the lieutenant walked away and said, "You can shoot if you want to."

Had the lieutenant not been explicit, I would have. I knew I could shoot safely. I had been an assault team leader on SWAT and was a firearms instructor in the FBI. I had plenty of high-speed, intense training and shooting time behind me. I knew there was no way my rifle was so out of whack that I would have been a danger firing it despite my not having had an opportunity to sight it in.

But the lieutenant had given an order, and I had to set the right example for his men.

I realized that, like most second lieutenants, Brewster was brand-new. His squad leader, in cautiously countermanding the lieutenant's order, was expressing a lack of confidence in his platoon commander.

The squad leader was a combat-savvy veteran of Iraq, and he was correct—technically. But like it or not, Brewster was in command of that platoon. And like every second lieutenant, he would have to earn the respect of his subordinates. I wouldn't make it any harder on him.

I had to obey his order.

I couldn't have known it at the time, but Lieutenant Brewster and I were destined to work together again in Afghanistan. He was to be in command of the FOB I supported. It's good that I didn't disobey him. We might not have been able to work together if I had.

Howell and Wolfe were ecstatic. I was fifty-eight years old and about to "kick my own ass," as they put it. They painted my face with camouflage grease. Lieutenant Brewster took one look, smiled slightly, and, with the impeccable etiquette he unfailingly displayed, said, "Sir, please don't do that again." I was the only member of 1st Platoon with a painted face. Howell and Wolfe were from 2nd Platoon.

Before we started out, one of the coyotes, not only noticing my personal camouflage, but my age as well, asked another, "What's with *that* guy?" The other responded, "Former Marine—moto." Moto meant "motivated." That was explanation enough.

It was tough going, but I discovered that I could still do it. I knew that it would be necessary for me to be fit in Afghanistan. I had no intention of remaining "in the rear with the gear" if Colonel Hall would allow me to move forward.

I ended up offering to help one of the Marines I was moving forward with. He had asthma and needed to suck on his inhaler. Wordlessly I wondered what he was doing there. I felt he should have been medically disqualified from deployment. But that was "outside my lane," so I said nothing about it. Anyway, noticing his difficulty, I offered to carry his pack. He was embarrassed and declined. I didn't mean to make him self-conscious—it was a genuine offer of help—one Marine to another. But what the heck—to him I was an old man, so of course he was uncomfortable.

While with Lieutenant Brewster's platoon, I also met the Bravo Squad leader, Sergeant Lance Holter. Roughly six feet tall (when you're my size—five foot, eight inches tall—everybody seems to be at least six feet) and wearing glasses, Sergeant Holter was very supportive of my efforts to teach street awareness to his squad. As a result, I spent more time with them than with any other squad.

In time buddying up with Sergeant Holter and his squad would prove to be a real godsend.

————

Finally Mojave Viper ended, and we all were billeted in Quonset huts at a place in the middle of the desert known as Camp Wilson. Quonset huts are long, one-room, dome-shaped metal buildings that became popular during World War II. They are quickly and cheaply built. Most of the Marines shared a single hut with a heck of a lot of other Marines, much like the squad bay of my OCS days. I shared one with a small number of officers.

It was there that I met one of our forward air controllers (FACs), captain Eric "D-Ring" Terhune. While shaving one morning, he became the first person to recognize the Marine officer's sword that's tattooed on my left shoulder. As a former enlisted Marine—a mustang— he had seen lots of moto tattoos, but mine was the first of its kind he had ever seen. He was highly personable and an attachment from outside the battalion—as I was. D-Ring and I had something in common. We became fast friends.

As a treat for a job well done, the battalion had steak night, and each Marine was allowed two beers. Long, long ago, in the very same desert during a similar respite from training, I had learned that it's very difficult not to become dehydrated in the desert. Also that a dehydrated man and alcohol do not mix. At that time in the old days I became intoxicated on very little beer. Thirty years is time enough to forget the lesson, however.

I sat with my CLIC Marines. Since Camp Wilson was a short drive to the main part of the base, which had a PX where beer was sold, and since I had my car parked at Camp Wilson, Howell reasoned there was simply no good reason why we "elite few" should be limited to two beers. He really enjoyed attempting to find "good reasons" to do things his way; he was a lot like me in that regard, and I liked him for it.

I said, "No way."

After one beer, my dehydrated body was feeling pretty good. However persisted. I still said, "Nay, nay."

After two beers I was beginning to think I understood how that Tarawa Marine felt when he joined my squad lo those many years ago. I was back with a squad, by God! One of the guys didn't want his second beer. I took it off his hands.

After downing it, my desiccated corpus decided Howell was something of a genius, and I probably had a duty or something to keep the tradition of zaniness alive in today's Marine Corps. I decided to show this new generation of Devil Dogs what it was like in the old days.

In short, I got loaded on three beers. My judgment went out the window.

I knew I couldn't drive—I'm grateful I had that much sense left—so I tossed the keys to Howell. At his height and weight, consuming only his allotted ration of two beers, he was safe behind the wheel. Off the two of us went to the PX. I sat in the car with our rifles, bayonets, and other items that flat out didn't belong there, as he bought the beer. Then we returned to Camp Wilson, where Wolfe and Lance Corporal Dave Blizzard were waiting for us.

The four of us piled in my car, in the Camp Wilson parking lot, talking, joking, telling stories about the Corps then and now, while rocking to Flogging Molly on my car stereo. Flogging Molly is an Irish rock band that was very popular at the time.

All was as delightful as could be until somebody said, "Hey, isn't that a car pulling in the parking lot?" It was.

"Who the hell could that be at this hour?" someone mused.

"HOLY MOTHER OF GOD, IT'S THE SERGEANT MAJOR!!!"

Geez, even I was scared. Sergeants major report directly to St. Michael the Archangel, whose duty is to keep Satan squared away in hell. St. Michael rarely gets involved—that's why he has sergeants major. We all ducked. I killed the music. And then, peeking timidly over the darkened dashboard, my blood froze. Howell, Wolfe, and Blizzard had left their rifles outside the car and leaning against the front fender. I saw my life flash before my eyes.

"Please, God, make those rifles invisible!" I fervently prayed. My prayers were answered. Invisible rifles are the only explanation as to why we would live to see another day.

After that near-death experience the party was over.

The next day God exacted payment. I was reminded how hungover a man who was dried out by the desert could be.

5

The Odyssey

The advance party was scheduled to leave the United States for Afghanistan on March 25, 2008. Major Helton would lead it; Lieutenant Colonel Hall would follow with the main force a little later. I volunteered to go. The major wanted to know what an LEP—essentially only an adviser on law enforcement matters in his eyes—would add to the mix. I knew I would be much more than that. My *real* job was to find a way—*any* way—to be value added. It's a very flexible concept and difficult to articulate.

To make matters worse, I had no solid idea of what my personal mission was. The battalion had to find some way to train the ANP, but I had still not been ordered to do that by Colonel Hall. Therefore, I had to discover for myself what my duty was to be, get Colonel Hall's blessing, and march on from there.

As a street law enforcement officer for twenty years I had learned to read the human terrain. I could look at many people and tell what they were up to. First, though, I needed to get the feel of the country. I needed to establish baseline behavior for the typical Afghan. Otherwise, how could I recognize atypical behavior? The sooner I got started, the sooner I could produce some results. But truth be told, I had waited my whole life for this; I couldn't wait to go.

I must have gotten my point across somehow, as the major decided to include me. Although I had only volunteered myself, he also included "Uncle Frank." Frank was good-natured about this turn of events, even though he would have preferred to have gone with the main body. He lived in California and he enjoyed spending his weekends at home with his wife.

I didn't get much sleep the night before leaving. The U.S. Army had been fully involved in the mountains of eastern Afghanistan for a number of years. But 2/7 was heading for the western desert. That area was a great unknown. And unlike Iraq, where I was a member of a group of protected VIPs, this time I was a full-fledged part of a Marine battalion.

I wasn't as nervous as I had been prior to leaving for Iraq, and I was thankful I had been there. I knew what it felt like to be in a place where an unseen enemy wanted to kill me. I think that had been an unconscious enervating source of stress for me while in that country. Even so, once again I had to come to terms with the prospect that I might not be coming home.

———

When I was a young law enforcement officer, decades before, I was cognizant of the possibility I could be killed in the line of duty. Rather than worry about it, I made my peace with God and resolved never to think about it again. For the majority of my career, I never did. Whenever it did cross my mind, I turned again to God.

Prior to leaving for Afghanistan, I revisited my Creator and put myself back into His hands. That being done, I never worried about dying while over there. Although every day upon waking, and especially "leaving the wire," I reaffirmed that I was in His hands. I'm not saying I was never afraid, only that if He wanted me, I was ready to go. I didn't *worry* about dying. I felt that—at fifty-eight—I had lived a good, long life, and if it was my time to go "home," there was no tragedy in it.

Losing the young Marines, on the other hand, was heart-rending. It was deeply painful when it happened. Life for them was just beginning.

I drew a pistol and an M16 from the armory. They would be in my possession almost continuously until we returned to the States. I had carried a pistol every day of my working life in law enforcement, so I was quite comfortable wearing it—and shooting it. The M16 and I became part of each other when I was on active duty as well as during my law enforcement career. I even owned my own AR-15—the civilian version of the M16. Therefore I was intimately familiar with both weapons.

Most Marines preferred the M4 short-barrel collapsible-stock version of the M16. It was lighter and shorter than the standard M16A3, which made it much easier climbing into and out of a Hummer. All the same, I asked for and got the M16A4. My rifle was longer than an A3. It had a solid stock and extra-long barrel. It weighed a good bit more, but I was "Old Corps," and I wanted a weapon that could really reach out and touch someone. During active duty I had been inculcated with the "one-shot, one-kill" mentality of a Marine rifleman. Contrary to what is depicted in the movies, it was always one shot at a time. The firing might be rapid, but it was not "spray and pray."

We assembled in the chilly predawn darkness at the designated departure point. Many wives, mothers, and girlfriends were in evidence, saying their good-byes. About half the battalion had already done a combat tour in Iraq. They were confident they could handle what lay ahead. The other half was new to the Corps, and they hid their apprehension as well as they could. From here on out, I'd be wearing the same desert "digi" camouflage uniform as the rest of the battalion. With one annoying difference—where the "U.S. Marines" tape should have been, mine read "DOD Civilian" (DOD stands for Department of Defense). As a man whose dog tags were older than most members of the battalion, that stuck in my craw. I was a MARINE, by God. I cut the offensive tape off shortly thereafter.

We were transported by bus to an airfield, each of us alone with our thoughts. When we got to the airport it was still the wee hours of the morning. I was surprised and delighted to see a large number of older men and women who were there to wish us well before we deployed. Thoughtfully, they provided us with cookies and soft drinks. Though tired, sleeping was out of the question due to the predictable nervous jitters.

We loaded aboard a commercial jet that had been leased from some never-heard-of airline. It was a large white aircraft, and I managed to sit in one of the first-class seats. The extra room was a godsend on the particularly long flight. We spent the next forty-eight hours on or near that plane before we finally disembarked for a couple of days. The captain and crew were all Americans and very cheerful. They treated us very well, feeding us sandwiches and soft drinks pretty much anytime we asked for them.

First we flew from California to Iceland. We got off the plane to stretch our legs while it refueled and walked on wet tarmac to the terminal. I didn't see much of the country, as the weather was overcast and foggy. However, I immediately noticed a tremendous scent of cold and snow. It seemed to smack me in the face the instant I got off the aircraft. I was born in the North and am no stranger to winter weather, but this was different. The air was so cold, so crisp, so moist—and so unforgettably clear. It bombarded my senses like winter never had before.

There was only one Icelandic official present, and he wasn't much of a conversationalist. It was too early in the morning for other airport employees or travelers to be out and about, so there was no opportunity to interact with native Icelanders. I was disappointed, as I have always been fascinated by the treasure chest of history and legend surrounding that country. But at least I got to breathe Icelandic air and walk through Iceland's puddles on an Icelandic runway. I would have loved to have stayed for a few days, but it doesn't take long to refuel a plane, and we were quickly called back.

When we reboarded the plane we flew nonstop to Budapest, Hungary. We again debarked and entered the terminal. This time we had to walk through metal detectors under the watchful eyes of several Hungarian security police.

One snack bar was open, but the line was so long that most Marines didn't have time to buy anything before being summoned back to the plane. Once again, there were no civilians about—except an overwhelmed snack bar employee. It was still too early in the morning. I ambled off by myself in the terminal—I've always been a rebel like that—and decided to shave in one of the lavatories. We'd been on the plane about twenty-four hours by that time and a shave felt good. Refreshed, I found my way back to the others.

One Hungarian guard gave me the evil eye as I approached the group from a direction other than where I should have been. Part of my reason for wandering off was to test the security of a once enemy country. During the Cold War, Hungary was Communist, and I had been an FBI agent. Old habits die hard.

After many more long hours aloft, we finally landed in Kyrgyzstan. I had never even *heard* of Kyrgyzstan prior to landing there. During the Soviet era, it was one of the Communist satellite countries. In fact, we landed at a former Soviet Air Force facility. Now known as Manas Air Base, it is a major U.S. Air Force conduit into and out of Afghanistan. This was as far as the civilian airline would take us. We would be billeted at Manas until military transport aircraft could be arranged to take us the rest of the way.

Kyrgyzstan had instant appeal for all of us. We were surrounded by steep, picturesque, snowcapped mountains. I noticed green pastures with grazing horses in the valleys below as the plane decreased altitude prior to landing. It reminded me of pictures I had seen of Switzerland. When we debarked, the air was crisp and clean-smelling. Not as starkly noticeable as in Iceland, but crisper and cleaner than anyplace I could recall at home. The weather seemed just perfect, very springlike, with green grass beginning to grow not just in the valleys, but everywhere. The sun was shining. I didn't doubt it was subject to extremely cold winters, but in that present moment, it was idyllic.

We were bused from the landing field to the base itself. As we drove, evidence of prior Soviet occupation was arresting. Many of the buildings outside the U.S. sphere were drab and dreary-looking. There were still high concrete walls with rusting barbed wire strung across the top. The present-day Russian Air Force had a jet fighter base only about forty miles away. That knowledge was not exactly comforting to a prior Cold War veteran like me. I had trained for years to kill those people and had resigned myself to what seemed to be inevitable—I would die in the process.

U.S. Air Force officials held on to my and Frank's passports. They were concerned that we might slip off the base and into a nearby town for drinks. Being a former federal lawman, willingly putting myself into a place where Russian agents might be lurking, or that Russian pilots might be visiting at the same time, was about as unlikely a prospect for me as anything I could dream of. But apparently some civilian contractors who had passed through before us did exactly that. To make the eventuality even more unlikely, neither Frank nor I had civilian clothing. We were definitely staying put.

Although the officers were assigned private quarters, and Frank and I were accorded officer status, we decided to stay with "our" Marines. All the Marines were housed in one gigantic dome-shaped tent covered in yellow waterproof material. The yellow color gave the interior a bright, cheerful air. The space was completely open and furnished with row upon row of bunk beds. I picked a bottom bunk in the very corner. At night I could hear the wind howl outside and the tent covering quiver and shake. It was strangely comforting while snuggled inside my warm sleeping bag in bed.

We stayed at Manas for several days. They were undeniably the most pleasant days of the entire deployment. Frank and I enjoyed trips to the

PX and to a little shopping area where native Kyrgyz sold items of interest to all the Americans who passed through. The Kyrgyz were very Oriental-looking. The girls working in the shops would cover their mouths with their hands and giggle for seemingly no reason at all. I had the feeling, later confirmed, that Genghis Khan had passed this way. His Mongols left their mark on the inhabitants.

There was also a gourmet coffee shop outside an Internet café. The shop sported an outdoor gallery. Frank and I and several Marines enjoyed endless hours sipping coffee in the beautiful spring-like weather while sitting comfortably on the veranda. The Air Force thoughtfully played pop music over the base PA system. Within sight of us were male and female Air Force personnel playing volleyball in stylish Air Force gym attire. I would wistfully think back to Manas many times in the coming months while enduring grim living conditions in the Afghanistan desert.

The Internet café was a real treat, since email was the link to home and the world. It was a pay-for-time establishment run by young, obviously Russian men and women. Unlike the other locals we had seen, they were completely European-looking. There were no Mongol ancestors in their family trees. They were on an American military base through which passed, into and out of Afghanistan, countless thousands of American servicepeople. If it wasn't a training ground for the Russian secret police, it should have been. Logically, they'd have been interested in what the gray-haired guy was sending and receiving, so I kept it as bland as cardboard.

All too soon, it was time to leave. We flew in a C-17 fitted with row upon row of seats. The trip to Afghanistan took several hours, but those wonderful C-17s have lavatories. We landed at Kandahar Airfield. Although it was only March 28, the heat that greeted us as we opened the doors of the aircraft was oppressive. Immediately upon stepping outside onto the tarmac, sweat began to pour from my body. In many respects the burnt brown mountains surrounding the base and stifling heat reminded a lot of us of Twenty-nine Palms in the summer. Since it was still springtime, I knew that summer would really cook. In only a few days we had gone from winter to spring to brutal summer heat. We had had no time to acclimate.

But we had arrived in Afghanistan.

6

Kandahar Airfield

Kandahar Airfield—known as KAF—was an extremely large base completely surrounded by impressive defenses. It was so large that when the enemy tried to rocket us, it was pretty much a foregone conclusion that their indirect fire would fall short. KAF was home to a variety of nationalities and branches of service. American soldiers and airmen, Canadians, British army and Royal Marines, Germans, Danes, and Dutch were already there upon our arrival. Now, for a time at least, U.S. Marines were added to the list.

Unfortunately, there was no more room for us in any of the "civilized" areas, so new ground had to be broken. But first it had to be swept for mines left by the Soviets during their ten-year war to add Afghanistan to the list of Soviet "republics." Areas that had not yet been swept were cordoned off by barbed wire with a sign that read ominously, "MINES." We were warned to stay on roads and not to wander off onto vacant land. A hasty tent city was built on the north side of the airfield.

Regrettably, everything of interest was on the *south* side of the airfield. It was a long, hot walk away. We were bused to our new battalion area, where large olive drab tents had been erected. Most had wooden floors, but the entire construction project was so hurried that many

Marines had only large chunks of gravel as their floor. Cots in rows completed the work.

Tents where sensitive equipment was stored were air-conditioned; most sleeping tents were not. It was still spring, so sleeping at night actually got chilly. It warmed up fast once the sun came up, though. Even I couldn't sleep past 8:00 a.m. due to the heat, and I have always had a high tolerance for hot weather. Typically, when I awoke, the tent was empty—my tentmates having been driven out from under the olive drab heat-soaking canvas sometime before.

Frank and I settled into our new digs in one of the wooden-floored tents along with a veritable menagerie of differing personalities. Our coterie included the chaplain, Navy lieutenant Russ Hale, known affectionately as "Chaps"; a battalion doctor, Navy lieutenant Adrian Miclea; Second Lieutenant Pat Caffrey, in command of a platoon of engineers; and three elderly Afghan gentlemen. The Afghans were extraordinarily polite and brewed *chai* (Afghan tea) every day; with unvarying courteousness they always offered to share. Like many Marines I had developed a liking for chai while in Iraq. I appreciated their civility.

The Afghans were rated as category one interpreters. Category one meant that their security clearance was first-rate; they were in high demand. Lamentably, not only were living conditions in our tent spartan, but also we were heading out to virgin territory where no established FOBs were waiting. Among other things, that meant no air-conditioning. It wasn't even full summer yet, and the heat was rapidly growing vicious. The gentlemen felt they were too old for such an environment, and they quit and went home very early on. With their security clearance and language skills, they could find highly paid work in Kabul, the capital of Afghanistan, with no problem.

Chaps was good-natured and upbeat—near the end of the deployment he acquired moto (motivating) T-shirts for the entire battalion. Doc Miclea had a wicked scar where a sniper in Iraq had tried to kill him by shooting him in the femoral artery. Uncle Frank was his usual comical self, and Pat Caffery and I had become acquainted back at Twenty-nine Palms, so I regarded him as a buddy. I could've had worse tentmates.

At the foot of my cot, inside the elastic surrounding my Kevlar (helmet in my day) I planted a "Do Not Disturb" sign that I had liberated from the Holiday Inn at Twenty-nine Palms. Draped on tent ropes at the head of my cot I hung an olive drab T-shirt—it showed a picture of an angry "Garfield the cat" and it read, *"You sent me to Afghanistan? You bastards!"*

When we first arrived at our forlorn billeting area, we were informed that the enemy would send indirect fire—known as IDF to Marines— every night. Usually it would be rockets, since the perimeter was extended so far that mortar rounds couldn't make it. For the first few nights nothing happened, and I thought the warning was an exaggeration.

Then, while lying on my cot alone in the tent, watching a movie on my computer, I heard it. *Whump, whump, whump, whump.* Four IDF rounds impacted about four hundred meters or so southwest of our position. I knew that area was empty land—so no harm done. I also knew that the enemy couldn't stick around and make a sustained bombardment out of it, as our counterbattery fire or air support would make short work of them, so I knew it was over. More proof that my time in Iraq was well spent after all.

Frank rushed into the tent to pick up his body armor and Kevlar helmet. I told him not to worry, that it was over. He asked, "Are you *sure?*" Well, I was sure enough for my own peace of mind, but there was always a possibility of error—so I replied, "I'm reasonably sure." Frank decided to play it safe. He donned his personal protective equipment and went looking for a bunker.

He needn't have bothered. They had erected our tent city so quickly that there were more lifeboats for passengers on the *Titanic* than bunkers for us.

I kept watching my movie.

Suddenly, in rushed the chaplain's assistant, a young Navy sailor. He had the "deer in the headlights" look. He was dressed in a Marine desert (diggie) camouflage uniform, with a "U.S. Navy" tape sewn on where "U.S. Marines" would have been. He was wearing every piece of protective gear he could get his hands on. He reminded me of a *Star Wars* storm trooper in tan camouflage.

He had a pistol on his belt. Additionally he carried an M16, and rather oddly, I thought—he had a bayonet. He *always* carried that bayonet throughout the entire deployment. I'll never know why. His job was to assist the chaplain. I don't think Chaps led a single bayonet charge in the 'Stan. Bayonets were only useful for jabbing in the dirt while listening and feeling for the hollowness of an IED.

He kept looking from me, the only occupant of the tent, to Chaps's vacant cot, and back to me.

I tried to reassure him, "It's all right." And "It's already over." But he never lost the thousand-yard stare and, like a spectator at a tennis match, jerked his head back and forth from me to the chaplain's empty cot. Then, wordlessly, he rushed back out into the darkness.

It finally occurred to me that somebody might be doing a head count to make sure there were no casualties, so I meandered down to where the company gunny was doing exactly that. Wearing only trousers, a T-shirt, and flip-flops, I felt as casual as I looked. I said, "Hey, Gunny, in case anybody's wondering, I'm still alive." Figuring the chaplain's assistant might be too rattled to check in, I told the gunny what had happened. In typical gunny fashion he bellowed, "What's *he* worried about? He's got *Jesus* on his side!"

I went back to my movie.

I was informed at a later date that the British Royal Marines had finally had enough of that particular IDF insurgent. He had been rocketing vacant portions of the base for some time, hitting nothing. The Brits were content to just keep tabs on him. Now he was getting a little too close to something. So they hunted him down and killed him.

There were no more IDF attacks made directly against our position after that.

Since we were so far from the main part of KAF, a bus would come by every twenty minutes or so and transport Marines back and forth. Right by the bus stop two Marines stood guard—around the clock. All too often, Lance Corporal Andrew "Whit" Whitacre and Lance Corporal Nick Harris were unlucky enough to draw the duty. It made waiting for the bus a lot more entertaining for me, however.

Whit and I had become friends during Mojave Viper, and through him I got friendly with Nick. Whit was possibly one of the most good-natured guys I ever met. He was twenty-one and stood about six feet tall with blond hair and boyish good looks. Whit could have been a recruiting sergeant's poster boy.

He had already been deployed to Iraq, with 2/7. He seemed to know everybody in the battalion, and everybody liked him. It was impossible *not* to like him. He had that kind of infectious personality that has been winning popularity contests since they were invented. He and Wolfe, one of "my" CLIC Marines, were best friends.

During Mojave Viper the cold and wind and overcast skies had teamed up with benign neglect from the Golf Company CO and first sergeant, and I was feeling rather low. During one phase of the training the entire company and I were bivouacked at a make-believe FOB. Training was being conducted at a small "town" a few miles away across the desert. I decided to see if the company "powers that be" would even notice that I walked alone across the desert and back each day. Not surprisingly they didn't. It didn't help my morale when Frank told me that he was chauffeured to and from the same place by the company he supported.

One gray morning as I stepped out of my tent into a biting, cold wind, I saw Whit walking with the first sergeant. Whit saw me at the same instant and spontaneously blurted out to the first sergeant, "I LOVE that guy!" It made my day.

Whit and Wolfe kept talking about a really great place for fun and frolic called Lake Havasu. It was a man-made lake on the Arizona-California state line. From the stories they told it must have been a blast. They both offered to take me there when we got back. In fact, they were obviously looking forward to showing the "old man" a good time. I didn't have the heart to tell them that I couldn't party like I did when I was their age, but I agreed anyway. I figured I must have at least one good weekend left in me. Harris and Howell and other guys I knew went there all the time as well. I was really looking forward to it.

It wasn't meant to be.

In retrospect, KAF wasn't a bad place. In fact, there would come a time when I would regard it as a veritable Disney World. But when we first arrived it took a lot of getting used to.

On March 31, 2008, after only a few days at KAF, I wrote to my old high school pal Lieutenant Colonel Jack McMahon, USMCR (Ret.),

Life is spartan and that's giving it something. This place makes 29 Stumps look good by comparison. We are the bastard stepchildren of this base. Can't wait to move on although things will likely get worse. My greatest enemy is morale. Gotta keep redefining my mission. Can't say what my latest personal thrust is, but I keep finding something useful to keep my mind occupied. Its gonna be a long haul. Austere. In the extreme. Knees fine. Shoulders (fine finally!) chest congestion getting better every day. Soon I hope to run and do pushups and crunches again. I lugged twice the baggage load yesterday. I'm a friggin' mutant. Nobody my age is supposed to be able to do what I do. Especially after double shoulder surgery. I'm sitting here at a computer after cutting out of my 879th IED awareness class. It's good to be able to jump from one side of the "civilian" line to the other. Ooh rah. Still. This life sucks.
PS But of course I'm not quitting.

The "civilized" part of KAF had a non-air-conditioned PX; an un-air-conditioned barbershop; several great semi-air-conditioned chow halls; a Dutch-run recreation canteen, which was open to all; and quite a few shops that sold electronics. KAF also had a non-air-conditioned recreation hall with pool tables, Ping-Pong tables, movies with free popcorn, telephones, and free Internet. The time on the Internet was seriously limited and the lines were prodigious, but the Internet was available. In short, most places were sweatshops, but interesting sweatshops. Most impressively, KAF had the Boardwalk.

The Boardwalk was a raised wooden sidewalk that formed a large connected hollow square. Over the sidewalk a wooden roof had been erected, thereby affording shade and escape from the burning sun. Around nearly three-quarters of the Boardwalk were shops of various kinds. A few were operated by Canadians, but most by local Afghans or some other interesting ethnic folks. The first thing one would see getting off the bus was a Tim Hortons coffeehouse staffed by friendly Canadian women. Gourmet coffee is always a welcome treat in an austere environment—no matter how hot it is. Additionally, there was an ice cream shop—when the ice cream machine was working; an outdoor hamburger joint; an overabundance of little odds-and-ends stores; and a very small Canadian PX, where I enjoyed warm Diet Cokes.

Dominating the Boardwalk area was a regulation-size hockey rink. Boldly emblazoned with the red Canadian maple leaf set squarely in the center of the rink, it was constructed inside the hollow square near Tim Hortons. When I first saw it I nearly dropped. I thought the Canadians had somehow managed, in blistering heat, to keep an iced rink right out in the open sun. I was soon disabused of the notion when the teams showed up to play wearing sneakers. Walking around the Boardwalk I could imagine the smell of a chlorinated swimming pool, the sounds of diving boards, splashing water, and happy swimmers. It was just my imagination. There was nothing in the center of the Boardwalk except the hockey rink and burning sand. There would come a time when I'd get used to sweating every minute of the day, but that time hadn't come yet. There was no escaping it. We lived inside an oven.

Happily, one of the shops did embroidery. I had them sew Velcro onto my diggie shirt where that offensive DOD Civilian tape had been, and slapped on a newly made three-inch-by-two-inch patch. It was tan with brown embroidery. The place of honor was dead center in the rectangle: it featured the eagle, globe, and anchor—venerable symbol of the Marine Corps. Across the top read "T. P. McGowan," and right under that "Once a Marine, Always a Marine." It had "1st Civ. Div." across the bottom.

Marine divisions are abbreviated 1st Mar. Div., 2nd Mar. Div., and so on. An inside joke is the "1st Civ. Div." Standing for "1st Civilian Division," it told all Marines that although I was technically a civilian, I had earned my eagle, globe, and anchor. I was still a Marine, by God.

I brought a name tape with me from the States that read "Secret Squirrel." I had been told in Iraq that whenever someone with gray hair, no rank insignia, and no name tape would show up, Marines would refer to them as secret squirrels. I liked the moniker and had Velcro sewn on the back. I didn't wear it until we pushed out. Then I wore it on my tactical vest.

Once the remainder of the battalion arrived, in early April, Frank and I engaged in frequent conferences with Colonel Hall. As noted previously, the battalion's mission was to train the Afghan National Police, known as ANPs. As we were former law enforcement, it was logical that the colonel would seek our input. Frank and I pondered the idea ad infinitum, preparing PowerPoint presentations laying out several proposed courses of action for the battalion commander to consider. With an AO consisting of thirty thousand square miles, Frank and I really didn't think we could do much by ourselves, but it was our duty to try to come up with *something*.

Personally, I was as strongly opposed to the idea of training the

ANP as I had ever been. Recalling the battalion commander's earlier admonition never to let him fall in love with his plan, I shared my misgivings with him. I voiced my belief that what they needed to be taught was how to survive in a war-torn environment. It would be years before they might need American-style policing skills. I pointed out that there were no courts up and running. Police make arrests. The suspects go to court. The court decides what comes next. With no courts, what is the proper role of police? Without a court system they weren't police, they were a militia. I think that bit of reasoning made sense to the colonel.

I held the view that the skill sets the ANP needed could be better provided by a Marine rifle squad than by Frank and me. The ANP needed to be able to handle their weapons and master rudimentary military tactics. A gentleman as well as an officer, Colonel Hall gave careful consideration to what Frank and I had to say. And, naturally, in the end we would do as he wished—personal opinions notwithstanding.

While the details of the battalion mission were being worked out by Colonel Hall and his staff, Frank and I decided to continue doing what we had begun back at Twenty-nine Palms: teaching Marines throughout the battalion how to read the human terrain, and continuing to coach our CLIC Marines. We arranged to use a classroom in the recreation hall to coteach one platoon at a time, rotating as many platoons through as we could manage. We would also gather our CLIC Marines, sometimes in just a shady corner of the battalion area, and continue working with them.

One day one of our CLIC Marines honestly admitted that he was totally unconvinced that the questioning techniques we had been teaching him would really work. I decided a case-in-point lesson was in order. So I told him that I was going to get him to tell us something embarrassing about himself. He wouldn't want to, of course, and I was telling him up front that I was going to get him to do it. He exhibited smug confidence.

I asked him what his hometown was. He said, "St. Louis." I replied that he surely must have gone up to the top of the St. Louis Gateway Arch. He told me that he had. I asked him to describe what it was like. His answer was as bland as uncooked spaghetti.

I had been to St. Louis; one of my best buddies in the Corps was from there, and I had visited him and his family. We had been to the top of the arch. It was nerve-racking. The elevator can't just go straight up; the arch is curved. So it bumps and bumps its way to the top. The top sways in the wind. It's an uncomfortable—and unforgettable—feeling.

I had him. I knew he was never up in that arch. He had lied.

So I began to hammer him, and like a boxer on the ropes he couldn't do much more than get hit. It wasn't long before he admitted that he wasn't from St. Louis, and it went downhill from there. Just at the moment when he was about to reveal something embarrassing about himself, I shut it down cold. The other guys were wild—they wanted him to continue—and curious as hell. But I had made my point, and that was as far as I'd let it go.

On another occasion, the "rock game" was invented. I noticed that Wolfe was bored and not listening. I wondered what new gimmick I could come up with to wake him, and the others, while still making a teaching point. The "rock game" came to me. I had six of the CLIC Marines file by one at a time, out of sight of the others, and I shook hands with each one. Into one hand I placed a rock. That rock was then put into the Marine's pocket when no one could see. With all six Marines standing in front of the larger CLIC group, I challenged the group to tell me which Marine held the rock.

I told them that they had all they needed to know—they had months of observation behind them—they knew each other's "baseline" behavior. So what was there about facial expression, or body English, that was different now? Who possessed the "guilty knowledge" that would be betrayed by a slight difference in expression? They each took a shot at it. Most got it wrong. In their defense I should note that some of the players were deliberately trying to look guilty. Howell, who knew Wolfe the best, was emphatic, *"It's Wolfe!"* There was *no* doubt in his mind.

He was right. Howell nailed it because he knew Wolfe so well. There was just the subtlest change in Wolfe's facial expression, and Howell was on it. The others overplayed their "guilt" and were eliminated in Howell's mind. Since Wolfe and Howell were my first "students" and had developed into my close friends, inwardly I beamed with pride. Most importantly, the point was made that one must establish baseline behavior for an individual or group of people and watch for telltale signs that *something* is different.

Frank loved the rock game and we started playing it with all the Marines as they came to us a platoon at a time. To make it more interesting I began to give one of them a folding knife. I believed a hidden weapon would help muster some deep-seated feelings of guilt or secret knowledge that might be observed more readily.

I admit that I also made it easier on the platoons by choosing six of the youngest, newest members of each platoon, Marines who would likely be intimidated standing in front of the group. I believed the new guys were more likely to betray their secret through expression and that they would be afraid to try to pretend they were guilty. We never had a 100 percent success rate, of course, but there were some members of every platoon who correctly identified the Marine with the knife.

In the interim, we seemed consigned to remaining at KAF indefinitely. The month of April, growing hotter with each passing day, really dragged. The colonel had ordered that all battalion Marines, with one loaded magazine on their person (not in the weapon), were to carry their rifles at *all* times. The only exception would be in the shower. The colonel, realizing that time weighed heavily on everyone's mind, didn't want his Marines to grow complacent. He felt that carrying a weapon and ammunition would keep the fact that they were war fighters foremost in their minds. That applied to Frank and me as well.

I have always liked to run. The heat never deterred me in the past, and it didn't deter me at KAF. So every other day, I would put on shorts and sneakers, carry my heavy rifle with fully loaded magazine at sling arms, and run. One Marine who saw me told me that seeing an old man like me running in that heat made him feel like a slug. I grinned hearing that. Truthfully, I reveled in the disbelieving looks I got. The temperature was noteworthy.

I met a former Navy corpsman, "Doc" Stacy McKinnon, at a veterans' function in Milwaukee. Since I learned that she had spent considerable time on the north side of the airfield, I asked her if she had seen an "old guy" with a rifle running during the heat of the day. She and her Marine pals had— they nicknamed him "Corporal Klinger," after the guy on the TV show M*A*S*H because they were sure he was trying to get sent home as a psych case. They joked that if running in the heat didn't work, the guy would wear a dress next. I told her I was Klinger. She couldn't wait to email her pals and tell them she had finally identified "Corporal Klinger."

Running in the fiery air served two important purposes aside from basic fitness. I got so used to carrying the rifle that it no longer felt heavy. There was no tremor in my arms when the time came to shoot it. Also, I became inured to the inferno we lived in. Although the temperature kept climbing, it didn't "seem" quite as hot. Running really helped me to adapt.

One day we had a sandstorm. I decided to run anyway. Howell and Wolfe advised against it in the strongest possible terms. I still went. I wore desert goggles and covered my mouth with a bandanna of sorts. It didn't work really well. My reddened eyes stung mercilessly and for the next few days I coughed up mud balls. I had to admit they had been right. Wolfe was fairly smug about it and took every opportunity to call to my attention that since he and Howell had deployed to Iraq they knew what they were talking about—and maybe I should listen to them more in the future. His point was well taken.

On Saturdays local Afghan merchants were allowed on one portion of the base. It was a bazaar in true Near East fashion. With ornate carpets laid out on the ground, or from tables they had set up, they sold anything they could get residents of the base to buy. But caveat emptor—let the buyer beware—they sold a lot of counterfeit merchandise. I nearly bought some supposed old U.S. silver dollars. Once I picked one up I could tell by its lack of weight that it was made out of aluminum. It *looked* good, though.

The bazaar broke up our week. It was something to look forward to. We passed row upon row of carpets, dresses, flags, swords, knives, bootlegged movies, metalware—everything, it seemed. Since we had access to a post office at KAF, I bought presents for my brother's kids and delighted in shipping the stuff home to them. My brother told me that when the boxes came, the kids were on them "like sharks on a chum bucket."

Pretty much every Afghan in the bazaar spoke English. It was necessary in order for them to conduct business. That's where the similarity among them ended, however. The personalities of the sellers were quite different from one another. Some were very forward and fast-talking, like the proverbial "used car" salesmen, while others were very quiet and very polite. I enjoyed spending time talking to the latter. Some of these gentlemen even offered me chai.

I came to discover that, as was the case in Iraq, the offering of chai was very proper behavior in Afghan society. Taking them up on their offer and engaging in polite conversation was an excellent way to increase my knowledge about Afghanistan and the baseline behavior of typical Afghans. I sat on the ground on carpets with them—chairs are not the Afghan way—under the shade of a makeshift tent.

Nevertheless, even the Boardwalk and bazaar got old after a while. Boredom became depressive. We were living in an outdoor oven, doing nothing of importance, it seemed, and just marked time, day after endless day. To make things worse, I was beginning to experience some discomforting mood swings. I'd be emotionally up one minute and very down the next. I've always had a good imagination, and my nighttime dreams have always been vivid. But during this period they were getting downright bizarre. I began to wonder if I could hack the deployment psychologically.

Then one day I was sitting in the mess tent talking to a Marine who told me that he had gotten up moments before I arrived and launched himself at his sergeant. He had beaten the hell out of the man. It seems the sergeant had been hitting on the Marine's sister back in the States. He said the guys around him had to pull him off the hapless NCO.

Incredibly, he also relayed to me that none of it really happened. His imagination "took over" while he was sitting at chow. He had just sat through a complete hallucination. He told me he had heard that the medication they gave us to prevent malaria caused weird stuff like that to happen. I considered that the meds might be the cause of my emotional discomfort.

When I dreamed I was in bed with talking turtles, I became convinced that he was right. Since a mosquito at KAF would have needed to fly around in a mini temperature-controlled space suit, I decided to quit taking the medicine. It worked. My mood swings—along with my oddball dreams—left me. Later, when we departed KAF, I began taking it again—I really didn't want malaria. But the strange mood swings and dreams did not return.

I took up space in the Dutch recreation center. I was there so often they knew me by sight and would wave a cheerful "hello" when I walked in. I began to call it my "office." I told Frank and other Marines if I wasn't around and they wanted me, they should check for me there.

The Dutch sold Internet time at a reasonable price. Getting signed up required assistance from one of the bilingual folks who worked there—the account was based out of the Netherlands, and all the instructions were in Dutch. But once signed on, hallelujah—there was the world of the Internet, with no lines, no rushing, and no waiting. Fortunately, the check signers had issued me a laptop.

The television was almost always on. Located in the middle of the center, surrounded by a couch and easy chairs, it was a large-screen color TV. Unfortunately, it broadcast Dutch television, and there were no subtitles. Still, it could be amusing to watch. Best of all, the Dutch made real milk shakes with real ice cream. They also had cool—not cold—Diet Cokes. I couldn't be certain that it was air-conditioned—as I would still sweat—but it was definitely cooler than any of the other places available for us to hang around in. Most importantly, the Internet helped me to beat the cruel boredom.

One night the entire base got a real treat. Toby Keith was doing a USO show and would appear at the Boardwalk. Since the Boardwalk surrounded a huge hollow square—except for the hockey rink—there was plenty of room for spectators. Although most servicepeople tried to get as close to the stage as possible, I reasoned that if a suicide bomber somehow made it past security that would be the best place to detonate, so I hung back out of range. Twenty years of street law enforcement work has left me a tad suspicious. On my job we used to say, "Just because you're paranoid doesn't mean they're *not* out to get you." My pictures were long-distance, but peace of mind made up for the loss of clarity.

I have to admit I was overjoyed. I had been hearing about USO shows all my life. Bob Hope and a long line of famous people had been entertaining troops overseas since World War II, and here I was—actually present at one. I will also unabashedly confess that I will be a Toby Keith fan for the rest of my life, out of gratitude.

I guess the Taliban were miffed that they weren't invited, because right in the middle of the show, the IDF sirens sounded. Civilians ran like hell for the concrete-and-steel shelters; rear-echelon troops followed at a brisk pace. Only Marines and a smattering of combat-savvy soldiers remained. We had already figured out that the sirens gave NO advance warning. They only sounded AFTER the incoming rounds had hit. The greatest danger from IDF at KAF was getting run over by military police racing by on dirt roads at about a hundred miles per hour. They had their lights and sirens on and were in an awful hurry to get God knows where. As an ex-cop I always suspected that they just wanted to drive hell-for-leather and that the incoming IDF sirens was an excuse.

Toby Keith and company were quickly surrounded and ushered off the stage. The rest of us stayed where we were and talked while we waited. We had a feeling he'd be back. This was a disturbing breach of discipline to the military police (MPs). They kept telling all of us that we had to go to a shelter. By then the sirens had been silent for about ten minutes and whatever IDF there had been was so far off that we never even heard the rounds hit the ground, but that made no difference. We were supposed to take shelter. The MPs were quietly ignored. They weren't Marine MPs.

Small pockets were finally persuaded to wander off, probably figuring the concert was over; most remained. Finally an Army major told us we had to move, and we obeyed. We crossed a dirt road to the nearest shelters only to discover that they were so full we had to stand outside anyway. Almost immediately thereafter, Toby Keith came back onstage. We raced back and enthusiastically applauded as he picked up right where he left off in the middle of a song. He finished the concert. I still really appreciate his efforts.

April turned into May. I had left the States on March 25. My morale was low. I spent more and more time at my "Dutch office," surfing the Web. It was the only bright spot in my day.

Finally we got word that we were going to move forward. I was not reluctant to leave KAF.

7

On to Bastion

Our next stop was to be the massive British base called Bastion. To minimize the possibility of ambush, each of 2/7's companies moved to Bastion separately, at staggered times and in the dead of night. From Bastion each company would move forward again to its respective area of operations.

I departed KAF with Golf Company. I wouldn't see Frank again until the very end of the deployment. We left in the modern replacement for the venerable Jeep Willy known as a Humvee or Hummer. I rode in an up-armored Hummer driven by Corporal Cory Becker. "Up-armored" meant it had extra armor as protection against bullets and rocket-propelled grenades (RPGs). Hummers remained vulnerable to IEDs, however. "Doc" Kody Watkins, our Navy corpsman, rode in the front passenger seat. Lance Corporal Mike Michalak manned the M240 machine gun in the turret.

I was designated by Sergeant Joe France, the squad leader, as Michalak's replacement on the gun, should Michalak become a casualty. It had been decades since I had fired a machine gun, and then it was a different model, the M60. I remembered the tactics of using the weapon, but I needed to be brought up to speed on the M240 model. Sergeant France grinned as he taught me. I'm sure he got a kick out of instructing a gray-haired fifty-eight-year-old former Jarhead on the gun.

I smiled inwardly as he did so.

I was the only passenger in the backseat. The only other rear seat had gear and water piled high. Water and MREs were carried everywhere, even tied on the outside of the vehicle. I'm only five feet, eight inches tall, and my knees were crammed against the metal support of the front seat. I had to sit semi-sideways to keep from banging them every time we hit a bump. I can't imagine anyone taller even fitting into the backseat, let alone remaining there for hours. Throughout the deployment I spent countless hours in a Humvee and I was never comfortable in the backseat.

We pulled out in the middle of the night. It was good to finally be moving forward. It was a tad scary as well. KAF was safe. The IDF they threw at us was akin to a lightning storm with only a couple of bolts striking the ground every once in a great while. The odds were definitely in our favor. Sure, people do get hit by lightning, but not too often.

———

Anybody who remained constantly behind the wire at KAF and brags about their combat duty is a BS artist. You can recognize them by the gaudy "self-proclaimed hero" T-shirts they bought at the Boardwalk. They'll read "I'm a Taliban Hill Fighter" and other such crap. I bought a couple of T-shirts because I thought they were funny. One read, "Operation Enduring Freedom, been there, done that, got the T-shirt." They fit my sense of humor but I almost never wear them.

At long last, we were leaving the wire. We drove through the city of Kandahar in the wee hours of the morning. Kandahar city is the birthplace of the Taliban movement. It spread from there to other parts of Afghanistan, but Kandahar is its heart and soul. Driving through its darkened streets was spooky. Now and again a pedestrian would be seen. They would stop and stare. Our convoy was a long one. We drove single file, one vehicle behind the other. I don't know how many vehicles were in it, but it was a *long* convoy. It must have taken the entire company, driving slowly, quite a while to clear the city.

Finally we were out of the city and on the open road. The pace quickened, but only slightly. A convoy that long can't travel very fast. The "accordion effect" kicks in. Think of rush hour in a city. The sheer volume of traffic causes drivers to slow down, speed up, then slow down again.

We traveled on what is known as the "Ring Road." It is the only paved road outside a major city in the entire country. It was built by the Soviets during their occupation. It rings around all of Afghanistan; hence the name, I guess. While conferring with international police at KAF I'd heard it referred to as "the *real* border of Afghanistan." The international forces bolstering the Kabul government have been trying to pacify all the districts around the Ring Road for some time. Too bad they didn't read the history of the Soviet invasion. The Ring Road was the only area the Soviets actually controlled.

They still didn't win the war.

I liked traveling on the Ring Road because it wasn't as bumpy as was driving off-road and was therefore easier on my knees. I also liked it because there was less danger from IEDs. It's difficult to dig through a paved surface, and unlike Iraq there wasn't garbage and junk alongside the roads—where IEDs could be hidden. There was very little that was thrown away in Afghanistan. It is a very poor country, and people would find some use for other people's garbage.

Also unlike Iraq, the IEDs were universally victim-detonated— meaning somebody or something had to put weight on the detonator. In Iraq there were mostly remote-detonated IEDs. Someone watching would decide when to blow it and send an electronic signal to the charge. Victim-detonated IEDs couldn't be placed on a paved road.

We drove on all night, hour after endless hour, out in the country, unable to see much besides the taillights of the vehicle in front, and the headlights of the vehicle behind. As dawn broke, so did one of the vehicles up front. The whole column came to a halt while repairs were made. Our vehicle was stopped very near a mud-walled settlement that came clear down to the road on our left. Off to the right side of the road there was nothing but a marsh. Replete with tall reeds, it was unusual to see standing or flowing water in the Afghanistan desert. A small stream that ran under the road and fed into the marsh was observable to our left rear.

Soon we attracted attention. Children and a very elderly adult male appeared. The very youngest were toddlers who paid us no mind. They played in the dirt like youngsters everywhere. I took some comfort from their presence. As long as they were there, we wouldn't be attacked. I studied the older kids and the older adult intently. I had yet to confidently establish baseline behavior for Afghans. In what ways were body movements universal? As yet I didn't know. I *had* to know in order to "read" their intentions with my eyes. The older kids were begging for candy or food. At first Michalak threw some to them; later, as time dragged on, their nonstop entreaties became annoying.

Another man appeared. He was younger than the first adult, but not a young man. I guessed he was in early middle age. I didn't like the look of him. He smiled with his mouth but not with his eyes. I had seen that look many times before throughout my career. It was usually not a good sign.

I got out of the vehicle and checked the nearest structure. Everything was made of adobe. It was empty but led to a corridor from which anyone could have approached us unseen. That did not make me happy. I felt vulnerable being stuck where we were. We had no room to move. There was a vehicle directly in front of us, and another directly behind. That building was the logical place for an enemy to engage us. It was much too close for my comfort. Later the company gunny gave Corporal Becker hell for letting me out of the vehicle.

Poor Becker. I didn't ask; I just got out.

I found out afterward that the gunny was with Doc Miclea in Iraq when a sniper shot the doc near his femoral artery. Doc had also gotten out of his vehicle back then. And he nearly bought the farm. The gunny didn't want to see that happen to me. What the gunny—and others— still had to realize was that I wasn't a VIP. I was an armed embedded member of the battalion. My life wasn't worth any more than the young Marines around me. Their moms loved them too. Moreover, I was a former Marine officer. I could read the battle space. If the enemy thought as I did, we would have been the first in the convoy to die.

But the children were still playing there a without a care in the world.

We were stuck at that place for a long time. Eventually the second man, who didn't smile with his eyes, said something to the older children. My perception was that he had told them to leave. One of them didn't seem to want to go. The man changed the tone of his voice to one of authority, and they all got up. Ominously, the older kids took the little ones with them. They didn't all jump up and leave at once. First the kids left. Then after a short time, the old man meandered away. Finally, the second man turned and walked away from us. Their manner of leaving struck me as staged.

Just prior to his turning a corner he glanced back and I saw it. The "felony look" was written all over his face. So it *was* universal after all.

Surprisingly, there are a lot of cell phones in Afghanistan. And the Taliban are known to use them extensively. I thought, "This guy is about to make a phone call." If there was going to be an attack on our position, it would have come from inside the building I had checked earlier. I never took my eyes off that place.

My apprehension was growing minute by minute.

Luckily, we began to move. We were fortunate in more ways than one. We had overhead air cover provided by the 101st Army Airborne Division. Their Kiowa helicopter gunships had been our guardian angels all day. Just as we started to move, the Kiowas made contact with the enemy on the ground. I wondered if the Taliban were responding to the "felony look" guy and moving toward us when they were spotted. It's very difficult to catch sight of people on the ground who don't want to be seen—unless they are moving. The human eye picks up movement very quickly. I was fascinated by the sights and sounds of the Kiowas attacking their targets. Kiowa machine guns could plainly be heard as well as their rockets being launched.

The enemy wasn't that far off.

The plan all along was for us to rest during daylight inside a small Canadian FOB astride the Ring Road and move out again after dark. The FOB was only a short distance away. After we pulled in, I was told that the Kiowas had taken hits. One had landed inside the FOB to inspect the aircraft but, deciding it was sound, the pilot took off again and rejoined the fray. I stood on the roof of a vehicle and watched. I could see the choppers going in for the kill and circling the target area. I could hear their machine guns chattering and watch their rockets swoosh toward the ground. I was told that several of the choppers had taken hits. Thankfully, there were no American casualties. The Kiowas must have done their work well, as we had no contact with the Taliban that day.

The Canadian FOB was typical of a small outpost. It was surrounded by Hesco barriers as walls. Hesco barriers were named for their inventor, I think. They were essentially huge, wide sandbags. They could stop anything the enemy might throw at them. The entire concept reminded me of the kind of temporary fortifications the Romans used to throw up whenever a legion stopped. Except the Romans did all the digging themselves, and we had machinery. The ground inside was covered with large gravel rocks. Since there were only a small number of soldiers stationed there, there were only a couple of buildings. Not nearly enough to get Golf Company out of the desert sun.

We parked our vehicles in rows inside the FOB, in baking sunlight, and there we stayed. We drank the water we had brought with us—it was all hot. And we tried to get some sleep. Forget about all that talk of heat back at KAF. The temperature there was delightful compared to what we experienced in the Canadian FOB. It was still only May but the sun was searing. The rocks radiated heat back up at us from the ground. Inside the vehicles the temperature was oven-like. Sleeping inside one of them was not an option.

Our gunny simply crawled under a vehicle and went to sleep on the gravel in the shade the truck provided. I decided that was a good idea, but with one modification. I unrolled my issue sleeping pad and lay on it. Back in my active duty days I had gotten used to napping whenever I could in the field, and I used my eight-point "soft cover" to block the light from my eyes. It also kept flies off part of my face.

The new-style cover is an improvement. The brim is slightly longer. The old one was just the right length to touch the tip of my nose as I breathed. That tickled and made it harder to sleep. The new one is per-fect. The longer brim also kept flies off more of my face. I secretly made a deal with the flies. I wouldn't swat at them as long as they stayed off my face. The rest of me was fair game. I would negotiate the same deal with many of their winged comrades in the coming months. Most of them cooperated.

As the sun began to set, its rays became horizontal and finally reached where I was sleeping under the vehicle. The heat woke me up. I don't know how long I slept, but I awoke refreshed. I drank some more hot water and ate an MRE. I swear the gunny slept at the position of attention—rocks and all. He was a gunny. He just changed his batteries from time to time and he kept right on going.

Shortly before dark we pulled out and continued our trek toward Bastion. In the remaining daylight I looked out at Afghanistan and marveled at the utter desolation. That people would fight over this country seemed absurd. Some Afghans actually thought we were trying to conquer them and take their land. If they had ever seen so much as a picture of the United States they would have realized how ridiculous that idea was. You couldn't pay an American to live where I was looking. The most desolate locale in the United States looked good compared to what I was witnessing. Soon enough it was dark again and there was nothing to see but taillights in front and headlights behind.

Then we came upon it. The strangest, most eerie sight I saw the whole time I was in Afghanistan. In total darkness we slowly, carefully, watchfully drove past two large burning trucks by the side of the road. The night was eerily silent. Naturally we suspected an ambush, but none developed. There was no sign of human life. There were bags and bags of rice and other foodstuffs scattered about on the ground. The mutely burning, abandoned trucks are etched into my memory. History repeats itself. It was as if we were a cavalry patrol apprehensively passing burning pioneer wagons in Apache country.

One truck afire might have been a vehicle malfunction, but two? I had to conclude that they had been destroyed by the Taliban. The fact that they left all that food, though, was perplexing. Maybe they just took what little they could carry and left the rest, bags torn open, strewn about—useless. I'll never know.

I also wondered what had become of the drivers. The convoy didn't stop to check.

As we continued on into the second night, fatigue really began to set in. I was feeling it and I wasn't even driving. Becker had been doing all the driving since we left KAF. The stop-and-go stuff was understandable and unavoidable. It was frustrating and fatiguing all the same. The sooner we reached Bastion, the sooner we could get out of these cramped vehicles and get some proper sleep. The inevitable occurred. During one long stop all four of us fell asleep. I came to when the glare of headlights reflected off the driver's-side mirror right into my face. It was the vehicle behind us coming up to see what was wrong. A look through the windshield told the story: the taillights of the vehicle to our front were a long way off.

I yelled at the top of my lungs, "WAKE UP!" But Becker was out cold. I had to smack him hard on the back of his Kevlar helmet to bring him to—an action he didn't particularly appreciate at the time. We caught up and stayed awake for the remainder of the trip. I later heard at Bastion that people falling asleep during the long stops was commonplace.

The sun rose and we were still driving. Finally, we turned off the Ring Road onto an obviously well-traveled sand road surrounded by miles of open, barren desert. That was comforting, as it would be unlikely that anyone in our convoy would trigger an IED. The dirt road led directly to Bastion. As soon as we had parked our vehicles and squared away our gear, we were taken to a large open air-conditioned dome-shaped building loaded with bunk beds. The whole company piled in, oblivious to the Brits already billeted there and whose space we were invading. We all fell into a deep sleep.

———

We weren't there long. We had maybe a week to enjoy air-conditioned sleeping, showers in a nearby building, and a small PX that sold ice cream a short walk away. Howell found the ice cream; he was good for stuff like that. I have no doubt that had there been beer he would have found it. We had to race the sun to see if we could eat the stuff before it melted. We had to eat fast. All too soon the days of air-conditioning would end.

Before they did, however, the company commander took a detail of armored vehicles and went forward to recon certain positions the company would be occupying. I had been sent to him to be an asset. But to be of use I had to get out from behind the wire, so the fact that he didn't take me along was exasperating. It wasn't the first time he had left me in the rear; he had done so at KAF several times. I could have been more useful to the battalion if I had gone with him rather than keeping the Dutch company. I had dropped all the subtle hints at my command, but obviously to no avail. Passive neglect was beginning to get to me.

So much for subtlety; I was incensed. Bastion was a huge base. I walked hours in the dark to find the battalion commander. I knew the long walk would do me good. I needed to calm down. I was extremely angry. I have never liked being someone's baggage. I didn't like it on active duty when I had to trot along with nothing real to do, and I didn't like it any the more in Afghanistan. Given the opportunity I will always find *some* way to make myself useful.

When I got to the battalion command post, the colonel was in a meeting. Major Helton asked me what the problem was, so I told him. I explained that I simply *had* to get "eyes on" the country to be of any use to anyone. I let him know that the "check signers" had all of us LEPs sign a memo of understanding that we were going to be in danger of death or serious injury where we were going. We had all accepted that fact. We simply were *not* VIPs. Now I needed the battalion to stop treating me like one. I used the analogy that I couldn't solve a bank robbery while sitting at my desk. The first step in the investigation was to get to the bank.

The executive officer seemed to understand and promised to speak with the company commander. He obviously did. The CO never left me behind again for the remainder of the time I was with him.

Since there wasn't enough room at the CP location, the companies that were pushing out for the hinterland first were assigned billeting closest to the CP. As they left, however, we were relocated. Our new digs were canvas tents with an additional layer of canvas on top to give extra protection from the burning sun. The flooring was made of black plastic interlocking mats. Moreover, every tent was air-conditioned. As had been the case in Iraq, I found I needed to sleep inside my British sleeping bag despite the outside temperature. The temperature inside those tents struck me as freezing. I sorely wished for a personal thermostat. I was certain that standing water would freeze inside the tent, and boil outside of it.

I ended up, coincidentally, in the same tent as Lieutenant Brewster and the staff NCOs who were going with him to Golestan. Looking back on it, our paths crossed so many times both in the States and in the rear in Afghanistan that I shouldn't have been surprised that I would spend most of my time in country with him. Personally I think Providence provides us with little clues as we make our way through life, if only we are tuned in to Him.

While the enlisted Marines all had cots to sleep on, we "privileged" few slept on the plastic deck. I, at least, used my issue inflatable sleeping pad. It was another prerogative of an old man, I suppose. The evenings were spent standing off away from the discussion and observing Lieutenant Brewster planning his checkpoints at the place he would be occupying. From what I could see of the topographical map, he was really going to be "out there." I was secretly relieved to discover that veteran gunnery sergeant Manny Mendoza was going with him. The gunny would bring experience to the young lieutenant's staff.

Several evenings Gunny Mendoza and I would sit outside our tent in lawn chairs drinking nonalcoholic beer and reminiscing about the "old" Marine Corps. He had joined roughly as I got out, so we both had common memories. We understood each other as only contemporaries could, and we spoke of the changes we had seen in the Corps. We also spoke of the Taliban and their tactics and how some of the Iraq veterans were in for a shock. The gunny resolved to shake them out of their comfort zone. Since he was a huge man, well over six feet tall and as wide as I was tall—all muscle—he cut an imposing figure. I had no doubt he could do it. In view of the fact that we later worked closely together, it's good that we got to know each other at that time. A foundation of mutual respect was laid while drinking those no-octane beers.

Also part of Lieutenant Brewster's staff, and in the same tent as I, was Staff Sergeant (SSGT) Justin Wells. SSGT Wells was the man on the ground who would guide aircraft onto any targets that might require air support. Since the air wing personnel all have nicknames, pilots had long since christened Wells "Noxious." I changed that to "Obnoxious." For his part, he reveled in referring to me as "Tough Guy Terry." I have no idea why, unless it's because a guy my age running around with that crowd needed a hard-hitting nickname to survive.

Lieutenant Colonel Hall and the battalion staff established the battalion command post at Bastion. The CP was named "Camp Barber," in honor of a Korean War captain and member of 2nd Battalion, 7th Marines who—with his Marines—had done the impossible and held off repeated Chinese onslaughts at the "Frozen Chosen." Captain Barber was awarded the Medal of Honor for his unbelievable feat. My uncle Bill had been just down the road from Captain Barber.

The battalion plan was to strategically place FOBs all over the battalion's area of operations (AO). Since there hadn't been much enemy activity in the Golf Company AO, it was determined that platoon-size FOBs would be sufficient. Golf Company, like all Marine infantry companies, had three rifle platoons. Ordinarily that would have meant three FOBs. However, there was a strategically important FOB under construction on the Ring Road just outside a town called Delaram. One of 1st Platoon's squads was to be sent there along with two anti-tank mobile units. Therefore, Lieutenant Brewster's 1st Platoon would be one rifle squad short. This caused grave concern later on—he was really out on a limb.

Undaunted, Brewster took his two rifle squads and attachments from Weapons Company and headed straight for Golestan. There was nothing waiting for him there. He'd have to dig in and deal with conditions as he found them.

Second Platoon drove the Taliban out of a town called Bala Baluk. Their success was so resounding after a short, sharp firefight that personally, upon arrival, I thought the fighting in and around Bala Baluk was over.

Third Platoon was bound for a place called Baqua. It was smack in the middle of opium-growing country and was known to be heavily saturated with IEDs. The company commander was taking 3rd Platoon to Baqua along with heavy equipment and engineers who would build the FOB. I joined his personal security detail (PSD) and went along.

8

Baqua

When we left Bastion I rode with a different crew. Lance Corporal Dave Demanske drove, with Corporal Justin Durham in the front passenger seat. Lance Corporal Brady Christiansen was in the turret. Demanske was a blond-haired, soft-spoken guy who was impossible not to like. Durham was the vehicle commander and seemed completely relaxed with me; I was glad of that. Christiansen was a zany character who reminded me of myself at his age—not necessarily a good thing.

The main road to Baqua was deemed to be too dangerous due to IEDs, so it was determined that we'd slip in the "back door." There really was no back door—we were going to make one. We'd use dry riverbeds as roads. We did that quite often throughout the deployment. They were much safer than the roads. It's hard to figure out where to plant an IED in a dry riverbed.

We approached Baqua in two stages. First, we left Bastion and once again drove on the Ring Road. Although we had some distance to travel, it was daylight and our column was smaller. The paved road made for good traveling time. Nonetheless, it took the better part of a day to get where we were going. We stopped for the night at an unpretentious U.S. Army position that was too small for us to get inside. We probably had twenty or thirty vehicles in our convoy. We pulled the vehicles into some kind of defensive position on another of those large gravel rocky areas that radiated heat back up at us. Then we waited.

The terrain we were going to cover was much too rough to traverse at night. We would leave the following morning. We ate MREs, drank hot water, and passed the time, glad to be out of the cramped Humvees. It was there that I sat on the roof of a Humvee looking down the open machine-gun turret to watch a movie being played by Lance Corporal Mike Trujillo. He played it on his laptop in the middle of the front seat area. Marines were also watching from anywhere they could, inside or outside the vehicle. The film was *Charlie Wilson's War*, a movie about U.S. involvement with insurgents when the Russians were in Afghanistan.

It was terribly ironic to be watching it in Afghanistan. I remember near the end of the movie the crowd was shouting *Allahu akbar!* It was displayed on the screen in English subtitles as "Thank you, America!" My God, I thought, how could the moviemakers be so ignorant? Although it is perfectly acceptable to say *Allahu akbar!* out of piety, it is often used as a war cry. And it's likely to be the last thing you will hear on this earth if you find yourself too near a suicide bomber. It means "God is great!" Most definitely *not* "Thank you, America."

It was also there that I began to spend more time hanging out with our forward air controller, whom I had first met back at Twenty-nine Palms during Mojave Viper—Captain Eric "D-Ring" Terhune. Although he was a fighter pilot, he was rotated to the ground side of the Marine Corps, as is the accepted routine. The Marine Corps long ago learned the immense value of close air support to the infantry, and there is no one who can better communicate with pilots in the air than a pilot on the ground.

D-Ring was older than everybody else except me, and like me, was an "attachment" to Golf Company rather than an assigned member. As such, and being an officer, he had few friends in the company. He was affable, and I liked the way he interacted with the enlisted Marines. He was their senior, but he treated them with decency. I like that trait in an officer. He was also older than most of the enlisted guys with whom we traveled—nowhere near as old as me, of course—and it was a pleasant change of pace to converse with someone with a bit more time on the planet.

The next day we moved out. Once again it was single file. Our convoy stretched quite a distance. We had Marine engineers with us by then, along with other attachments. I was in the second-to-last vehicle; D-Ring was behind me—dead last. The terrain was no doubt worse than expected. Vehicles, especially those pulling trailers, kept getting stuck. The short, steep inclines of dry washes that crossed our front were particularly troublesome. The soil of western Afghanistan was rocky, sandy desert. What the rushing water from a bygone rainy season had left behind *were* loose sand and gravel. We spent a lot of time at a dead stop while vehicles somewhere out of sight were extricated.

Although it was still only spring, the heat was on the rise with each passing day, and also with each passing hour. We had packed what was felt to be plenty of water, but the trip was taking much longer than we had anticipated. We gulped the elixir of life down at a prodigious rate. To beat the boredom, whenever we stopped for a long period, I would get out of my vehicle and walk back to D-Ring's. He had a radio and could hear the company commander's communications with various elements of the convoy, so D-Ring had a better idea of what was going on than the rest of us.

During one such stop I asked him to take my picture. Against a backdrop of pure desert desolation, standing in a dry river wash, there I was—sunburned, flak jacket open, soft cover on, wearing a pistol and carrying a rifle. I was probably the only Marine in the battalion to carry a Vietnam-era magazine holder. I was carrying twelve magazines instead of the issued seven. I have always held to the "better too much than too little" theory when it comes to ammunition. The look on my face says it all. It was hot; we were burning up, thirsty, and tired. We still had a long way to go.

After hours of slow movement we had to refuel our Humvee. Demanske and Durham used five-gallon cans to refill the tank. Since we had topped off before leaving that morning, this was not a good sign. Hour upon hour the motor march continued at a snail's tempo. We were still sucking down water at an alarming pace. We were getting low. During many of our frequent stops, somebody in the vehicle would approach other Humvees to see how they were stocked with water. It wasn't good. Everybody was running out. We just kept hoping Baqua wasn't much farther.

As we neared our destination we passed uncountable acres of poppy fields. They had already been harvested, but what the crop had been was unmistakable. I had been told that Afghanistan produces 96 percent of the *world's* opium. Seeing that vast expanse, I could believe it. Afghanistan grows poppies like people in Nebraska grow corn. That's all we saw for uncountable miles. We also passed pile after pile of dried poppy plants. They were the pods piled up in odd-looking mounds.

Marines asked me what they were looking at. I explained that they were next year's seed crop. The fields would be sown with the contents of each pod. During one stop, I broke one open and ate the seeds. My companions were aghast. They acted like I was doing drugs. I explained that what I had just eaten was exactly what they ate on a poppy seed bagel or hard roll. It takes an evolutionary step-by-step process to turn the plants into a drug.

It took thirteen and a half broiling, thirsty hours to reach Baqua. Long before we got there we had run completely out of water. We were parched. The water may have been hot, but it was wet. Thirst in a superheated desert cannot be described in words. We sat in our vehicles and roasted.

Michalak, in another vehicle, had gotten some dirty ice before leaving. He bought it from a local Afghan who hadn't used clean water. There was actually dirt visible in the ice. Michalak had kept it in a cooler attached to the outside of his Humvee to keep the contents—water and soda—cool. The ice had long since melted and the contents were long gone. He drank that dirty water right out of the cooler, deciding he'd take his chances on getting sick later.

When we finally reached Baqua, D-Ring stormed forward to confront the company commander and find out why the men had not been given a water resupply. His flushed face was not entirely due to the heat; he was livid. His body English magnified the effect. A stocky, muscular man, he would have been a formidable opponent in a fight. Of course he was not going to fight; he was a Marine, and the CO was in command. But D-Ring was clearly in a bad mood. I learned later that he and the company commander had gone head-to-head in a heated exchange. D-Ring was a Marine's Marine. To him, the troops came first.

D-Ring told me the company CO had said the men could wait. He also told me that the CO had water for himself. That kind of self-centered behavior was so unlike a typical Marine officer that I had to see for myself. I walked forward, and sure enough, a one-liter bottle of water produced at Bastion was sticking out of that man's carry pouch. The Brits at Bastion bottled their own water from their own wells at the base. The plastic water bottles have a distinct look. Since I had personally observed him bumming water, cigarettes, and food from his men during the trip, I have to assume that he had been out of water and had just gotten some.

I'll be honest. I never liked that man. I still don't. But after that incident, I lost all respect for him as well.

D-Ring had also learned that somebody had screwed up. What was supposed to be a trailer full of water had mistakenly been left behind. The trailer that was believed to be carrying water was not. There would be nothing until the next day, when the Army would come to our rescue. A scant few bottles of Bastion water were found and passed around. About twenty of us shared a one-liter bottle. A few short swallows is all anybody got. It was all the water we had. It was all there would be until the next day.

It speaks well of the continuing tradition of brotherhood in the Corps that no one supervised the passing around of that lone water bottle. Everybody just took a little and handed it to the Marine next to him. We were all excruciatingly thirsty. Yet there were no selfish Marines in the entire group. The guys who drank first probably took the least. There was no complaining. Marines tend to take the worst conditions in stride. Still, I remembered the lesson I had learned in 1977—the desert heat can kill a man.

The Army guys from the small FOB we had just left, unencumbered by a long convoy, made better time than we had. By 10:00 a.m. the following day they came to our rescue with as much hot water as they could spare. Although I would pass the summer months at another location, the hottest I ever was in Afghanistan—or anywhere else on this earth, for that matter—was at Baqua.

Later, when I found myself sitting in front of Lieutenant Colonel Hall's desk, I was sorely tempted to "drop the dime" and tell him all about our company commander. But I just couldn't bring myself to do it. Nobody likes a snitch, and I didn't want to be one.

Baqua was the name of an old—probably historic—ruin. Rumor had it that it had once been the fortress of a king, or the residence of a wealthy merchant. Allegedly it sat astride what was a major caravan route between Europe and the Far East in the distant past. Its days of glory were long gone. It was nothing more than an unoccupied adobe-walled ruin with huge cracks in its parapets and crumbling mud buildings within. It squatted in the middle of the desert floor—baking in the glare of the relentless sun.

The vehicle I was in, and others, took up a defensive position behind the ruin. A very large crack in the wall was there, big enough for a man to pass through. The vehicles were arranged in a semicircle around that fissure. Each Humvee had a turret with an automatic weapon. The turrets were manned around the clock. The Hesco FOB was to be built outside the ruin, but until it was completed, the old walls were our protection. And we were guarding the rear entrance.

The Marine officer in me felt compelled to check out the terrain for myself. I went for a walk alone. Most of my professional life I have operated on the "forgiveness is easier to obtain than permission" theory, so I just went without asking anyone. I could see a walled Afghan civilian compound not far off, which could easily have served as an assembly area (a place for the enemy to gather). Not visible unless the ground was actually walked on, as I was then doing, was a concealed avenue of approach—an irrigation ditch. The furrow was shallow but deep enough for a man to crawl in—unobserved. A smaller ruin—a beaten-down adobe barrier and a few old buildings—obscured our ability to see the logical exit point from the ditch.

An enemy could have entered the minor ruin unobserved and moved through its crumbling buildings to an adobe barricade. It was a mere twenty-five yards from us. From that point, the Taliban could have been on us in seconds. Once they had overrun *us*—guarding the "back door"—they could have entered the large crack in the wall. It would have provided them with easy access to the upper ramparts—the "high ground." From that position small-arms fire and rocket-propelled grenades could have been rained on the Marines inside the ancient fortress. It goes without saying that I was deeply concerned about our tactical disposition.

I pointed this out to the NCO in charge of the position (not Corporal Durham) and advised him to alleviate the problem by moving our vehicles and us inside the minor ruin. From there we could observe any enemy exiting the irrigation ditch and cover the crack in the wall as well. It had the additional advantage of providing an adobe wall around our position. He wouldn't do it. He was afraid of the company commander. I told him to ask permission. It was an eminently reasonable realignment—surely the CO would see that and agree. The NCO wouldn't do it. The company CO was considered highly unapproachable by his men.

So once again I went off by myself. I took up a position inside the lesser ruin, from which I could observe the potential avenue of approach. I was prepared to stand solitary guard all night. The NCO was distraught. I didn't care. I was right to be concerned. Lance Corporal Tim Perkins found me in the dark and told me there was no way he was going to let me stand guard alone.

I knew if push came to shove I could explain myself to the battalion commander. I had already photographed the assembly area, the irrigation ditch, the small compound, and its relationship to our position—as well as the crack in the rear wall. I had also taken pictures from the top of the walls looking down at vulnerable Marines inside the old fortress. The investigator in me was prepared to go to trial. I felt sure the battalion commander would agree that our rear was inadequately protected and that I had done the right thing. Alternatively I was prepared to accept responsibility for my actions. But Tim risked perdition from the CO. I will always respect him for that.

The whole affair created another "white knuckle" internal struggle for me when I sat with the battalion commander in days to come. I badly wanted to tell him how tactically inadequate our CO was. But as much as I respected the colonel, and as much as I believed that he valued me and would have listened, I just couldn't bring myself to squeal. I still wonder if I was right to withhold the information.

In December 2008, at a memorial service for battalion Marines killed in action (KIA) during the deployment I learned for the first time that the company commander had been relieved of duty—fired—by Lieutenant Colonel Hall while still in Afghanistan. I was overjoyed.

Finally the NCO in charge asked me if there was some other disposition he could make that would satisfy my instincts and not cause him to move the entire unit. By moving one armored vehicle to the corner of the main ruin, observation could be kept on the potential avenue of approach—its existence now known. It wasn't the best troop disposition that could have been made, but it would do. He made the change on his own initiative and Tim and I returned from our solitary post.

As I recall, the NCO was highly put out because I had questioned his judgment. He felt things were fine the way they were. After all, he said, this wasn't his first "rodeo"—referring to a prior deployment to Iraq. The rodeo analogy didn't persuade me. I had been a captain. I was trained to attack. What I saw alarmed me because it was how I would have taken our position if I were the enemy. Willful blindness and/or a desire to be popular were not going to impede my usefulness to the Marines I was in Afghanistan to support. I kept things as low-key as my conscience would allow and stayed "inside my lane" as best I could. But some things were blatantly wrong and I would not stay silent. Throughout the entire deployment there were many times when it was difficult for me to keep my mouth shut.

As Lieutenant Brewster would later put it, I had to "walk a fine line."

———

I had learned a lot since my own Iraq experience. Prior to entering *this* country, I had diligently studied the Taliban and their tactics. I realized how differently the Taliban fought than the enemy in Iraq did. Afghanistan wasn't Iraq. This was going to be an entirely different kind of war. Ironically, the "boots"—the new guys, green and untested—were all ears.

At one point I asked my buddy Lance Corporal Steve Jorgensen how many firefights he had been in during his Iraq deployment. He told me seven. I asked him to guess how much time all seven had taken. He guessed about an hour and forty-five minutes. When the Taliban attacked our FOB at Golestan, they kept at it for three hours. When a "firefight" lasts that long, it's no longer a firefight. It's a battle.

Afghanistan was definitely *not* the same "rodeo."

Meanwhile, back inside the semicircle, we slept on the ground, ready for instant action. I tried to sleep with my rifle under my right hand and wore my pistol all night. My flak vest was my pillow. None of us changed clothes or washed up for the whole time we were there.

I left my boots on day and night for so long I developed ringworm. It was the first and only time in my life I had gotten it. Doc Watkins gave me some ointment to put on it. The ointment worked. Doc admonished me to return the ointment to him, as it was the only tube he had. Long after we had gone our separate ways, I realized I still had it.

Sorry, Doc.

It didn't take the Taliban long to react to our presence. They began to launch rockets at us pretty much every evening just before dark. I'm sure their reasoning was that if they got into trouble, the coming of darkness would assist them to escape. I stood on the very top of the walls and yelled "INCOMING!" when I saw the telltale yellow smoke trail the rockets left behind. The Marines had been ordered to take cover. I stayed on the walls wearing no body armor and only a soft cover (hat).

Another reason I stayed on the walls was because the ANP were up there. They were all armed. So was I. I didn't trust them one bit. The Marines were below them, so I stayed on the same level. I had learned how to watch someone without their knowledge in my law enforcement days. I used my peripheral vision and keenly observed their expressions and movements. I wasn't wearing body armor, but neither were they. I was also mentally ready to take them on if necessary. Whether I was completely successful or not, it would have bought some time for the Marines below.

I was beginning to enjoy my newfound freedom of action. With independence came flexibility. I could not only think outside the box, I could act outside it as well. I wasn't limited to a military approach. I could utilize my entire life's experiences—military and law enforcement—as a synthesis. I had tacit authorization from the battalion commander to place myself in positions where I could observe what I needed to. My personal safety was no longer a hindrance.

The enemy rockets were very inaccurate. They never even came close. I could follow the path of their smoke trails and tell where they were going to land. We had two 81mm mortars set up inside the ruin, and they returned fire. It's impossible to know if they had any effect; the insurgents were firing from a concealed position, and it was a long distance away. Although I still remembered how to call for fire on a target, I couldn't be of any help to the mortarmen. The enemy was too well concealed in flat, featureless terrain characterized by chest-high brush. I could see, in a general sort of way, where the rockets were, but I couldn't quite tell where our mortar rounds were landing. Hence I couldn't suggest any adjustments.

Oddly enough, I reveled in it all—yellow smoke pouring from incoming rockets, the 81mm mortar crews answering the enemy's call to fight—the possibility of ANP betrayal, being exposed on the high wall. It may be insanity, but at the time, I enjoyed the danger. I had waited a lifetime for the experience. Somewhere deep inside me, a part of my psyche breathed an unfathomable sigh of relief. It can't adequately be explained; it has to be felt.

A patrol of experienced war fighters led by the company gunny went out each evening hoping to ambush the rocket-firing insurgents, but they had no luck. I asked the gunny if he would take me along, and he promised to do so when the time was right. I knew what he meant. I might have been an albatross around the neck of the patrol. I was still inexperienced when it came to combat. The patrols were actively seeking a fight with an enemy known to be close at hand. That was not the time to bring me along. Unfortunately, the gunny and I parted before I had a chance to go with him. I greatly admired and respected him and would undoubtedly have benefited from his guidance.

In the interim, the real work was being done by engineers and 3rd Platoon. The group I was with had guard duty—at the "back door." Since the guard was rotated, those who were not on duty spent most of each airless, blazing-hot, oppressive day trying to find shade. I soon discovered the "bat cave." It really *was* a bat cave; there were bats in residence. But I liked the tongue-in-cheek allusion to Batman and played it up.

Down the "hall" of that inside man-made cavern was a windowless, dark "room." It was a secret place, its existence revealed only by searching for it with a flashlight. It had obviously been occupied in the not-too-distant past because it contained mounds of blood-soaked bandages and empty boxes of antiseptics. I wondered if the previous occupants had departed in a hurry when they saw our dust cloud approaching. I could tell that the rust brown blood wasn't terribly old. I wondered if the room had been a hidden Taliban "hospital" of sorts. I didn't hang around any longer than necessary to take it all in. Dried blood gets into the air, and disease can be contracted simply by breathing it in.

During the hottest part of the day, I would lie on a shelf—away from the hidden "room"—which was carved out of the inside adobe wall. There I would take a nap. It was probably ten degrees cooler inside the bat cave than outside. Although it was still awfully hot, it felt terrific to lower the thermostat of hell by ten degrees. I justified that daily nap as an old man's prerogative. It was a glorious way to break up the stifling boredom. It didn't take the rest of the Marines I was with very long to congregate there. Officer status notwithstanding, D-Ring would join us as often as he could. The guys enjoyed the opportunity to talk to an approachable officer.

Lance Corporal Perkins was our version of TV in the bat cave. A natural-born comedian and philosopher, he kept us entertained with jokes and stories. Corporal Bryan Stuart would frequently quip that he came to Afghanistan to "PAR-TAY!" and Perkins would keep Stuart going on about it. It was incongruent enough to be humorous. This was no place to party.

Perkins also liked to challenge me on intellectual abstractions. He wasn't being confrontational—he relished the opportunity to present some of his ideas and elicit a response. From my perspective, I'm a teacher by nature. I enjoyed the pensive side of his personality. That this repartee should have taken place in an environment so hostile to life itself speaks well of mankind's innate awareness of *something* greater than ourselves—although I doubt that Perkins would agree. Whether he realized it or not, I believe Perkins was a Platonic ideal in vivo. And he was—ironically enough—then in Hades.

Once the sun came up, sleep was impossible due to the roasting heat. After a few days, however, we would leave security to the guards in their armored turrets and sleep inside the ruin up against the eastern wall. The rising sun took longer to reach us there, so we got a bit more shut-eye. D-Ring joined us every night, sleeping right on the ground fully dressed and ready for instant action—just like everybody else. He was a true Marine officer. Finally the time came to leave. The Hesco FOB was already taking shape. Before we shoved off, however, a small Army contingent departed, led by a major. I shook hands with him and wished him luck immediately prior to his parting. They weren't gone long. The major's Humvee hit an IED. Fortunately it only killed the vehicle. The major sustained no more than slight wounds.

The area around Baqua was literally salted with IEDs. They seemed to be everywhere. Engineers with metal detectors constantly swept the dirt roads and the areas adjacent to the roads. All that we ever found were the victim-detonated IEDs mentioned earlier. Those IEDs were constructed of wood with two copper metal contacts. The contacts were separated by springs—apparently bedsprings—until sufficient weight was applied. At that point the contacts would join. Power was supplied by a motorcycle battery. The contacts were connected by wire to the explosive charge, and it would detonate.

With victim-detonated IEDs and vehicles, it was all a matter of luck. The charge was separated from the contacts; therefore the enemy had to guess which direction the vehicle would be coming from. If the vehicle came from that direction, as the weight of its front wheel caused the metal plates to close, the explosives would be directly under the crew cab of the vehicle. Seldom were there survivors, and those who did endure were horribly burned.

If, on the other hand, the vehicle came from the opposite direction, the front wheel set the charge off sooner, and it blew up the front half of the vehicle, where the engine was. That's what happened to the major's Hummer. And that's why he and the others in that vehicle lived to tell the tale. If a man stepped on the detonator, it would be a miracle if he survived regardless of direction of travel.

Since we were also about to leave Baqua, the reappearance of the bleeding major and the ruin of his Hummer were sobering sights. When our time came, we left by a different route from the one we took to get there. There was no road—we traveled cross-country—and we encountered no IEDs. Each driver did his absolute best to stay in the tire tracks of the vehicle in front of him. If the first one hadn't set off an IED, most likely the follow-on driver wouldn't either. It wasn't always possible to stay in the exact tracks of the previous vehicle, however. Therefore, driving in IED country—even when none is encountered—is stressful. One never knows from instant to instant if an IED is about to go off.

Sergeant Joe France led the column from the first vehicle. Often we would stop, and Sergeant France would inspect a suspicious spot of ground personally. His was the most dangerous position. The first vehicle was the most likely to hit an IED. Unfortunately, at a later date, when I wasn't with him, his vehicle struck one of those homemade mines. Thank God only the vehicle was killed. But for Sergeant France and Lance Corporal Mike Michalak, it was their third combat-related concussion. Anyone inside a vehicle that hit an IED could expect a concussion at the very least. Fearing permanent brain damage if either Marine struck another one, medical personnel pulled both of them off the line. They were sent to the rear for the remainder of the deployment. Neither was happy about that.

D-Ring was still traveling with us, and our convoy was down to only a few vehicles. Therefore we made good time. Once we reached the Ring Road we pushed on. Our next stop was 2nd Platoon at FOB Bala Baluk. The FOB was on a paved tributary off the Ring Road. That made traveling to the position relatively safe. Second Platoon Marines were colocated with an Afghan Army FOB. They shared the same Hesco outer perimeter, although the Marine portion was separated from the Afghan Army on the inside. Putting aside trust issues involving the Afghan Army, the FOB struck me as unassailable. Since the Marines moving into Bala Baluk had dealt the Taliban a severe blow, I still thought the fight there was over. Maybe if I had stayed more than one night I'd have felt differently.

I was looking for a place where I might be utilized to the greatest advantage. I didn't think Bala Baluk was the right place for me. D-Ring was ordered to remain. It was difficult to leave him, Whit, Nick Harris, Howell, and Wolfe. They were my buddies by now, but I enjoyed a freedom I had never had when on active duty. I had the trust of Lieutenant Colonel Hall to find my own way to be value added. So the day after I arrived at Bala Baluk, I left. I got on board a convoy en route to another FOB on the Ring Road—in Delaram.

9

Delaram

Afghanistan is administratively divided into districts overseen by governors. Each district is organized into subdistricts. Delaram was the capital of one of the subdistricts, and it was administered by a subgovernor. It was the subdistricts along the Ring Road that the Allied planners were trying to pacify. They felt that if they could surround the interior of the country with secure, prosperous communities, all connected by the Ring Road, that the happy people living there would prevent the Taliban from returning.

Delaram was astride the Ring Road where commerce ought to have flourished. It didn't. Delaram was impoverished. It was beyond poor; it was squalid. Lining the Ring Road on both sides were small shacks assembled with anything the people could find to use as construction material, including discarded cardboard. Men sat by the side of the road selling sticks of firewood. There was an air of desperation about the place.

There were old cars, and there was a run-down gas station or two, but it was a shockingly beggared town. No happy, prosperous people were living there. I don't know where the billions of dollars of aid we and other countries have been pouring into Afghanistan has been going, but it hasn't been filtering down to the ordinary Afghans I saw. Those people were living on the precipice of life. The worst American slum would have seemed like paradise to the community I saw living in Delaram.

Immediately outside the west side of the town were poppy fields. Forget the highly touted poppy eradication stuff the media get from the government; nobody was lifting a finger to eradicate anything that I could see. From my perspective it was just as well. The dirt-poor farmers who worked those fields lived as sharecroppers. Poppy was their only source of income, and their families would have starved without it. The land was owned by a few rich Afghans. Besides, the overwhelming majority of opium that's grown in Afghanistan finds its way to Iran and China. The heroin that makes its way into the United States comes from Mexico. As far as I was concerned, Chinese and Iranian addicts are none of our business.

A river with very steep banks spanned by a solid bridge formed the boundary of the east side of the town. ANP buildings were inside the town on both sides of the road overlooking the river well below them. The structure on the north side of the road was made of adobe. It looked indefensible from the north and west sides.

As had been my custom in law enforcement days, I wandered around and took in small details. In this case, I examined the trash pit and saw a plethora of hypodermic needles and other impedimenta indicative of heroin addicts. Clearly, the cops had a large number of junkies in their ranks.

The defensibility of the ANP building on the south side of the road was another story. It was made solidly of rock and concrete and was surrounded by razor wire. Machine guns were posted on the roof. The building was pockmarked by bullets, but none had penetrated the stone construction. The open space of the road provided clear fields of fire to the north, and the south overlooked a steep, dry tributary, which ran down to the main river. The west was protected by stone walls with lots of razor wire. As mentioned earlier, the east overlooked the river, a steep climb after crossing the wide waterway. No attacker could approach from that direction. The subgovernor maintained his office and residence inside these ANP defenses. But there were needles in that trash pit as well.

Across the river from the town on the east side of the river was another steep bluff. Gazing menacingly down to the river valley below was a large Hesco FOB, which was occupied by the Afghan Army. Immediately next to that was another FOB, occupied by a Spanish army unit. Connected to the Spanish defenses, but not to the Afghan Army, Americans were busy building an enormous Hesco FOB. It was ridiculously huge considering how few Americans were stationed there. Obviously somebody above my pay grade was looking to the future.

We had no running water and no toilet facilities. We shaved and washed up using bottled water in outdoor sinks with a couple of cracked mirrors gazing back at us. Solid human waste was disposed of in small bags called "WAG bags"—I have no idea what that acronym really stands for—and burned. Long PVC pipes about five inches in diameter were driven deep into the ground. That was for urine. The smell by those pipes could've driven away a vulture. Periodically the ground around them was sprinkled with lye—nobody's aim is perfect.

The only source of water aside from bottles came from a single hand pump inside the Spanish army perimeter. The Spanish I was forced to learn in high school came in handy. *"¿Donde esta la agua?"* got me to the well. To wash clothes, we carried a bucket into the Spanish army's area, pumped water. then sloshed the clothes with a stick. The process was repeated until the brown water turned tan. Nothing got cleaner than that. We, ourselves, were always sweaty and dirty. Our "washed" uniforms dried stiff from the dirt still embedded in them. Gritty socks and underwear were a real treat to put on.

Much later a Navy engineer strove valiantly to provide us with functioning showers. They worked for a short while until some technical problem shut them down. But while they were serviceable, I would walk into the shower with my uniform on and stand under the flow, staring in wonder at the dark brown water running down the drain. As with the bucket method of washing clothes, once the water turned tan the laundry was done. The clothes simply weren't going to get any cleaner than that without a professional-strength washing machine—which we didn't have. Then I would peel the uniform off layer by layer and repeat the process of watching the dark water exit the shower. In the end, I washed me. It was glorious while it lasted.

There were enough olive drab canvas tents to house the Marines stationed there, with camouflage netting for shade behind them. I tossed my pack on an empty cot inside one and called it home. There's something about the smell of a hot canvas tent that never changes. The scent reminded me of my days in the field when I was an active-duty battalion staff officer.

The eating area was terribly small but sheltered from the ruthless sun by more camouflage netting. It was in a narrow space between two large metal storage boxes such as one would see on freight trains. A Hesco wall completed the claustrophobic dining ambience. We had to wait for a place to sit or just eat standing up. There wasn't enough room for everybody at the same time. The food was bland and predictable. Sometimes I could barely choke it down. I would have much preferred MREs. The chow made me wish for the return of "C rats"—which is really saying something. I'm an avid milk drinker, but what passed for milk, some kind of "can't spoil" white-colored liquid in cardboard containers, didn't taste like anything that came from a cow. I drank it anyway.

The dirt constantly blowing inside the FOB was called "moon dust" by the Marines. It had the consistency of talcum powder and got into everything. Since the sides of the tent were mosquito netting only, when I awoke in the morning, I was covered in it. So was my gear. We lived in dirt, breathed dirt, and ate dirt. Living conditions were about as austere as they could get. It goes without saying that there was no

PX, no Internet, and, of course, no air-conditioning. Summer was fast approaching, and the temperature kept rising. Second only to Baqua, Delaram was the hottest place I have ever been—on the planet.

What I *liked* about Delaram was the sense of intrigue that enveloped it. It's the reason I chose to locate myself there. The leaders of the police didn't trust the subgovernor. They told us he had been captured by the Taliban and released a short time later. Since normally the Taliban will assassinate such government functionaries, I didn't trust him either. As for me, I wasn't getting good vibes from the ANP second in command. Many of his answers to our questions felt contrived and designed to mislead. I had been lied to by experts in my law enforcement days, and he fit the bill. Since it was nearly impossible to get a straight answer out of this guy, his evasion was troubling.

I found evidence of an Afghan Army heroin overdose victim while on foot patrol across the Ring Road directly opposite the Afghan Army FOB. A primitive needle was lying very near a complete Afghan Army uniform—right down to underwear and socks. I'm convinced it was a fatal overdose because Muslims remove the clothes a dead person was wearing; they are regarded as unclean. Had the soldier not been dead, there would have been no need to undress him. So, in short order, I had garnered evidence of hard-drug usage among both the ANP and Afghan soldiers. I was sure there were other secrets waiting to be discovered as well.

We had a lone Marine counterintelligence operator with us—covertly, of course. We were kindred spirits, so he revealed himself to me. The "two heads are better than one" cliché kicked in. We were both anxious to map Delaram's human terrain. He's still in the Corps, so I'll just call him "Staff Sergeant Striker."

One of our interpreters, called "terps" for short, immediately aroused my suspicions. One evening I was sitting with Staff Sergeant Striker when that particular terp came to talk. Among other things he complained that his fiancée lived in Iran and he needed to call her every day. She was young and beautiful, he said, and he was nearing middle age.

He expressed concern that she would leave him for another if he didn't continuously call. Woefully, he would lose his last chance for love and happiness. Striker wasn't buying it, so the guy kept going on and on. I just sat and listened—wordlessly.

At one point, Striker asked the man how many languages he spoke. The terp rattled off a long list. Arabic was not one of the languages he listed. I remembered all those grade-B World War II movies where escaping English-speaking soldiers or airmen would be nailed by the Gestapo. The Gestapo would speak to the man in English and receive an automatic reply in English.

So I said to our terp, in Arabic, *"Ente taki Arabi?"* Instinctively he replied, *"Arabiya, nam."*

He had corrected my mispronounced word for "Arabic" and answered "yes" in Arabic.

I asked him why he hadn't listed Arabic as one of the languages he spoke. He became flustered. Not actually knowing, but acting on my street investigator instincts, I asked him how long he had lived in Iran. He answered twelve years. Since Iran is Shiite Muslim while Afghanistan is Sunni Muslim, I let it slip that I knew he was of the Hazara tribe (a Shiite tribe in Sunni Afghanistan). Since he *was* a Hazara, he became completely rattled and began to open up. More and more it became obvious that this terp was a spy for Iran. The phone calls to Iran to his "fiancée" were more likely to his "handler" than to a paramour.

Iran at that time was deeply concerned that moving Marines into western Afghanistan was a prelude to a two-pronged American invasion of Iran—from Iraq and Afghanistan. There was some concern that Iran might launch a preemptive attack into western Afghanistan. Since we weren't preparing for an offensive in Iran, making that paranoid country more nervous didn't seem judicious. Staff Sergeant Striker was in charge of counterintelligence, not me, so once I offered my advice I simply let it drop. However, I'm pretty sure he decided to calm Iranian fears by letting the "love-struck" spy call his "girlfriend" often.

In addition to counterintelligence, two other Marine missions were going on—simultaneously. "Alpha" Squad—the rifle squad from Brewster's 1st Platoon—had the onerous task of patrolling Delaram on foot and of training the ANP. It was the same squad I had run Range 400 with back in Mojave Viper. It was a plus for me that I knew those Marines from the States—particularly the squad leader—as I was welcome to go on foot patrol with them whenever I liked. I wanted to get outside the FOB at least once a day.

Next, there were two full-blown mobile antitank units led by a first lieutenant who reminded me of John Wayne. Not that anybody was expecting Taliban tanks, but the battalion had the vehicles, so it used them. Lieutenant "John Wayne" was tall, athletic, and charismatic. He was an experienced officer from the Iraq campaign, and his Marines loved him. He was self-motivated and aggressively searched far and wide for the enemy. If we could have changed out his armored vehicles for horses I might have been in the presence of a cavalry troop inside a fort in the old Southwest. "John Wayne" and I got along famously. He welcomed me to go along with his patrols at any time.

So I had plenty to do, and diversity of work to stave off boredom. All I needed was running water, indoor plumbing, a washing machine, air-conditioning, an Internet connection, palatable food, an absence of "moon dust," cooler weather—and life would have been perfect.

I went on my first foot patrol at Delaram, going out with Alpha Squad. Summer was nearly on us and it was a waltz through Dante's Inferno. I hadn't yet ditched my heavy bullet-stopping ceramic armor plates. Among them, water, my rifle, pistol, and full magazines, I was carrying quite a load for a fifty-eight-year-old guy in that indescribable desert heat. All that heaviness settled on the very top of my shoulders—the trapezius muscles. They adapted with time and built themselves up, but in the beginning, I was pretty sore. To the delight of "Brownie"—a young, very likable Marine—I never fastened the chin straps on my Kevlar helmet, letting the straps just hang. He referred to that as the "'Nam look."

Lance Corporal Curt Bartz was tasked by the squad leader to be my personal bodyguard my first time out. There were some interesting things during that patrol that really caught my attention as an investigator, so relatively frequently I stopped to examine minutiae and use my camera to capture details on the ground. Quite often it's the small things that add up in the law enforcement world. Moreover, attention to detail was reinforced during my active-duty Marine Corps time.

Unfortunately, frequent stopping meant falling behind the rest of the squad. Finally, I snapped out of my introspective analysis of the Afghanistan countryside and noticed that Curt and I were alone. Curt had never left my side. Nor did he utter one word of complaint or appear ruffled in the slightest. Bartz was a solid Marine and an Iraq veteran. That's one of the things I liked about being with a Marine battalion. I knew he would stand by me if the "5th Taliban Horde" came over the hill.

By the time Curt and I rejoined the squad, the squad leader was ready to head back. I pretended not to be as dog-tired as I was. Referring to me, the squad leader made some offhand comment to the effect, "Well, he's still walking," so I put on my best "game face." I don't know if I fooled anybody; I was dead beat and worn-out from the heat. Later, as I went on foot patrol more frequently, I became better accustomed to the physical demands. In time most came to regard me as a Marine—albeit an *old* Marine—or at worst, a halfway competent civilian. Then there was no more special treatment. I had a rifle just like everybody else. I was expected to take care of myself and those around me—just like everybody else. As far as I was concerned, I was back in the Corps.

Often on patrol several ANP came with us. It was one of the ways the squad fulfilled its training mission. It enabled the ANP to see how Marines behaved while on patrol. Our squad leader wisely never crossed the river using the bridge. The river was wide but shallow, and we sloshed through the water. Since there was no way to avoid wet feet, we all just sucked it up and traversed it as if we were on dry land. There was one young ANP cop who must have thought if he ran fast enough he could cross it without getting his feet wet. It was highly comical to watch him. He sort of combined a hop and a run. He never did master the art of running on top of the water. He also never quit trying.

When Staff Sergeant Striker augmented Alpha Squad outside the wire, it added an interesting dimension for me. He and I were always looking for something useful to his counterintelligence operation. Details can't be revealed, but an anecdote is instructive. One day at the ANP station, Striker asked to borrow my camera. "Moon dust" had killed his. He meandered around for a while, then returned the camera. Back at the FOB he showed me a picture he had taken of the ANP second in command. Warning bells had gone off in Striker's head about that man, as they had in mine. The man obviously didn't realize his picture was being taken. He had a look on his face as though he were trying to bore a hole in someone's head and see what was inside. It was not his baseline smiling look.

When I saw that picture I asked Striker, "Who the *hell* was *he* looking at?!"

Looking me dead in the eyes, Striker replied, "You."

I was always wary around that ANP leader. I never let him get behind me unless I knew Striker had my back. Only Americans knew my last name, and everybody called me by my first name. I was even introduced as "Mr. Terry." Apparently my gray hair and lack of a name tape or rank insignia had generated a lot of interest from that particular ANP chief. His interest, in turn, generated heightened awareness from Striker and me. It was natural for people to be curious about me, but that man's unease smacked of self-preservation.

Every now and again, in the dead of night, one of our sentry posts would be shot at by a person or persons down in the river valley below. Fortunately, they never hit a Marine. Striker and I would join Alpha Squad the next day, looking for signs of the shooter or shooters. As had become custom, several ANP cops would join us. Two of our regular trainees were obviously and always stoned on opiates. I say "obviously" because unlike most abused drugs, which cause the pupils to dilate, opiates cause the opposite effect. The pupils become pinpoint small.

Their behavior was another giveaway. The stoned cops were as annoying as stoned people anywhere. They decided they liked me and kept coming to wherever I was to give me a hug. They also kept calling to me in a language I didn't understand, babbling happily about who-knows-what. The fact that they were armed with AK-47s didn't contribute to any sense of well-being on my part. It was particularly irritating because, like everyone else on patrol, I needed to be alert to any sign of an IED or an ambush. My particular purpose being on those patrols was to focus my policing skills on looking for clues regarding the shooter or shooters. The cops were a major distraction. It goes without saying that I didn't trust them one bit and tried as best I could to never let them get behind me. Often that wasn't possible without losing contact with the rest of the patrol.

Fortunately, Striker was always behind them, watching. He had my back.

Stoned cops notwithstanding, we were fortunate we didn't have the mission of training the Afghan Army. I had been told in the States that the Afghan Army was coming along nicely and that they liked Americans. All we had to do now, the brass had said, was to train the police. Then everything would be fine and the country could take care of itself. That's not what I saw in my little corner of Afghanistan. The Afghan soldiers on the other side of the FOB wall rarely missed an opportunity to hurl insults at the Marine sentries and to remind them that we were interlopers in their country.

———

In the meantime, "John Wayne" kept up his relentless hunt for the enemy. Second only to physical discomfort, monotony generates the greatest amount of misery on a deployment. I developed a pattern to help me with that. One day I'd go on foot patrol with Alpha Squad and the next day I'd roll out with John Wayne and his "cavalry." Wayne searched far and wide for the enemy; he was spoiling for a fight. He'd set night ambushes—we had night-vision goggles, so we could see in the dark—and visit isolated towns and farms far from Delaram. The lieutenant was trying to run into the enemy head-on, forcing them to come to blows. Alternatively, he strove to develop intelligence as to their habits so he could figure out a way to get at them.

He was the epitome of a Marine officer. He liked having me along so I could read the human terrain and give him my take on some of the people we interacted with. Often he, Striker, and I would put our heads together and try to figure out some way to ruin the Taliban's day. I was still learning about the country and its people, so I'm afraid I wasn't quite as useful as I would become in the not-too-distant future.

We were definitely not there to eliminate poppy farming, but the Afghans couldn't be sure of that, so they steadfastly denied any involvement. I got a really solid feel for baseline Afghan lying behavior while the lieutenant was interviewing an old farmer. The Afghan's body English, his facial expressions, the tone in his voice—all indicated friendliness and sincerity. Surely he was telling the truth. Then he said he grew only wheat, not poppies. The field to our immediate left was a harvested poppy field. At my feet was a poppy plant. I picked it up and, smiling, showed it to the lieutenant.

I learned that when they chose to, Afghans can lie very convincingly. But I also began to notice subtleties that would enable me to crack their "code." I just needed a little more time. Knowing how people look while lying is a skill set a street investigator needs. It would come in handy later on.

Meanwhile, intelligence reports came pouring in with ominous news. The Taliban had a suicide bomber lined up in Pakistan, and his target was Delaram. Some intel indicated the individual might dress like a woman so as to blend in better and be able to get closer to our patrols. One day while mounted—that is, in Hummers—a couple of us saw a "woman" covered from head to foot in a black Muslim dress complete with burqa and face covering. "She" was out at a time of day when women were usually not. "She" also moved like a man, in my opinion. We tried to get closer to get a better look, but "she" disappeared. There is no way of knowing if that was our guy or just some modest woman who made haste to get home when she noticed us watching her. But it added to the sense of unease that permeated life outside the wire.

It also highlighted the complications of working in a country where it was considered bad manners to even look at a woman, let alone to approach one or to talk to one without her husband present. God forbid there was some genuine need to search her. None of the female issues would have been a problem at all if the enemy didn't exploit our sensibilities and those of the Afghan people on the issue.

As an example of the culture—in Iraq as well as Afghanistan—it was considered to be bad form to ask a man how his wife was, or how his daughters were doing. One could ask how his *family* was or even how his *sons* were, but to even mention a female was very rude behavior. Women were supposed to be invisible. One should not even "notice" a woman on the street. Naturally, I paid close attention—but only with my peripheral vision. We all did our best to conform to the dictates of the society in which we found ourselves.

On foot patrol one day, through the dense, narrow streets crowded with people, a major who was assigned to the public affairs section was rapidly approached by a man with what appeared to be a detonator in his hand. The major recounted that he knew he had no time to do anything, and his heart stopped for a moment. It turned out that the man approaching was holding up a ballpoint pen. With his thumb on the retractor, it looked just like a detonator.

Fortunately, it was another false alarm; it was also another example of stress outside the wire. Had the man actually been the suicide bomber we had been anxiously awaiting, the major wouldn't have had the time to say good-bye. Half the squad and a score of innocent civilian men, women, and children would have been blown to atoms. I wasn't too far behind the major. I would have gone to God without ever knowing what hit me.

Finally, after I had left Delaram, the suicide bomber did in fact show up. Or rather two of them arrived. One detonated himself next to an armored vehicle belonging to the Spanish army. He didn't scratch the paint, just made them wish there was a drive-through car wash somewhere nearby. The second blew himself up right outside the Alpha Squad leader's Humvee. The explosion blew the front bumper off, and also made a nice, gory mess on the vehicle, but only the bomber was hurt. I'll bet the occupants of the vehicle were more than a little shocked when the guy turned himself into pink mist. Our intelligence reports were quite correct.

Naturally, I made friends while in Delaram. Lance Corporals Steve Paine, Bobby Harless, and Cody Peterson were fellow tentmates. They had also been friends for quite a while before winding up in my tent. The banter between Payne and Harless in particular was comical and entertaining in the extreme. Payne never let an opportunity to bait Harless pass. And Bobby responded with righteous indignation every time Payne did so. I have to admit I got in on the act.

Everybody in that tent, except me, was awaiting transport to one of the platoon FOBs. Transport came when it got there—it could be a long time coming. In the meantime the Marines had no responsibilities, so they were constantly thinking up ways to amuse themselves. One Marine, in a state of utter boredom, lit himself on fire with alcohol-based hand sanitizer just to amuse the rest of us. It was uproarious. A couple of others got in on the act. Bored Marines are like lit cherry bombs. It's just a question of when they will go off and how much damage they will do. Frequently, during downtime the antics in that tent reminded me of being a kid at summer camp. I think I was actually starting to enjoy myself in spite of the hellish heat and moon dust. I was adjusting to the discomforts, growing acclimated to the physical demands, and managing to enjoy a few good laughs every day.

Reality came crashing down on our heads soon enough. On June 14 Sergeant Michael Washington's vehicle struck an IED that killed him and three other Marines. Another Marine was very, very badly burned. The badly burned young Marine was a newly arrived replacement. He had left our tent at four o'clock that very morning. Although he had been with us for days, I hadn't even taken the time to get to know his name. He mostly lay on his cot, with a book on his chest. He smiled a lot, I remember, but I took no notice. The initial reports indicated he suffered burns to his lungs. I believe he survived, but it was touch and go. If his lungs were burned on the inside, I can only imagine what happened to the outside of his body.

Although I had known any number of law enforcement personnel who had died in the line of duty, I took Sergeant Washington's death hard. He wasn't the first 2/7 Marine killed in Afghanistan, but he was the first person I actually knew. I felt anger at anything and everything as I walked into a large empty storage box and silently cried. I also vented out loud to a couple of National Guardsmen who were cops in "real life." They were older than the typical soldier or Marine, and they understood how it feels when a younger guy gets killed.

I ranted while wondering why Sergeant Washington was where he was when it happened, since we all called that stretch of road "IED Alley." I was angry that I hadn't been in a position where I could have protested to him—or whoever ordered him to go where he died—that IED Alley was no place for them to be. I suppose a bit of survivor's guilt was present. My duty, I felt, was to keep young Marines alive. I had just failed in that obligation—or so I believed at the time.

My mood changed completely. It wasn't summer camp anymore. A grim, humorless determination replaced the lighthearted camaraderie that had begun to characterize the deployment.

10

The Alamo

Colonel Hall frequently left the comfort and safety of his battalion command post (CP) and ventured far and wide to check on his troops. Therefore I got to see him, and talk with him, wherever I was—from time to time. In like manner, whenever a convoy was going back to the battalion CP from the Golf Company AO, it stopped at Delaram. I often hitched a ride with them and dropped in to see the colonel.

During one such visit he expressed concern about the intelligence reports that were coming in concerning FOB Golestan, where Lieutenant Brewster was operating with an understrength platoon. The reports were dire. The enemy was believed to be massing with the intent of overrunning the Marine position. When the colonel told me he was actually worrying, I volunteered to go up there and see what I could pick up on my "street investigator radar." He looked at me quizzically but approved my request. It was probably on or about June 15, the day after Sergeant Washington and his Marines were killed in action.

Lance Corporal Brett Miquelon, a Marine from California, was part of the colonel's personal security detail (PSD). Brett and I had become acquainted when we were all still back at KAF. With a face full of freckles and a shaved head, he stood out. He also stood out because he had an infectious sense of humor. Whenever Colonel Hall showed up, Brett was there also, and we would kid around. On the day I was leaving for Golestan, probably around June 16 or 17, the colonel and his PSD stopped at Delaram. Miquelon and I engaged in our usual round of mutually insulting tête-à-tête.

Colonel Hall approached me and—eyeing me with what I took to be a friend's concern—said, "Don't get yourself killed up there." Miquelon had just been busting chops, calling me an "old man" immediately prior to the colonel's appearance. I replied, "Don't worry, sir. I'm not too young to die, but I haven't heard my last 'old man' joke yet." Then the colonel pulled out, en route to another FOB.

Payne, Harless, and Peterson were slated for Golestan. That same day a resupply convoy was heading there, and they were driving up with it, in a Humvee. Since there were only the three of them going in a vehicle that sits four, with Peterson in the machine-gun turret, I hitched a ride with them. Payne just assumed I would be the vehicle commander—he definitely didn't regard me as a civilian—and since the other two didn't object, I assumed the role. "Technicalities be damned," I thought.

Supply convoys were sent to FOB Golestan about every ten days to two weeks. I figured that was plenty of time to nose around and see what I could come up with. I still felt that Delaram was the right place for me to operate for all the reasons I stated earlier. Therefore I took only my assault pack with me, leaving other gear behind. I brought shaving gear, three pairs of skivvies, three olive drab T-shirts, and three pairs of tan boot socks. Those were the only luxuries. Kevlar helmet and body armor, magazines for my rifle, first-aid equipment, spare batteries, my uniquely Marine, personally owned Ka-Bar knife, and my check-signer-issued laptop completed the inventory.

The convoy pulled out of Delaram at about dusk. It was led by a "minesweeping" truck—a vehicle that had a metal arm in front of it attached to a large heavy "roller." If an IED was encountered, that should have set it off with no casualties. Much of the trip was in country that those in charge of the convoy would later come to know intimately, but they hadn't yet been afforded the opportunity. Therefore, once darkness closed in, we got lost several times.

When the countryside we were traversing changed from flat open plain—with excellent fields of vision and clear fields of fire—to narrowing mountains, I began to perk up. I always looked at us as I would have if I were the enemy. It didn't make for a relaxing journey.

We were hours into the trip, with many hours yet to go when we took the wrong fork in a road. We ended up dead-ended in a remote mud-walled village. Several times we tried to get straightened out and exit the village, only to discover we had gone down another village byway. At one point the entire convoy did a U-turn in some poor farmer's field. I'm sure that didn't endear us to the locals.

Finally the convoy just stopped, strung out in a long line of vehicles, right in the middle of the village. There is no electricity in rural Afghanistan, so people go to bed early. They live pretty much from sun to sun. In fact, the first call to prayer is at sunrise. So when I observed two men walking parallel to us about a hundred yards away, in the middle of the night, my awareness heightened. It was way too late at night for men to be out for a stroll. That sort of thing just wasn't done in rural Afghanistan.

We remained stationary way too long for my comfort. My demeanor was intense. I had been laughing, joking, and playing around with these three Marines for some time prior at Delaram, but not now. Payne was behind the wheel, watching intently. Harless was edgy, muttering his displeasure under his breath. Peterson was in the turret, saying nothing— his absolute silence reminded me of the lull before the storm. I exited the vehicle and took a tactical walk around, getting the lay of the land. The "Lone Ranger" stuff was getting to be a habit.

We were close enough to structures that an enemy could have materialized at almost any point and cut into the column. I discovered a square walled-off area a very short distance from where we were stopped.

It had just enough of an entranceway for our vehicle to enter—but barely. Otherwise it was a completely enclosed empty space. From the middle to the walls was approximately twenty yards. The walls were about five feet high, made of bullet-stopping, rock-hard adobe, and if we were in the center no one could approach us without getting shot. Peterson's armor-protected turret was higher than the stockade; he could still engage an enemy and help protect the convoy. That enclosure would have afforded us much better protection than where we presently were.

I briefed my companions on what, in my day, would have been called an "immediate action drill"—that is, something that would be done without any hesitation. I pointed out the walled area to Payne and told him that if we were attacked and I gave him the word (in the absence of orders from the convoy commander, of course) he was to drive our vehicle into that protected area. Peterson was to engage any approaching enemy with his belt-fed machine gun, and Harless was to keep him well supplied with belts of ammo. The rest we would play by ear.

Like being on patrol when no suicide bomber approaches, or no IEDs are encountered, even when something *doesn't* happen, it's nerve-racking.

On that night, to my immense relief, nothing happened.

We got moving again. However, with the passing of hour after hour, Payne was finally getting too tired to drive. I drove the damn Humvee. I sure as hell wasn't supposed to. I had no military driver's license, had not been trained on the vehicle, and was technically a civilian. But I drove anyway. As we climbed higher into the mountains, we encountered ever-narrowing trails with many switchbacks. A steep climb on one side was offset by a steep drop-off on the other. I enjoyed myself enormously. I'm a rebel like that. Finally, as the night dragged endlessly on, even I became too tired to drive. Harless took the wheel. Peterson stalwartly manned the gun in the turret for the entire trip.

Thirteen and a half hours after leaving Delaram, we arrived at FOB Golestan. The sun was already up. It was on or about June 18.

A cursory look around was all I needed to realize why Colonel Hall had been troubled. The place reminded me of the Alamo. It was not a Hesco walled fortress, like most FOBs. It was a partially enclosed adobe position with openings in the enclosure and obvious terrain features favorable to an attacker. I took it all in quickly. I recall thinking that I could take the place with twenty-five Marines and I wouldn't need all of them. I would have kept five in reserve.

I was exhausted, the trip had been harrowing, and my patience was not what it otherwise might have been. I mutely wondered if the platoon commander, Lieutenant Brewster, had been made aware of the intelligence reports battalion was picking up. The Taliban meant to attack in strength and annihilate him. I was there because the battalion commander was worried; now I was worried as well. There was no time for gradual diplomacy. The captain in me, like the Wolf Man during a full moon, came out with fangs showing.

I stood with a deliberate posture of authority and eyes to match. I motioned to Brewster and said, "We've got to talk."

Much later, when Lieutenant Brewster and I had developed both mutual respect and friendship, each of us chuckled as he spoke of his first impression of me at Golestan. He said he thought, "Who does this *old guy* think he is to summon *me* to talk ten minutes after arriving at *my* command?!"

Ever the gentleman, although thoroughly peeved, the lieutenant began to dialogue with me. I won't bore the reader with the details. Suffice it to say that it took some time before he and I were at ease with one another. Considering our contentious beginning, it's a near miracle how splendidly we began to work together over time. As it dawned on me that many of the shortcomings at Golestan were not of Brewster's making, I began to appreciate the steps he took to alleviate them. Before the deployment was over, I would describe him as audacious. Audacity is a virtue in an outnumbered military commander. Robert E. Lee was the soul of audacity. Brewster, I came to realize, was made of the same stuff.

That would come later, however.

Once the initial confrontation with Lieutenant Brewster was over, I spied Sergeant Holter of Bravo Squad. We were both glad to see each other, and we met like old friends. He quietly expressed his reservations about the precariousness of the platoon's position. He articulated the hope that my arrival might cause change for the better. I knew I needed to know more about what was going on in the area around the FOB, so I asked him to take me out on patrol and he agreed—we would be leaving the FOB at midnight that night.

Next I spotted Gunny Mendoza. The gunny's frustration was visible. I could read it on his face and see it in his body English. I could hear it in his voice. He told me that his advice to the lieutenant had been falling on deaf ears. Knowing that the gunny was sent to Golestan specifically because he had the experience to guide a new second lieutenant, my concern for the safety of the platoon ratcheted even higher. I silently cursed the fact that I had no secure way to communicate directly with the battalion commander. I was certain that things were worse at Golestan than he knew.

Gunny Mendoza understood. We had fifty-six Marines in a porous defensive position, with excellent covered and concealed approaches accessible to an enemy should that enemy avail himself of them, and we were more than thirteen hours from reinforcements. Unlike the typical Marine Corps battalion, which had indigenous air assets, we might have to rely on aircraft from another country—if we could get air support at all. In other words, we were really way out on a limb, on our own, and according to the battalion intelligence section, the dogs of war had gotten our scent and were swiftly closing in.

Together, I promised the gunny, we would talk to the lieutenant. There were some things that could be done to improve our position, even though it would still be vulnerable. First, though, I was anxious to get out on patrol with Sergeant Holter. I needed to see more of what lay around us. I needed to know just how close the enemy was. I believed the people of Golestan would provide me with that information without saying a word. That's why I was there—"street investigator radar."

Finally I flopped on an empty cot—whose I don't know—and got what sleep I could in the stifling desert under an olive drab canvas covering. It offered a little shade but really soaked up the heat. At an altitude of approximately four and a half to five thousand feet above sea level, the FOB was noticeably cooler than Delaram. Still, a few sweat-soaked hours of nap time were all I could manage. Whereas it had been about 140 degrees or so at Delaram, it was still a good 130 at Golestan. Ten degrees cooler was nice, but it was still bloody hot.

When I got up, stiffly, I took a good look around. To the west was a high, mountainous ridgeline that ran from north to south. Colored only in varying shades of brown, it was burned to a crisp by the unrelenting sun. Between the mountain and our position was a bone-dry riverbed. Comprised of smooth gray stones and grayish sand, it was used as a road by one and all. Quite wide, I supposed at some point in time it must have hosted a rushing torrent of unstoppable water.

Before the riverbed, immediately to the west of our western adobe wall—fifty-five steps, in fact—was a thick, solid four-foot-high rock wall that surrounded several concrete and stone buildings. It was known as "the clinic," since it was meant to house an Afghan doctor who, theoretically, would provide medical services to the local people. In point of fact, the "doctor" barely had step one first-aid training. His buildings and walls caused me the greatest concern.

If I were attacking the FOB I would have commenced in the dead of night when all the Marines, except for posted guards, were asleep. I would have had my men crawl low, unobserved, to that bulletproof wall. Then to start the attack I would have dedicated two rocket-propelled grenade (RPG) launchers and two belt-fed (RPK) machine guns to each of the Marine bunkers opposing it. The operant definition of "fire supremacy"—as I was taught lo those many years prior, at TBS—is a state whereby any defender foolish enough to lift his head to shoot at the attacking force stops a bullet. At that close range, coupled with the element of surprise, the RPGs and RPKs would have guaranteed fire supremacy.

My first troops over the wall would have carried ladders or boards and thrown them on what paltry razor wire there was, allowing subsequent waves of attackers to pour in. On the west side of the FOB, at the lowest point, our wall was only about five feet high. At fifty-eight years of age, I was able to get from the rock wall, through the razor wire, and vault that wall in seventeen seconds. It took me thirty seconds to get from the nearest cot, don gear, pick up my rifle and Kevlar helmet, and reach the same point. Do the math. Theoretically, the enemy could have poured into the FOB in force. The fighting would have been hand to hand.

I was deeply concerned.

The west wall was not the FOB's only weak point. The south wall was no more than about four feet high and was adjacent to a solid, bulletproof, concrete boys' school. Although sandbagged Marines were posted on the roof of the school, and the school area was surrounded by razor wire, a gulley ran in an east-to-west direction from the dry riverbed to a point on a dirt road over which our wire crossed. That point was low ground—below our line of sight. Therefore, both the gulley—an avenue of approach—and the spot where the dirt road and wire met were unobservable. An enemy could have cut the wire unseen and launched an attack from the south at very close quarters.

Both the clinic and the school had been constructed by some prior Allied force for the good of the community. Razing them did not seem to be an option. Although from a military standpoint that would have afforded the FOB clear fields of fire and denied cover and concealment to the enemy, counterinsurgency strategy requires winning the hearts and minds of the people. Destroying a school and clinic was not likely to further that cause. Yet the FOB was vulnerable precisely because the school and the clinic remained standing. They posed a real dilemma.

If the enemy had sufficient manpower—and subsequent events proved he did—and if the enemy attacked both from the west and the south, taking advantage of the terrain as described above—which he did not—we would most likely have made history—just as the defenders of the Alamo had made it. Lieutenant Brewster's name would likely be toasted at formal military functions along with that of Lieutenant Travis—the commander of the Alamo. Two lieutenants overwhelmed by superior enemy forces after a desperate battle to the last man. Marines don't surrender; the Taliban doesn't take prisoners. Not exactly the kind of history I wanted to make. Obscurity is much to be preferred—at least in my pragmatic old mind.

Golestan should have been a priority for the company commander. He was Lieutenant Brewster's immediate commander. He should have gone to the battalion commander and articulated serious concern while proffering potential solutions—not the least of which could have been to pull the platoon back. Knowing the colonel as I came to know him, I have no doubt that very idea was percolating in his mind.

It was also the company commander's job to allocate company resources—he could have reinforced Brewster, for example, from another part of the company. He might have sent Brewster his missing rifle squad, even if he needed battalion approval to do it. But just as the CO had demonstrated a lack of tactical acumen at Baqua, he seemed apathetic about Golestan. Brewster was on his own minus one rifle squad with no equipment to construct a typical Marine FOB, and only fifty-six men—some of whom had just arrived on the same supply convoy that brought me.

So I found myself in a poor defensive position with a pissed-off lieutenant, a frustrated gunny, an out-of-touch company commander who was somewhere far away—and no means of communicating with the man whose concern had brought me to Golestan in the first place.

I was not a happy camper.

When I awoke, after another all-too-brief nap, I looked around some more. To the north we looked pretty secure. A waterless offshoot that emptied into the main north-to-south river ran east to west at the base of a steep drop-off. That dry riverbed provided us with excellent unobstructed fields of fire. Across the dried-out waterway were high ground and a wooded area. I wondered how a patch of woods came to be when it was bordered on two sides by bone-dry rivers—especially since everywhere else was parched desert. Later I realized that all the runoff from wells, irrigation, and so forth in the village of Golestan ended up at the low ground, where the trees were. Still, they were separated from the FOB by a wide stretch of open ground—the dry watercourse.

Also atop high ground, on the north side of the dry tributary and situated right outside the village, sat an adobe-walled "FOB" that had been constructed and occupied by the Soviets. It was being used by ANCOP, which stands for Afghanistan National Civil Order Police. While the ANP were off receiving formal training, ANCOP took their place. When the Soviets had garrisoned Golestan, they stationed fifteen hundred men there. As previously noted, we had fifty-six. I would guess there were about fifty ANCOP.

To the immediate east was a lot of open land that gradually became foothills and mountains. Therefore, there were great fields of fire facing east, and that direction didn't concern me. I was a little apprehensive about what I called "Russian Hill." It was to our south and east. When the Russians occupied the country they had fortified a position on top of that prominence. The rock-lined entrenchments they had built were still there.

The hill was about eight hundred meters high and very steep. There was no cover at all on its sides from which to assault should the enemy man the peak. Moreover, the fortifications could only be taken out by a direct hit from a mortar or by an air strike. All the same, it was pretty much too far away to threaten us directly, and our armored vehicles should have been more than a match for any Taliban foolish enough to

Afghan National Police station at Delaram. The walls
of the building were riddled with bullet holes.

An Army Humvee that had just left Baqua. The vehicle hit
an Improvised Explosive Device (IED). No one was killed.

A typical "side street" in the sun-scorched village of Golestan.
Only mad dogs and Marines walked around in the midday sun.

"Blocao el Malo" was painted on an adobe house before we got there.
It is the place where Bravo Squad and I were billeted.

Two up-armored Humvee vehicles assigned to the platoon. They form a barrier of sorts against attack. The green tent behind them is the command post.

Seen from inside the "Alamo." The letters WWLBD are spray-painted on the lower layer of mini Hesco barriers. The troops did it. The letters stand for "What Would Lieutenant Brewster Do."

The trees are an anomaly. All water from wells in the village of Golestan ended up there. Hence the "woods." It was from this tree line that the bulk of the attack on the "Alamo" occurred.

The "Alamo" was thirteen hours away from the nearest supplies over land. We began to be supplied by airdrop. This is a picture of supply pallets being kicked out the back of a cargo plane with parachutes deploying.

Me sitting on my cot cleaning my pistol, rifle propped against my leg. The dirt and dust were so bad that weapons had to be continually cleaned.

The platoon adopted a puppy. Pampered by the Marines, in this photo she's sticking her head right over an ammo belt leading from an ammo can to a "ready to fire" machine gun.

On the left is Scott Brown. I am on the right. Scott and I rode
up to the battle of Feyz al Bad in one of these trucks.

Lance Corporal Jonathan Zequeida. He was shot through
the leg by a machine-gun round in an ambush outside Feiz al Bad.
Lance Corporal Daniel Hickey got the Silver Star for braving
enemy fire and saving Zequeida.

Lance Corporal Jeremy Boucher, nineteen years old.
He was later shot through the leg during the ambush at Feyz al Bad.
He refused to leave his machine gun. He received the Bronze Star.

Lance Corporal Daniel Hickey. After saving Zequeida, he then
stood out in the open and went head-to-head with an enemy
machine gunner. He received the Silver Star.

The author at Feyz al Bad. We began going house to house shortly after this picture was taken. For reasons known only to God, I was smiling.

2nd Battalion, 7th Marines at the memorial service for those killed in action, Marine Corps Base, 29 Palms, California. Tragically the battalion has lost more men to suicide since returning from Afghanistan than it did from enemy action.

wish to engage us from that site. However, it afforded the enemy an excellent observation post from which to look right down into our FOB.

There would be no secrets from the Taliban.

On one of the patrols to a village known to be pro-Taliban prior to my arrival, Lance Corporal Dustin "Butters" Housley—one of the CLIC Marines—took a picture of a strange drawing on a wall inside one of the houses. Nobody knew quite what to make of it. It had a circle in the center and spokes radiating out from the circle. I took a long, hard look at it and then up at the parachute we were using for shade over the command post (CP) area. I started pointing out the various positions inside our FOB that were depicted on the sketch. It was a representation of our position, parachute and all, from a position above us. Clearly the enemy had been on Russian Hill and had mapped out our FOB in detail.

Combined with the intelligence garnered at battalion, I was sure we were in for it. The only question was when.

That night at midnight, I was assigned to Lance Corporal Jonathan Zequeida's fire team by Sergeant Holter. The patrol was Bravo Squad, and while I didn't know it at the time, Bravo Squad's destiny and mine were about to become one. I still harbored the notion that my stay at FOB Golestan was temporary. I expected to return to Delaram on the next supply convoy, in ten days or two weeks.

Although I was really fatigued from the trip to the FOB and badly needed sleep, I was energized by the act of leaving the relative safety of the position—in the gloom of night. Even though I had been outside the wire on patrol at Delaram, foot patrols took place in broad daylight. We had also been comfortably within "cavalry to the rescue" distance from Lieutenant "John Wayne." This patrol was different. We might have run head-on into several hundred Taliban en route to attack the FOB.

Fortunately, we all had night-vision goggles. They enabled us to see in the dark, albeit in a world incongruently consisting of various shades of green. We moved on foot in staggered column formation, across the wide-open dry riverbed to the north and into the nearby village of Golestan.

One of the positive changes since my time on active duty—in addition to the night-vision goggles—was the addition of small "cop-like" radios that connected each fire-team leader with the squad leader. During my tenure, we had relied on silent hand and arm signals. I would very much have liked to have had one of those radios. Later I would become Sergeant Holter's rifle partner, and no radio was necessary, but this was my first time out with the squad. Without a radio, I was merely an old rifleman, despite my personal agenda. All the same, that was strangely satisfying.

Silently we patrolled the empty dirt streets of Golestan, hushed except for the occasional barking dog. I had to get used to the night-vision goggles. They conveyed no depth perception. Stepping up or down while wearing them was a skill I had to develop—and fast. Sergeant Holter thoughtfully passed the word back to me that the merchants of Golestan, having been victimized by burglary at night, had hired a "security guard" and that that individual carried a shotgun. Good to know. Seeing an Afghan materialize out of nowhere, at night, with a long gun in his hands might have had tragic consequences.

The night was long and uneventful. It was also instructive. I had wanted to get the feel of the area outside the FOB, and I was getting it. Sometime prior to the coming of American Marines to the area, an Allied force had constructed a nice concrete school for girls surrounded by high solid walls. The Taliban took exception to educating girls and tried to burn it. While concrete doesn't burn, people got the message. The place was abandoned.

We positioned ourselves on the roof and watchfully observed the town come awake. As the first gray streaks of dawn lightened the dark sky, a local cleric began to sing his call to prayer. It was as exotic as anything I experienced in Iraq. The singsong melodiousness of the cleric's voice was entrancing. It was not at all like a Western melody, but it appealed to me in an indescribable way. Perhaps it was the knowledge that theological differences notwithstanding, I was hearing a call to prayer—a call to pray to the same Supreme Being, regardless of what name people called Him—and to whom I prayed as well.

A girls' school of sorts was reinitiated near a tribal leader's personal "fort" by his intrepid daughter-in-law. The man's son, her husband, had been killed fighting the Taliban. Defying many death threats, she relied on her father-in-law's influence and Lieutenant Brewster's dogged determination to protect the school. Not a day passed while Brewster was in command that Marines didn't show up unexpectedly and at unpredictable times at the "new" girls' school. The Taliban surely knew that if they were caught by Marines in the narrow alleys and byways of the village, Marine close-quarter battle ethos and firepower would have made short work of them. The new girls' school stayed open as long as Marines remained in the area.

At that latitude, the sun rises early in the summer. It was probably about 4:00 a.m. when we no longer needed our night-vision goggles. We remained—unnoticed, we hoped—on the roof of that concrete bastion for sometime more. As I watched the town come alive, the "street cop" in me took it all in. I compared what I saw and heard with the "baseline behavior" I had developed in other parts of Afghanistan. Finally, about five hours after commencing the patrol, Sergeant Holter had us move out back toward the FOB. Still in staggered column formation, and still part of Zequeida's fire team, I was eager for an up-close look at the people. Among other things, I wanted the opportunity to observe their expressions as they saw us.

We proceeded straight down "Main Street"—so called not because it remotely resembled anything an American would regard as a street, let alone a "Main Street," but because it was the busiest dirt avenue in the town. Small shops lined it, and a primitive gas station and "restaurant" were at the far eastern end. As we made our way back through the village, I heard music. It was Afghan music, but it didn't have the intonation of Islamic religious music; it was obviously for entertainment purposes. I noticed its origin inside one of the shops we passed. It was emanating from a battery-powered cassette player.

I knew right then that there were no Taliban in the immediate vicinity. The people had wordlessly told me what I had gone on patrol to find out. The Taliban are ultrastrict fundamentalist Muslims. While they tolerate religious music, they will painfully beat anyone caught playing nonreligious music. The Puritans had nothing on the Taliban.

We still had some time to prepare. It was June 19.

At Gunny Mendoza's invitation, I grabbed a cot in the uncrowded staff NCO tent. It also served as a supply dump where stacks of rations were kept. We were adjacent to the command post (CP) with its out-and-out forest of antennae. Lieutenant Brewster set up his cot immediately outside the CP, where he slept—I have no doubt—with one ear open all night long, listening to anything that might come over the radio.

After our initial challenging discussion, Brewster had promised to walk the perimeter of the FOB with the gunny and me and to listen to what we recommended. There were some points that the gunny and I both felt strongly about, and Brewster heard us out. One issue was the placement of claymores. A claymore is an explosive charge connected to a detonator by wire. When detonated, it sends numerous shotgun-like pellets at an approaching enemy.

The FOB had only two, and they hadn't yet been emplaced. Claymores were widely used in Vietnam. "Dummy" claymores were still very much part of the training when Gunny Mendoza and I were on active duty, and we both wished we had more of them at Golestan. They were positioned on the west side, facing the "clinic"—our most vulnerable side. Other suggestions were made, and a general three-way discussion of weak points and tactics ensued that mollified the frustrations of the gunny. He felt he was finally being heard.

I learned that much of the material needed to strengthen the FOB had only just arrived on the same supply convoy that had brought me—like badly needed sandbags and razor wire, for example. Hence there was much that Brewster couldn't have done prior to my arrival that contributed to my original impression that he was responsible for the deficient defenses.

I began to rethink my initial assessment of the lieutenant when he stated that if he ordered his Marines to work on the FOB twenty-four hours a day, seven days a week, it would still be vulnerable. I concurred with his opinion. Further, he declared that his defensive plan was to keep the enemy off balance through constant and unpredictable patrolling. Given the totality of the circumstances, I had to agree that his reasoning was sound. I was beginning to see the lieutenant in a more favorable light.

Gunny Mendoza was given a much more active role in shaping the FOB's defenses, and the matériel that had just arrived was emplaced with a palpable sense of urgency. The gunny had that effect on people. Things were improving—rapidly. The clinic was still troubling.

We had an unmanned aerial vehicle (UAV), which Lance Corporal Housley was able to fly. Think of it as a very large model airplane that was controlled from the ground. It had a TV camera mounted in the nose and could relay the image to Housley and others on the ground in real time. I was very interested in getting that thing up and running. Housley saw to it. Unfortunately, it crashed somewhere north of the village of Golestan. A mounted patrol was sent out to retrieve it, with no luck.

Bravo Squad and I went to town, looking. I questioned, through an interpreter, a large number of merchants—none of whom knew a thing. I got the same look I used to get in Brooklyn—sort of a "Who, me?"

Having established baseline behavior for lying by Afghans back at Delaram, I was skeptical. One merchant who looked particularly guilty said, "I have no idea what you're talking about but I will ask around."

I told him I would pay one hundred American dollars in cash if I had it in my hands no later than noon the following day. The currency of Afghanistan is called *afghani*—and one afghani was worth about two cents. One hundred American dollars was a lot of afghani.

I no sooner got the words out of my mouth than he said, "I'll have it here by then."

He said he knew who had it. He candidly confessed that he was going to try to sell it for whatever he could get for it. Obviously the prospect of one hundred dollars cash in hand was more attractive than getting what he could from whom he could when and wherever he could.

At noon the next day, sure enough he had the UAV. And I handed him a hundred bucks out of my own pocket. A lot of Marines thought I should just seize it, since he had lied initially, and it was U.S. government property, but I decided that keeping my word was more important than the money. Lying to the locals was no way to win their hearts and minds. In the end, I was reimbursed—thanks to Lieutenant Kyle Slocum and the U.S. Army's deep pockets.

I was interested in the UAV's recovery for several reasons: I didn't want it falling into enemy hands; it costs a hell of a lot more than a hundred dollars; and Lieutenant Brewster was ultimately responsible for lost property and could have been punished for its loss. Last but far from least, I had ideas regarding the use of that camera.

The back side of the troublesome clinic could not be seen from anywhere inside the FOB. It was the logical path of approach for an attacking enemy. I reasoned if we could mount the UAV on the roof of the clinic facing downward, we could monitor that avenue via the TV camera in its nose. We experimented with it at length but were finally forced to abandon the idea. The battery simply would not last long enough. Although additional batteries were requested, if they ever arrived I was not aware of it.

It's too bad, because knowing what was behind that clinic would have afforded me immeasurable relief.

Work continued at a feverish pace for days. That was good because the dogs of war were closing in.

11

The Coming Storm

Late in the day—still on June 19—the FOB was informed that 2nd Platoon had just been in a major engagement with the Taliban outside Bala Baluk. Captain Erik "D-Ring" Terhune had been killed in action (KIA), and Lance Corporal Andrew "Whit" Whitacre had been shot in the head and critically wounded. Whitacre had been medevaced to a British hospital at Bastion by helicopter. Whit was personally known and very well liked by all but the newest Marines in the battalion. The veteran Marines at Golestan had all been in Iraq with Whit, and they were deeply affected by the news.

I tried to console the sorrowful Marines by reminding them that Whit hadn't been called in as a KIA. During my twenty years in law enforcement I had known of many individuals who suffered head wounds yet lived. I told them I didn't want to raise false hopes, but the jury was still out. There was good reason to hope.

I was wrong.

A short time later we were informed that he had been pronounced dead at the hospital. As darkness enveloped the FOB, small groups of mournful Marines gathered in out-of-the-way corners and grieved Whit's loss. In their own way, they were conducting a wake.

Only this time I felt "survivor's guilt" too. I had chosen to leave D-Ring and Whit at Bala Baluk, believing the place was totally pacified. I was horribly mistaken. Other Marines didn't have choices. They went where they were ordered and stayed where they were ordered to stay. But I had made a choice. They had been my friends, and I wondered if I had let them down. Maybe if I had been there things would have been different. Maybe they wouldn't have been killed. I felt I should have been by their sides and shared their fate. I was racked with guilt and grief at the same time.

I felt estranged from the others. Unlike them, I could have been there.

It also bothered me deeply that nobody seemed to be mourning for D-Ring. All they talked about was Whit. That was natural and I understood—consciously. They all knew Whit from the barracks and Iraq. D-Ring was an officer and a Johnny-come-lately to the battalion. They really didn't know him.

But I did. He was my friend. And emotionally I felt that I was the only one to grieve for him. That set me apart from the others as well. I left the group and went off by myself.

I can't cry in public for some reason. I haven't been able to since I was a small boy. So I found an out-of-the-way spot between the latrine and the west wall, sat down, buried my face in my hands, and silently sobbed. I believe I sat there—my back against the exterior of the latrine—and cried for hours. An Army reserve officer who was then at the FOB happened to notice me. Possibly I wasn't as silent as I thought I had been. In the darkness he couldn't tell it was me. He told a pair of young new Marines that "one of your guys is behind the latrine and he's not doing very well."

It was dark and I'm not sure who they were. They came over and I told them in an emotionless voice that I was okay. I don't know if they knew it was me, but they seemed relieved to be able to get out of there. Once they left, I cried some more.

Since that day I wake up every June 19 and cry before my feet hit the floor. This was the fourth consecutive year. I know I'm not the only one.

During the remainder of the deployment, and even after returning to the States, I pieced together what had happened. A small group of insurgents found themselves in a gun battle with Marines at Bala Baluk and got the worse of it. Several were wounded and tried to get away on foot. Marines followed the bleeding enemy's blood trail into a shallow valley with high ground and bullet-stopping walls on each side. It was a trap.

They had walked into a killing box.

The enemy was secure behind the walls on both sides of the Marines and they opened up with AK-47s and RPKs (machine guns). Since the Taliban were on high ground on both flanks they were shooting down into the Marines. That meant they had no concern about friendly fire—or sending bullets into their own ranks.

Struggling to seize the initiative from the enemy with suppressive firepower, the Marines fought back. It wasn't happening. The enemy was too well positioned and there were too many of them. Some Taliban were spotted bringing up extra ammunition to their comrades. That they could resupply during the fight confirmed that this was not Iraq. This was not hit-and-run; it was not a firefight. It was a platoon-versus-platoon battle that lasted for hours. Armored vehicles were called up, but the terrain was impassible. They could only fire from long range and with seriously impeded vision.

Attempting to break the impasse, Captain Terhune made a mad dash forward. He was cut down by a machine-gun bullet in the abdomen almost immediately. The bullet entered below his body armor. As an experienced investigator, I have always been able to get people to tell me things even when they shouldn't. I was told that the bullet had severed an artery and that D-Ring had died very quickly.

Knowing Whit as I do, I believe he wanted to get D-Ring from out of the bullet-spattered spot where he still lay. So he left the comparative safety of the wall and rushed to take cover behind a tree, closer to D-Ring. The tree was savaged by incoming fire. As he cautiously glanced out from behind it, a machine-gun bullet struck him in the head. He was mortally wounded, although he still had a pulse—hence the initial report that he was still alive. Whit was dragged to cover by Marines who braved a torrent of incoming fire to get to him. It took much longer to get D-Ring—enemy fire was too intense.

Whit was evacuated from the battlefield back to the FOB, where his best friend, newly promoted corporal Zack Wolfe, lovingly cradled Whit's head in his lap while awaiting the medevac chopper. When it arrived, Wolfe helped get Whit on board. Finally, Marines were able to retrieve Captain Terhune's body. Lance Corporal Kyle Howell helped load his remains on the chopper. At last Marines got the upper hand and the enemy was driven off.

It will always seem like yesterday.

June 20 dawned at Golestan bright and clear, with the promise of another blistering desert day. The FOB was blessed with a venerable hand-pumped well such as the Spanish army had at Delaram. Marines "washed" clothing using the familiar "slosh stuff around in a bucket" method. Soap powder was available, but I'm not sure if that was a blessing or a curse, since the "rinse cycle" was the same as the "wash cycle." The soap was never completely rinsed out of the clothes.

Thin olive-drab-colored nylon cord was strung anywhere and everywhere, and wet clothes were thrown over it. If anything, the wind blew even harder at Golestan than it had at Delaram. As a result, fine particles of sand were power-driven into hanging laundry. I'm convinced my uniform could have stood up by itself once it was dry. Periodically clothes would be blown off the line, where they would lie drying in the dirt until someone picked them up.

By some miracle there was actually a lone tree inside the FOB. It survived because of its proximity to the hand pump. Runoff water nourished it. Its branches were decorated like a Christmas tree with socks and underwear. Little things take on exaggerated importance in a world as severe as the Afghanistan desert, and that tree came to mean a lot to me.

Sadly, it was right next to our mortar emplacement, and it was cut down. It interfered with the angle of fire. I missed that solitary tree. All the same, I would not have traded it for the mortars. We only had two 81mm tubes and one 60mm, but they did wonderful work for us when the time came.

The world began to heat up almost immediately after sunrise and only got hotter as the day wore on. Marines worked hard making good use of the sandbags and razor wire that had just been delivered. Extra wire provided a welcome buffer between us and the bulletproof "clinic," and the claymores were set up facing in that direction. A sandbagged bunker was constructed atop the concrete latrine, which also faced that worrisome area of approach. Claymores are detonated by a "clacker" connected by wire. The clackers were placed inside the new emplacement, which immediately became known as the "shithouse bunker."

Quietly Gunny Mendoza took me aside and asked if I would man the shithouse bunker. He wanted someone with maturity hovering over the claymore detonators. I was only too glad to agree. I had already identified that bunker as the key terrain inside the FOB. Not only did it face the dreaded "clinic," but also, turning around, one could see the entire interior of our position. Whoever held it controlled the core battle space. The emplacement included boxes of fragmentation grenades, an M240 machine gun, and lots of extra rounds. A handmade wooden ladder was the only way to access it. Kick the ladder over and whoever was up there was in about as good a defensive position as one could find.

I would have gone there anyway. Privately I had cautioned Payne, Harless, and Peterson that if things fell apart and their leaders were dead, they had to hold that bunker. If the enemy had already taken it, they *had* to take it back. No one could survive inside the FOB if that critical terrain was lost. I promised that if I were alive, that's where I would be. Things started to improve.

That was good, because the place still reminded me of the Alamo.

I got in the habit of going on patrol with Sergeant Holter and Bravo Squad pretty much every day. Some days we went out by vehicle and swept the area around Golestan; some days we walked through town. They often went out twice in a single day, and in the beginning I tried to do the same. But at fifty-eight years old, I really didn't want to burn myself out. I kept it down to one patrol a day. To lighten the heavy load I was carrying, I ditched the bullet-stopping armor plate that covered my back. I stowed it under my cot. That helped a little. Nevertheless, by midafternoon, I was nearly worn-out. I would pull my Marine eight-point cover (cap) down over my eyes as I lay on my cot and take a siesta. I called it a prerogative of an old man.

Initially some of the squad would turn to me and ask what I wanted them to do. It was natural, given my age and their knowledge of what my rank had been. I always pointed to Sergeant Holter and said, "*There is your squad leader.*" Sergeant Holter, a veteran of the Iraq War, proved himself time and again to be an outstanding Marine NCO. I had no qualms whatsoever about following his lead.

I soon morphed from being an "old rifleman" to being Sergeant Holter's "rifle partner"—meaning I covered his back. Instead of being assigned to a fire team, I went with him. It was eminently logical, since an interpreter, called a terp, always accompanied him, thus enabling communication with the locals. Being within earshot of the terp I was privy to the superabundance of verbal information being exchanged. I was also welcome to interject with questions whenever I felt the need. It was the right place for a street investigator like me. It was why I had come to Golestan.

Besides, I really wanted to cover his back.

There were two kinds of Afghan police—the ANP, or Afghan National Police, and ANCOP. ANCOP stood for Afghan National Civil Order Police. They were the elite. Unfortunately, there were only a relative handful of them in the entire country. During formal training of the ANP, ANCOP would rotate into the ANP's districts and hold things down until the ANP returned, nicely trained and equipped— theoretically.

When I got to Golestan, the ANCOP were in residence. Although my initial impression of the inadequacies of the ANP never changed, it didn't take long to realize that ANCOP were a completely different breed. Comparing them to the ANP would be like comparing Marines to the Boy Scouts. Well led, intrepid, and highly motivated, they earned my respect as well as the respect of the Marines around me. In time we even learned to trust them. That was a gift never bestowed upon the ANP.

They were all battle-hardened veterans. Their leader was a major. Of average height and build, he had streaks of gray in his black hair and beard. His countenance exuded confidence without arrogance. He appeared dignified but approachable. He issued orders quietly with the poise of one who was used to being obeyed. His men obviously held him in high regard.

The second in command was a lieutenant who spoke very good English. He was a member of the Tajik ethnic group. The Tajiks are a minority of the people who comprise the Afghanistan population, the majority being of the Pashto tribe. Like many Tajiks, he had a some-what Oriental look about his eyes. Taller than average and with a slight mustache, he was very friendly and also highly competent. He inspired his men. They loved him. I came to like him very much and regarded him as a friend.

I was a real anomaly to the ANCOP, as the lieutenant explained. They were amazed at my gray hair and obvious signs of age. Standing five-foot-eight, I was still lean and in pretty good shape. Weather-beaten though my face was, I looked a lot younger than my years, but still a bit too old to be out doing what I was doing. As we all got acquainted, the lieutenant translated the question that seemed to be on everybody's mind: just how old *was* I?

When I told them they appeared astounded. They all started slapping me on the back and with broad smiles spoke to me in a language I didn't understand. I got the impression, though, that it was the functional equivalent of "good man!" The lieutenant then told me that his men had just nicknamed me "the strong man." Maybe if his English had been perfect it would have come out differently—I was surrounded by young Marines who could've lifted up a car to help someone change a tire; I needed a jack.

It was as amusing to Bravo Squad as it was to me.

Joint patrols with ANCOP were a pleasure. They did not need us to train them. They were highly capable from the start. Moreover, their presence legitimized our being in Afghanistan. We were there to assist the rightful Afghan authorities and not to enforce our will on the inhabitants. It was their country and we were helping them to police it and keep the enemy at bay. As long as they were with us, people could not say that Americans were there to conquer. People everywhere were much friendlier toward us when accompanied by them. In addition, they spoke the language. The populace was a good deal more forthcoming with information for them than for us or—later—for the ANP. ANCOP were professionals, whereas the ANP I encountered were anything but.

The people respected ANCOP, but not the ANP. If the ANP were nearly as good, the war would be won.

As a consequence of the excellent working relationship we developed with ANCOP, we jointly patrolled far-off villages. We got to interact with communities who otherwise might have hidden themselves at our approach. Together we vigorously sought out the Taliban. Acting on tips garnered from the common people, we searched for hidden trails over the mountains and unknown water sources. We expanded our patrols on an ever-widening arc around the FOB. The knowledge of the terrain thus garnered would stand Marines in good stead when the ANCOP were gone.

They also made it clear that they were in charge. On one occasion, in a remote village, a member of the local population behaved with obvious disrespect toward them. They displayed their disapproval by arresting him on the spot. One of our Marine leaders thought they were being a bit too harsh on the man and sought to intervene on his behalf. The English-speaking lieutenant firmly let him know that this was *their* affair, not ours. *They* were the police, not us, and they would handle things their way. In the end, having received an apology from the miscreant, they "unarrested" him and let him go. It was as it should be; it was their country, not ours.

———

The ANCOP were stationed in what used to be the Soviet FOB across the east-to-west dry riverbed from the Marine position. Their site was much nearer to the grove of trees than was the Marine FOB, but it was where the Soviets had put it. It was there, so it was utilized. Besides, it was fully enclosed by high, bulletproof adobe walls. In that regard they were better off than we were. Nor did they have the bulletproof "clinic" to contend with. The inside was rather primitive, and I doubted that much had changed since the Soviets had abandoned the place. They slept on old spring beds with shabby mattresses. Sadly, the ANP were due back to Golestan soon, and the ANCOP would be leaving. Before they left, however, they would prove their battleworthiness.

We had no way of knowing it, but even then the Taliban were approaching in force. They were coming over the mountains on trails too narrow for anything but a man on foot with a donkey. Our reliance on vehicles was a hindrance. It was rather like the cavalry versus the Apaches in the American Southwest. Our vehicles kicked up a huge dust cloud sure to be seen when still miles away, and the Taliban were secure in their mountain strongholds. It would take time to move as much ammunition as they would need—with no modern conveyances—to staging areas near the chosen point of attack, but they had all the time in the world.

The dogs of war were moving in for the kill.

——————

Work on the FOB continued. One sergeant, a skilled carpenter, preferred to work at night, when it was cooler. Sleeping through the sound of a skill saw tearing wood, and the loud "whump" of a board flatly hitting the ground wasn't too difficult as tired as I was. However, a generator was kept running day and night to power the command post and provide minimal light for working. Since the FOB was very small, there was no escaping its constant noise. The fumes were pervasive as well, and I began to wake up with headaches. I believed it was due to sleeping in close proximity to the exhaust, so I started looking around for another place to bunk.

I felt myself a member of Bravo Squad and sought out their company for typical Marine banter when duties provided an opportunity. It was natural, therefore, that I'd look to their billeting area for my new digs. They were quartered in a six-room adobe structure with dirt floors and covered by a thatch-and-mud roof. That another nation's army had been in residence there in the past was obvious by the name painted on one side in large white letters *BLOCAO EL MALO*. We guessed it meant "The Evil Blockhouse" or something. It seemed appropriate.

There wasn't much room left inside, but Sergeant Holter and the squad were all for the move. The guys enjoyed busting on the "old man" as much as I enjoyed busting back. Fortunately, there was a National Guard lieutenant from my home state of New York in residence. A cop in the "real world," he belonged to a Military Police unit and was exiled to Golestan to help with the ANP when they returned. Six-foot-two or so, comfortably middle-aged, and naturally bald, Lieutenant Kyle Slocum graciously shared his hovel with me. It was much less hot inside—brutally hot but less so—and farther from the generator.

One night Lieutenant Brewster decided to call an unannounced readiness drill. It was late, and any Marine not on guard duty was asleep. Suddenly the call went out, "STAND TO!" Practice makes perfect, and the initial chaos was replaced by swift execution after a few more such drills. I climbed the ladder to the "shithouse bunker" and joined Bravo squad's lance corporals Bryan "Davey" Davidson and Rory Compton. Brewster ordered a head count over the radio. As position after position called in, it was our turn.

Compton had the radio. He confidently replied, "Two Marines, one civilian."

I went off like a mousetrap.

"CIVILIAN!??? CIVILIAN!??? I WAS A MARINE BEFORE YOU WERE BORN! MY DOG TAGS ARE OLDER'N YOU ARE! HELL, MY DOG TAGS ARE OLDER'N YOUR DADDY! I MIGHT *BE* YOUR DADDY—IS YOUR MOMMA GOOD-LOOKIN'?!"

It was typically Marine, totally good-natured, and Compton knew it. Even so, when Brewster held his next drill and called for a head count, Compton called in,

"Two Marines and uh, uh, uh . . . TERRY!"

Okay, I could live with that.

Lieutenant Slocum and a couple of soon-to-be-leaving Army officers and NCOs occupied an armored truck bed that had somehow been placed atop a huge metal storage box. It was right next to the "shithouse bunker," although separated by a chasm of about eight feet. It too faced the west, in the direction of greatest concern, the "clinic." That made for a total of four fortified positions now capable of fighting an enemy from that direction. I was beginning to breathe a little easier.

We couldn't have known it then, but when Lieutenant Brewster ordered a makeshift stand constructed for the Stars and Stripes, it was a last touch.

Since I had packed a standard-size Marine Corps flag with me, I offered it to be flown next to the national banner. They were to be planted side by side atop a hollow-shell partial Hesco barrier on the east side of the FOB. It really was hollow—there had been no time to fill it. Hopefully the enemy wouldn't know that because it wouldn't have stopped an incoming round from a BB gun.

Unfailingly gracious, the epitome of an officer and a gentleman, Lieutenant Brewster offered me the privilege of raising the colors for the first time. I was the "senior Marine" present, he said.

For about four months out of the year, the wind in western Afghanistan blows strongly and continuously. It's called "the season of wind." The strong, constant wind kept both flags flying straight out every minute of the day. Clint Eastwood, Tom Hanks, or Steven Spielberg couldn't have asked for more if they were making a movie about the place. It was all the more dramatic because it was real.

Pretty much every night I would lie on my cot, staring up at the mud-and-thatch ceiling, before falling asleep. Every once in a while a clump of dirt would fall. I felt a low-grade fear in the pit of my stomach and I often thought that I could never watch a movie about the Alamo again without realizing that I knew how those men felt. Or rather, how they felt before Santa Anna showed up.

Like them, I knew we were in a vulnerable position. Like them we were relying on adobe walls and thrown-together defenses in case of attack. Like them, we were hoping to survive and make it home. Every night since arriving at Golestan, I wondered if our fate would be the same as that of the men of the Alamo. Wearing only boxers, I drifted off into an exhausted sleep, cooled by a pool of my own sweat.

Although it had been my intention upon arriving at Golestan to remain only until the next supply convoy, then return to Delaram, I had already changed my mind. How could I live with myself if the FOB was overrun after I left? Like the Alamo, there would be no survivors. I decided to stay. It may sound trite, but the truth is I felt it would be easier to die than to live with the knowledge that I had abandoned all those fine young Marines just to save my own old hide.

At 11:30 p.m. on July 1, 2008, I quit watching a movie on my laptop, which was balanced precariously on my chest, and laid the computer down. Slocum was sleeping the sleep of the just and snoring slightly. The man was a rock. I dozed off pleased with the knowledge that I didn't have to get up early the next day; I could sleep until the heat woke me.

An hour and a half of downtime was all I got.

12

The Attack

I bolted awake. "What was that?" I asked myself. "Was that our carpenter sergeant working late again? Did he just drop a flat board?" I sat up on my elbow and listened intently. I looked at my watch. It was 1:00 a.m. on July 2.

WHUMP! WHUMP! "Okay, I know what *that* is!" It was the sound of rocket-propelled grenades (RPGs) slamming into the sandbag-reinforced adobe walls.

As I jumped up barefoot and half naked on the dirt floor I yelled to Slocum, "WAKE UP! THIS IS IT!"

I pulled on my pants—although in retrospect I don't know why I bothered—strapped on my war belt with pistol and extra rifle magazines, and yelled at Slocum again, "WAKE UP!" Then I threw on my tactical vest with the "Secret Squirrel" logo proudly displayed on the front, grabbed my Kevlar (helmet) and rifle, and gave Slocum one last chance to fight for his life.

"WAKE UP!"

"Umm huh?" he stirred.

"STAND TO! THIS IS NOT A DRILL!"

Marines were already blasting away with rifles and machine guns. RPGs were still hitting our perimeter.

Slocum is the most unflappable man I have ever met. He nearly slept through a war.

I bolted out the entranceway of our room and heard Compton yelling at the top of his lungs, "Should we set off the claymores?!"

I thought, "Holy Christ, they must be coming over the walls!"

Still barefoot and bare-chested, I ignored the rocks under my feet and climbed the wooden ladder to the shithouse bunker, where Compton and Davidson were manning their guard post. Muzzle flashes from enemy machine guns and AK-47s lit up the woods to our northwest like fireflies on a summer night, but I saw no human wave coming from the clinic. Davidson was manning the M240 machine gun. Compton turned to me.

"Should we set off the claymores?" he asked.

"Not NO—but HELL NO!" I told him. "Gimme those!"

He was holding the clackers with the safety latches disengaged. Both claymores were ready to go.

I put the safeties back on and told him, "These will be set off if and *when* I say. If I have to let the lead elements get past to inflict the most casualties, I will! *Nobody* sets these off except me!"

I understood why Gunny Mendoza wanted me there. He and I had been trained in many of the tactics used in Vietnam, including the use of claymores. We knew what claymores were good for as well as what they weren't. Although both Compton and Davidson were experienced combat Marines, having been in firefights in Iraq together, they had never used claymores. They thought setting them off would level the clinic and afford us clear fields of fire from that direction.

Not so. Claymores would rip apart human flesh, but they wouldn't have done more than chip away a few surface rocks from the wall of the clinic. If the enemy did assault from that direction, I planned on maximizing their effectiveness—*if* the wires from the detonators were still intact, that is. I asked where the case of fragmentation grenades was. I wanted to be ready to toss them like baseballs at the enemy, especially if shrapnel had cut the wires to the claymores.

Our mortars were launching parachute flares in an arc from west to northwest. Combined with the night-vision goggles, it turned black night into bright, green day. I had a little difficulty getting my rifle into a good shooting position. The heavy bullet-stopping plate on the front of my vest was an impediment. I quickly decided I'd have to get creative and held the butt of my rifle dead center against my vest. It wasn't easy to aim that way, but at least I could shoot back. Since I knew where our critical vulnerabilities lay, I grabbed the radio. I wanted to be able to alert Brewster immediately if I saw trouble developing.

I explained to Compton and Davidson what to look for and why. Compton peered at me quizzically. This was a side of me he had never seen before. I was the wisecracking old man who joked around with him and the rest of the guys every day.

He said, "You talk like a lance corporal, but you see with the eyes of a captain."

Inwardly I smiled. "Well, no big surprise there," I thought.

I stood outside the bunker on the unprotected portion of the shit-house roof. Compton asked me if I didn't hear the shrapnel as it whizzed by. I did, but I felt I needed to be able to carefully watch an opening due west of us for any signs of movement to the south. It could signal a flanking maneuver by the Taliban. I couldn't see it from inside the bunker. I also felt the need to keep a sharp eye on the clinic compound. Being so very near to us, it still caused me grave concern. My old law enforcement survival mechanism had kicked back in. I felt no emotion. Hence I could think clearly.

Surveying our position, I reaffirmed my belief that if the worst should develop, the shithouse bunker was the place to be. We could shoot in any direction, and as we were atop a concrete building, all we had to do was duck—and cover would be available. Grenades could be tossed wherever they would do the most good. Close by to our right, Slocum had joined his Army comrades in the bed of an armored truck. He was in the fight. I was glad.

I would have hated to wake him the next morning to tell him what he had slept through.

Although ANCOP did not have night-vision goggles, the light from our flares—as in all night battles prior to the invention of night-vision goggles—would have to do. ANCOP were fighters. Combat veterans with a desire to defeat the enemies of their country, they fought courageously. The muzzle flashes from their compound never let up throughout the clash. If the Afghan Army and ANP fought half as well, there'd be no need for us in Afghanistan.

I spotted three Taliban on a hill north of us and across the dry riverbed. I took aim—clumsily, thanks to the armor plate. I had barely squeezed off a shot when a blinding flash of light emanating from the middle of the trio blinked off my night-vision goggles. It was caused by an 81mm mortar round from one of our tubes. Our mortar forward observer, Sergeant Justin Gauthier, was a lot better at placing IDF than the enemy was. When my night-vision goggles came back on, only an instant later, the three Taliban were simply—gone. There is no way they could have run out of my field of vision fast enough even if they had survived the blast.

They were atomized.

Lance Corporal Alex "Little Red" Allman, a short, ginger-haired, freckle-faced, scrappy young Marine, looked up at me from ground level inside the FOB. For the past few days I had been teaching him how to say "Kiss my butt" in Irish Gaelic. There's no use denying it: Red looked like a leprechaun.

He yelled, "Hey, Terry!"

"Yeah, Red?"

"Pog mo thoin!" he called, grinning ear to ear.

"Hey, good for you, Red, you finally got it!" I yelled back.

Immediately after that verbal exchange, he moved to the northwest corner, where the incoming and outgoing fire were heaviest. Due to his lack of height he stood on a stack of cardboard-boxed rations so he could fire over the wall. I heard a loud BLAM BLAM! Red was blasted off his perch and launched backward. He was dragged off to the aid station semiconscious. I didn't know how seriously he was hurt.

Although medevaced to the hospital the following day suffering from a severe concussion, he ultimately returned. He was only eighteen or nineteen years old but he had just earned the Purple Heart along with the Combat Action Ribbon.

To this day he has no recollection of the "kiss my butt" exchange between us.

Realizing that our defenses were surrounded by razor wire, and remembering lessons taught by Vietnam vets, my immediate concern—upon hearing the explosions that rocked Red's world—was that the enemy was blasting our wire so they could assault on through.

I called Lieutenant Brewster on the radio and said, "Be advised possible sappers in the wire."

Brewster told me later that he smiled when he heard that. My age was showing.

Compton turned to me and asked, "What's a 'sapper'?" My age really *was* showing. It turned out to be a one-two punch from RPGs. We weren't in 'Nam without the jungle.

Marines never lose their sense of humor no matter what the circumstances. Making the rounds of the fighting positions, one of the NCOs—I'm really not sure who in the dark—called up to us,

"You guys need ammo?"

"No, Sergeant," Compton answered.

"Got enough water?"

"Yes, Sergeant."

"Terry, you need batteries for your pacemaker?"

"Naw, I brought extra, thanks!"

"Is this ladder wheelchair-accessible?"

"We'll find out in a minute!"

Camouflage netting had been set up around that corner of the FOB as shade from the wicked sun. Incoming was still whizzing about. The next day we could see the holes in the net the shrapnel had made. The net also caught all the ejected cartridges from when Compton and I were firing to the northwest. There was a lot of spent brass.

Time dragged on and the fighting ebbed and flowed. This was no Iraqi hit-and-run raid. It was a different rodeo entirely. Battalion intelligence had been quite correct. The enemy came in force and intended to fight it out.

The mortars kept the area around the FOB well lighted. As soon as one flare sputtered out, another would be launched. The light on the ground caused by parachute flares can be deceiving. As the flare slowly floats back to earth, it rocks back and forth. That can cause shadows on the ground to appear as if they are moving. Still watching the opening leading to the south, I thought I saw figures moving but I wasn't certain. I turned to Compton and asked him, "Did you see that?"

He said, "I sure as hell did!" and opened fire. Davidson let go with his machine gun.

I called in the sighting to Lieutenant Brewster, who had ordered the mortars to be preregistered on that dangerous area. In nothing flat the 81s blasted the hell out of whoever might have been congregating down there. Brewster also ordered a mobile reserve to move toward the area. If the enemy had any intention of exploiting our weakness on the south side, it was thwarted.

For the most part we fired at the tree line in general, and at muzzle flashes in particular. I have no idea if I hit anyone.

During a lull in the incoming fire, Lieutenant Brewster boldly sent a squad outside the FOB and into the clinic's compound. He needed to know what I was straining my eyes to see—if the enemy were massing there. If they were, Marines would be depending upon their ferocious "in your face" fighting style to survive the sudden encounter.

One squad against an unknown number of Taliban. I held my breath.

We all watched intently through our night-vision goggles. I don't think I started breathing again until they reemerged from the interior buildings. It's a wonder I didn't pass out. There were no enemy in that compound; the squad returned to the relative safety of the FOB.

―――――――

The eastern sky was showing the first hint of sunrise as the enemy's fire slackened, then stopped. It was 4:00 a.m. The attack had lasted three hours. Brewster ordered his reserve to mount their up-armored Humvees and seek out the enemy before they could retreat to the safety of the mountains.

"A counterattack," I thought. "Perfect!" And the timing was ideal as well. It was inspiring.

Throughout the entire three-hour engagement I held a radio. I listened to twenty-three-year-old Second Lieutenant Benjamin Brewster calmly and intelligently handle everything that came his way. His tone of voice never wavered; it remained even and calm. He must have instilled confidence in his subordinates.

Frankly, I was amazed. Not that Brewster himself was that good, but that *any* twenty-three-year-old second lieutenant could be that professional their first time under fire. I was all the more impressed after the battle when I realized the first RPG rounds sailed right through the command post where he was standing. The antenna farm gave away its location. One RPG round passed right between Brewster and his radioman. Brewster never batted an eye. The radioman was still wide-eyed with the "deer in the headlights" look hours later.

Another of the first of the incoming RPGs hit boxes of MREs, which had been piled high in the staff NCO tent—where I had been living only a few days prior. It splintered into metallic fragments. One piece hit the Kevlar (helmet) the platoon sergeant was wearing. It knocked him cold. Another round tore a hole in the canvas immediately over where my cot had been. It would have been interesting to have been lying on my cot when that thing ripped through a few feet above my face.

Since those incoming rocket grenades were the very first to be fired at the FOB, the mortar crews were still asleep. That's a good thing, because one of the rockets had passed straight through the mortar pit, struck a metal chair, and blasted a leg of the chair into an adobe wall with such force that we couldn't pull it out. Somebody would've been KIA if they had been at their posts a moment sooner.

Taking advantage of the letup, I scurried down the rickety wooden ladder and retrieved my boots. My bare feet were killing me.

Back up at the shithouse bunker I watched as the eastern horizon began to lighten. The sun had not yet come up, but the outlines of our two flags could be dimly seen as dark banners against a darker background. I realized it was July 2. Two days before the Fourth of July. I got goose bumps as the sky slowly continued to lighten.

"O say can you see by the dawn's early light what so proudly we hailed at twilight's last gleaming?"

Yes. I could see the Star-Spangled Banner, and it was still waving proudly. The enemy had been planning our utter annihilation for weeks if not months. They had thrown what they had against us for three hours, commencing in the dead of night. But our flag was still there.

The sun crested the mountain horizon, a blinding yellow-white orb casting gray shadows where its rays had not yet touched. And the vivid red, white, and blue colors seemed ablaze against a background of dull desert tan and brown. The wind kept the flags unfurled. They flew straight out—proudly—as if standing at attention.

I can never listen to the national anthem again without remembering that moment.

The Taliban were beginning to learn what enemies of the United States have always learned. Marines are not easy to defeat.

The enemy had no better luck against the ANCOP. They also held.

Some months later, one of the Taliban leaders who had been in on the attack was captured at another location. He revealed that upward of 250 men had been involved. That meant they outnumbered us by about five to one. He said the Marine response was so immediate and devastating that a proper attack could never be made.

The enemy spent all their time dragging off their dead and wounded. Their losses were significant.

He also revealed that they returned the following night with more men and a desire to redouble their efforts. They were determined to overrun the FOB and kill every last man. They wanted to demonstrate that the interior of the country could not be held. A drone was heard flying overhead. Believing that they had been spotted, and fearful of a devastating air strike, they pulled back.

All we knew at the time was that we could hear a drone flying over our airspace and that no one had notified us—a breach of military etiquette. Much later I learned that it had been sent on the orders of Lieutenant Colonel Hall, our battalion commander.

Having been informed of the attack, our colonel was still worried about his Marines at Golestan.

———

Gunny Mendoza was the first to point out two shrapnel holes in my USMC flag.

I now have it framed with a plaque commemorating the accomplishments of a handful of Marines in an obscure part of the world. It's mute testimony to the Marine Corps' history of fighting in "every clime and place where we could take a gun."

Brewster's counterattack came to naught. The enemy withdrew through the small—but densely populated—village of Golestan. Our vehicles had no business in the narrow alleyways, where the tactical advantage would shift to the enemy. Wisely, the NCO in charge returned to the FOB.

Two squads went out on foot and covered the ground from which the enemy had mounted its attack. Naturally, I went with Sergeant Holter and Bravo Squad. We were amazed at the complete absence of dead or wounded. I, for one, was sure—even then—that the Taliban had suffered significant losses. Yet the only thing we found was an occasional pile of spent enemy brass.

I looked carefully at the ground where I had observed the three Taliban disintegrated by the 81mm mortar round. The round had struck so precisely in the middle of the three, who were close together, that there wasn't even blood on the ground. They really had been atomized.

A vehicle patrol had swept the open country surrounding the town. Since the enemy was not spotted, they had to be inside the village. There is no way they could have made it back to the mountains before they were intercepted.

Brewster was determined to give battle. He mustered every Marine that could be spared without leaving the FOB defenseless—about two-thirds of the available force—and personally led them into the village. As the second in command, Gunny Mendoza probably should have remained behind in command of the base. He wasn't having any of that. We were expecting to come to blows. He accompanied Brewster.

I went also. And since I had finally gotten fed up with the extraordinary weight a Marine has to carry these days, I stuffed my heavy, bullet-stopping front plate under my cot. It could keep the rear plate company. Since I couldn't eat it, drink it, or shoot it, I left my Kevlar helmet behind as well. I was still intent on carrying as light a load as possible in that infernal heat. I trusted in God and my ability to move quickly—more quickly without all the weight—to keep me safe from bullets.

I wore my soft cover to shade my eyes from the sun; I never wore sunglasses outside the wire—I wanted to be able to discern the subtlest variations in shades of tan and brown. The gear vest was designed primarily to hold the armor, but I wore it anyway because most of my spare magazines were affixed to it. Besides, in that way no one but me would know I didn't have the armor plates; the vest's appearance didn't change.

There was a sense of expectancy in the air. We felt that the enemy was close by and probably in the town. We were primed and ready for a brawl. Although no one had gotten any real sleep in more than twenty-four hours, every one of us was as alert as men expecting combat around any corner could be. By leading Marines into a town the enemy had to have occupied, Brewster in effect threw down the gauntlet. Our presence there was a challenge.

We tactically moved through the village, questioning anyone we met. We told them to get word to the Taliban that we were more than ready to meet them face-to-face. We deliberately remained for a long time, daring them to come out and fight. In retrospect, that might have had something to do with the Taliban's decision to return to try again that very night. They had lost face in the eyes of the populace.

I read the expressions of the people and heard the tone of their voices. They had only just come to realize that Marines were not like the soldiers of previous NATO countries that had been at Golestan. Marines didn't stay hunkered down behind walls. Marines sallied forth in search of the enemy.

The community was flabbergasted at our presence in the middle of the town in broad daylight, only a few short hours after a prolonged attack. It was a phenomenon that was being repeated all over the battalion's thirty-seven-thousand-square-mile area of operations. Captured Taliban universally expressed amazement at the fighting spirit of Marines.

We met more than a few men who quietly lavished thanks and praise on the Marines for not firing into the town the night before. The Taliban had told them that we would raze it to the ground with air strikes. Although we had taken sporadic fire from the enemy coming from the village, as evidenced by muzzle flashes seen during the battle, Brewster would not permit counterfire in that direction. Throughout the deployment, he was always solicitous not to cause civilian casualties.

If further confirmation were needed, we discovered brand-new holes carved in adobe buildings with piles of spent cartridges on the ground. The town was spared, and people were grateful. They knew the Taliban were deliberately trying to entice us to cause casualties among them.

Marines won their respect that day.

After a long and unhurried hunt in Golestan, Brewster led us back to the FOB. I was delighted at the reduction in weight I had managed to effect by ditching the armor plates, and loved the long brim of my soft cover as opposed to the Kevlar helmet. It shielded my eyes from the sun nicely and kept my head much cooler. Unfortunately, the lieutenant—still marvelous with his gracious manners—turned to me and said,

"Terry, the next time we go out expecting to make contact with the enemy, please do me a favor and wear your Kevlar [helmet]."

At least he had finally called me "Terry."

I promised I would. In my Marine Corps world a request is still an order, no matter how tactfully it is phrased. Thankfully, he didn't realize that I wasn't wearing my armor plates. I never wore them again.

I knew I had come across as stern to the lieutenant when I first arrived at Golestan, so I didn't want to miss this opportunity to tell him what I thought of his leadership during the battle and its aftermath. I unequivocally approved. He had remained composed, clear of thought, and courageous throughout. His tactical decisions were flawless. I don't recall exactly what I said to him, but I'm certain that I made those feelings known. "Captain" McGowan's final words were words of praise.

From that moment on, I ceased to be a "captain in disguise" watching over a young lieutenant, and became Brewster's aide-de-camp. Our working relationship continued to improve steadily throughout the remainder of the deployment. Moreover, we evolved into friends. I was content; FOB Golestan was in good hands.

After about thirty-six hours of heightened wakefulness, I managed to take a nap. It was a good thing, since the lieutenant had the entire

FOB standing to all that night. I was back with Compton and Davidson in the shithouse bunker.

I'm sure the Taliban were disappointed that their attack the second night was foiled by the sound of a drone overhead, but they were no more disappointed than we would have been had we known they were coming and had turned back. The previous night most of the garrison was asleep when they struck. That night, we were waiting, all of us— awake, alert, manning the defenses—and itching for another go at it. Had they come at us they would have walked into a perfect firestorm of shock and awe. Not even the proximity of the clinic would have helped them. They would have been slaughtered.

Much later—back in the States—I learned more about the mystery in the sky that night. Unknown to any of us at the time, Lieutenant Colonel Hall made sure we had Harrier (Marine fighter-bomber) support the night following the attack. Since there was only one Marine Harrier squadron in Afghanistan at that time, it had to have been borrowed from the Twenty-fourth Marine Expeditionary Unit (MEU) being held at KAF. What the drone we heard overhead saw was our position about to be swarmed with more than a hundred men setting in place for another attack. When the drone was brought in lower for a better look, the enemy heard it and bugged out. By the time the jets arrived, they were gone.

Naturally, we were more than a little vigilant in the ensuing days after the attack, but things remained quiet. Patrols, both mounted and on foot, were increased. The Marines were doing up to three patrols a day—and strengthening defenses in between. They were nearing exhaustion. But no one complained, and all did their duty. After the attack I had firmly resolved to remain at Golestan. I sent for the gear I had left at Delaram. It would arrive by convoy whenever a convoy arrived. I had been living out of a small pack and in the clothes on my back for more than two weeks.

During this postattack period Brewster demonstrated exceptional creativity in planning his patrols. One night after dark—and soon after the attack—Bravo Squad was sent out to circle wide and sneak into a position behind Russian Hill. I went with them. While the armored vehicles and Marines waited out of sight, Sergeant Holter and I sat at the topographical crest of the hill. We could see for miles in every direction. Our night-vision goggles gave us a terrific leg up over Marines from previous wars.

I had brought a pair of high-powered binoculars with me to Golestan, and I had them with me that night. Holter and I took turns using them to intently scan the approaches to the FOB. Even with night-vision goggles men on foot might slip into an attack position if we weren't careful. Brewster's plan was obvious to me. If the enemy attacked the FOB, Bravo Squad—automatic weapons mounted in turrets atop armored vehicles—would swoop down on an exposed flank.

At about 2:00 a.m.—with only approximately two hours of darkness remaining at that latitude—Brewster ordered Sergeant Holter to daringly sweep down into the town and cut into the last concealed position from which an enemy could have massed. There really wasn't much time left for the Taliban to mount an attack that night, but Brewster was taking no chances. As always—not knowing if all hell would break loose—we were primed and ready for what might come. When no contact was made, the squad was ordered back to the FOB. The sun would soon be up.

13

The Outside World

Although our only source of electricity was a generator, we did manage to get an Internet connection going. It would be sporadic at best for a good bit of the time, but it was something. To an old Cold War Marine like me, it was unbelievable. We were on the opposite side of the world from home, so emails were nothing like real time, but we could pretty much write back and forth in about a day.

Bill Osborne, the former Marine whom I had met before we left the States, resumed sending me information about Afghanistan that he had gleaned from the Web. Only now it contained a lot about us—the battalion. I really had no idea what was going on outside Golf Company, and it was great to get some news.

Bill sent me an article from a Marine Corps publication written by Corporal Ray Lewis, who was a combat correspondent for his MOS. I had met Ray before pushing out and remembered thinking, "Wow, we still have 'combat correspondents'—flash to World War II!" Corporal Lewis wrote about Lieutenant General Helland's visit to Delaram. It was interesting to fill in the gaps and realize how things were progressing where I had left. The article was illuminating. Now we were augmented by soldiers, airmen, National Guardsmen, and civilian contractors who specialized in police operations. That last part tickled me. "Uncle Frank" and I had been with the battalion even back in the States.

The general went on to say that 2/7 was the first to go out at the platoon level in an open environment with the bad guys right outside the gate; I could sure identify with that part. The article concluded by noting that General Helland had convoyed to FOB Delaram and described it as one of the unit's most austere locations. I grinned when I read that. By this time I had come to think of Delaram as one level to the rear.

In my mind, there was no question. FOB Golestan was the tip of the spear.

From Bill, I also learned that Fox Company had a real fight on its hands going house to house, clearing a Taliban-occupied town known as Now Zad. I knew those guys, of course—the company commander was a heck of a nice guy, as was the first sergeant and company gunny. I knew the executive officer, all the platoon commanders, and many of the NCOs and other Marines.

Lieutenant Pat Caffery, an engineer by MOS and my tentmate from KAF, attached himself to Fox. Pat told me later of the company-size night attack they had made. It sounded like something we used to train for back in active-duty days—except now they had night-vision goggles, which enabled them to see in the dark. Fox Company was able to take about half the town. They just didn't have enough men to finish the job. There were no civilians living there—they had long since left—and the Taliban hung on tenaciously. The Marine battalion that relieved 2/7— 3rd Battalion, 8th Marines (3/8)—would finish the job. So for the rest of the deployment, "Fox" and the Taliban went nose-to-nose continuously.

I heard about Commander Jim "Fighting Doc" Hancock, a U.S. Navy doctor, and how he got his nickname at Now Zad. He had pioneered an extremely far-forward surgical "operating room" atop an armored seven-ton truck. Then he personally went on foot to find wounded Marines. On occasion he had to shoot his way to them. I heard that he was credited with two confirmed enemy dead in his zeal to save young Marines.

Much later on, when I was back at the battalion CP at British base Bastion, I spoke with Fighting Doc. He told me that he had realized pretty early on that the usual tent setup wasn't going to work too well at Now Zad. Worse, the trip to KAF or Bastion would take way too long. Knowing there would be a need for immediate trauma care, he improvised. He decided that a large heavy metal shipping container would have enough room for his surgical team and himself and would provide good protection. He had one put on the back of a seven-ton truck and then decided what he wanted placed inside. With the help of a team of welding contractors, it was done. The cost: "a couple of bags of Starbucks."

He told me that it "saved lives, no doubt about it."

Fighting Doc estimated that a couple hundred Marines were treated within about a hundred meters of the fighting—the trauma unit was within two to three minutes of the front line. No one who got there died. The good doctor was rewriting doctrine for shock trauma platoons when I spoke with him. He decided that current doctrines don't favor this particular war zone.

"If we don't get to the wounded fast enough, they're dead," he said, and "we've got to push the trauma unit to the front."

Fighting Doc had to use his rifle straightaway. It was on his first patrol. The terrain was bad, and he knew that the usual casualty evacuation vehicles or helicopters couldn't have gotten in there.

So he decided to go on a patrol to see for himself what Marines and Navy corpsmen were up against. He immediately realized that if they took a casualty in that environment, it would get really serious very quickly.

The patrol turned a corner and got hit by heavy ambush; immediately two Marines were cut down. Fighting Doc saw one of the enemy stand up with an RPG, aiming at Marine machine guns. He couldn't get anybody's attention, so he put two rounds in the Taliban's chest. He was pretty close—only about 150 meters.

But he explained that he "grew up a country kid, so I've been shooting since I was old enough to walk."

Fighting Doc recounted that June 23 was one of worst days "of my life as a physician." It was at Now Zad. The first casualty lost both legs; then another casualty lost his legs shortly thereafter. Doc remembers that he had to "get to those guys to stop the bleeding."

An IED went off under the lead vehicle. When it blew, Doc was up to six casualties. So he and Fox Company's first sergeant and a corpsman "tried to get to the kids with their legs blown off." They no sooner got to the makeshift operating room when he heard another explosion: another IED had just blown off yet another Marine's leg. Doc recalled, "I just knew we were gonna die right there."

Somehow they made it through the heavy fire.

Meanwhile, as Doc went back to treat yet another casualty, a Taliban gunner showed himself. Doc put two in his neck.

He was treating a casualty inside his homemade emergency room when the vehicle struck yet another IED. The blast threw him around pretty hard. It knocked him out. It "took a while" to get his senses back. While he was unconscious, a Navy nurse handled a Marine who had his intestines blown out.

The Fighting Doc and six other Navy medical personnel all got the Purple Heart that day.

All wars are different . . . and in 2/7's vast area of operations, I realized that each company's war was different as well. The battalion was really spread out.

We began to eat dinner in a hastily constructed mess tent made of the usual olive drab canvas but with a wooden floor and homemade tables with benches attached. The tent kept out a good bit of the dirt we had been ingesting with every meal. Something called "T rations," or "T rats," as we referred to them, made their appearance. T rats were aluminum foil trays of precooked food. Invariably dinner was chicken and rice. I mean it was *always* chicken and rice. Standing in line I used to quip, "I wonder what's for dinner. Gee, I really hope it's chicken and rice!"

Of course it was. I used to love chicken and rice. Now I never want to see it again.

It sounds delicious, and compared to C rats or MREs, it was. But thinking about it, it was only marginally better than roadkill. Truthfully, if the label hadn't said chicken, I wouldn't have been sure what I was eating. It was some kind of meat, I supposed, although there were times when I thought they had changed things and served fish and rice. Nope, it was still chicken; I read the label. The rice didn't move, so I figured it really was rice—probably. It didn't matter; I would have eaten it no matter what it was.

I was hungry. I was always hungry.

Because it was such a long and arduous trip overland, the powers that be began to resupply us by parachute—I mean shades of World War II. A C-130 propeller aircraft would fly over a drop zone outside the FOB and kick pallets out the back. The chutes would open and the sky would be filled with floating stuff. It really reminded me of old war movies. Our ground-air controller, Staff Sergeant "Obnoxious" Wells, talked to the aircraft and coordinated the drop. We were in "Apache" country, so first the drop zone had to be secured. An outer ring was set up with armored vehicles.

To my way of thinking it was more fun than watching bored Marines pit camel spiders against scorpions in gladiatorial contests inside the wire, so I accompanied Wells pretty much every time a drop came in.

One can only acquire just so much via cargo plane, however, and the corporal who hovered over the food in the mess tent scowled menacingly if anyone took anything like a full plate. Besides, if we ran out, I wondered if the guys at the end of the line would have to go without. I know I never took as much as I would have liked. And with all the walking we were doing, we were burning up a lot of calories. I was rapidly losing weight, and so were the guys around me.

So on one particular stomach-rumbling day, I emailed Bill Osborne, "The rations we get 'way out' here just don't provide enough. We're all skinny as hell."

That set in motion a chain of events that was nothing less than extraordinary.

You may recall that Bill and I had met when we were both Civil War reenactors and that he still was. In addition to reenacting, however, he and his wife, Becky, belonged to a group out of Milwaukee called the West Side Soldiers' Aid Society. It had been founded in 1862 to assist wounded Union soldiers who came home from the war. The society had been resurrected from the dustbin of history in 2003. Patricia Lynch, also a Civil War reenactor, was a volunteer at the Milwaukee Veterans Administration (VA). She was moved by the many wounded returning from the war in Iraq and reached out to her Civil War reenacting circle for help. They became today's West Side Soldiers' Aid Society (WSSAS). They are still dedicated to the ideals that motivated the original society of 1862. When they're not actively helping at the VA they continue to do living histories and attend Civil War reenactments. Bill told them about us, and they wanted very much to help. They adopted FOB Golestan.

Bill wrote back and told me to get him a wish list of what we would like. He reported that the WSSAS was solidly on board, and conventional Civil War reenactors were already contributing money for food and postage. The Internet connection at that time was in the staff NCO tent. I looked up from the computer where I had just read Bill's message and told Gunny Mendoza what he had said. The gunny was enthusiastic. On the spot, I emailed back:

Hi Bill,

The Gunny is sitting here and I just popped the questions to him. He said any kind of dry seasonings, mustard! Ketchup! Garlic and the usual suspects—INSTANT PANCAKE MIX! A skillet . . . to throw on a grill or fire. BBQ sauce (I'm typing as he speaks) the hot wing sauce, VINEGAR would be huge. Food—Doc [Hospitalman First Class William "Doc" Zorrer] is napping. [I'll get with him later.]

We asked for other impossible-to-get things too—things that didn't always come in family-sent care packages in sufficient quantity, such as socks. We could never get enough socks and there was no PX to buy them. Then, once the ball got rolling, every time a C-130 would start kicking pallets out the door, we knew the WSSAS goodies were floating gently to earth. It was Christmas over and over again.

Bill also asked me if I wouldn't mind writing about some of the guys of 1st Platoon. He felt it would really help the folks back home if they could get a feel for the young men they were supporting. I began to send what I called human interest stories, focusing on one, then another of the Marines at Golestan. Within the limitations of security, I would also tell them what was going on. Those human interest stories became the seeds that grew into this book.

We were very lucky to have Corporal Terry "Cookie" Huggins at our FOB; he was actually a trained cook. He made the most of the stuff that was sent. With some seasoning he could even make chicken and rice taste like—well, almost like—chicken and rice. For my part, ketchup makes anything taste good. Chicken and rice with ketchup—yum!

I made an Internet introduction and put Gunny Mendoza in direct contact with the home front. Not too long ago, I got an email from WSSAS member Tom Arliskas. He and his wife, Terry, are key members of the group. Tom wrote about those days:

The Marines needed and requested as I remember, socks, spices for cooking, lip balm, anything that could be mixed with water to eat like soup, "pancakes" and pots and pans to cook with. The West Side went to work. Donations poured in, sundries, candies, and everything requested was packed up and sent out to the "FRONT" . . . the WSSAS had their own personal group of Marines—they belonged to us—and we made sure our Marines were taken care of.

The gunny had been in touch with Tom, who still remembers:

Gunny Mendoza and his Marines just got back from a patrol and he told his men to get something to eat. They were tired, hungry, dirty, and miles from home. MREs were on the menu again. . . . Gunny Mendoza heard a commotion in their bunker, he walked in and saw heads bobbing and elbows working to shovel in the "PANCAKES"— "Where the hell did you get pancakes?"—the Marines pointed to the boxes from the "West Side Soldiers' Aid Society." There, have some Gunny. Mendoza went outside. Tears came to his eyes. I [Tom] talked to him afterwards on the phone and only he really knows why a Gunny would get so emotional. I guess it was the feeling that his Marines were not going to go hungry—eating "PANCAKES" in the middle of Afghanistan.

Bill's wife, Becky, told me that Patrick Lynch's ninety-three-year-old mother and Becky's three-year-old grandson used to help with the packing. From three to ninety-three—that was quite an age spread. I felt humbled at the realization that these total strangers cared so much. I also felt—and feel—deep gratitude. They were taking care of "my kids." I cared about those young Marines. I realized how much the home front was involved on a special level when I received an email from Laura Rinaldi, another of the WSSAS key people and VA employee:

I as an individual, and occasionally with groups, had often contributed items for troop packages, or money to ship them. You feel good about doing it, but could only wonder at who was receiving what, if they really needed it, or if they received the packages at all. This was the first time that the "troops" had names and faces. This was the first time that we had a firm picture in mind of the types of goodies that would really be welcomed by these young people. We were on a real mission when we hit the stores this time!! And to find out immediately what the reaction was to the smell of pancakes on the griddle—made me cry . . . still does!

The irony struck me like a thunderbolt. There we were, fighting in the most modern war to date, with technology I couldn't have dreamed of thirty-five years prior when I was an active-duty Marine, being supported with food and essentials—by the Civil War Soldiers' Aid Society. The past and present, the Civil War and the Afghanistan War, collided and coalesced at a tiny, obscure military post in the western Afghanistan desert. The conduit between the two conflicts was the West Side Soldiers' Aid Society.

Helping hands had reached across time.

14

Counterinsurgency

The lieutenant had a pretty clear idea of what he wanted to accomplish in his platoon area of operations (AO). It wasn't merely keeping the Taliban at bay, or even pursuing and defeating them. He had straight-forward notions of what it would take to win the war, and that was COIN—counterinsurgency operations. First among COIN principles was security for the population. That meant we continued to hunt for the Taliban and push them farther and farther away from the village of Golestan.

Second, he wanted to get the Afghan governmental officials reen-gaged in running their own country. They had pretty much gone to ground years before, but they still held their positions, even if it was in name only. In furtherance of that aim, we made an unannounced visit to the residence of the subgovernor. The man, and all Afghan civilians hereafter mentioned, will be known only by a nom de guerre.

"Ibrahim Khan" was the hereditary leader of one of two tribal sub-groups that dominated the platoon AO. Unlike the tribes of Iraq, Afghanistan tribal leaders did not have autocratic power. They exercised control through personal influence only. Ibrahim Khan lived far to the south of Golestan in his own private compound. Everything was still made of baked mud, but he had a fine-looking irrigated garden behind his house. It was beautifully green and provided the ambience from where we would sit and talk—under shade-providing grapevines. I loved visiting that place. He even had corn growing.

Ibrahim Khan was reputed to be playing both sides.

We had been told that he had been host the previous evening to one of the two principal Taliban leaders operating in the Golestan valley. Therefore, our unexpected visit created quite a stir. He didn't know whether we had come to take him away. He was an older man with gray in his hair and full beard, and had fought in the war against the Soviets along with his longtime friend "Hajji Mohammed." (Hajji throughout most of the Muslim world refers to an individual who has made the "hajj," or trip to Mecca. In Afghanistan it was often a simple title of respect.)

Despite being equally old, equally gray, and somewhat overweight, Hajji Mohammed met us armed with his AK-47; he never left Ibrahim Khan's side.

Notwithstanding his suspicions about the subgovernor, the lieutenant demonstrated a level of statesmanship that is rarely found in one so young; he hid his reservations well. He also managed to remain in charge despite the fact that his leadership status was completely mind-boggling to the Afghans. In that country, gray hair rules. Time and again the subgovernor would look at me—with my gray hair—and appear confused. Brewster was doing the talking for all of us Americans. In time, they would get used to it. Meanwhile, the lieutenant assured them that our visit was purely social. We had come to get acquainted only.

Introductions were made over chai—Afghan tea—and small talk was the order of the day. I was introduced as Brewster's "political adviser." Not to be outdone, the subgovernor introduced his AK-47-toting friend as his "security adviser." The old veteran of the war with the Soviet Union regaled us with tales of his days fighting the Communists. I knew he was trying to impress us with his status as a warrior so we would think twice before attempting to make off with his comrade, but his stories were entertaining and I enjoyed them.

They were particularly in character coming from a guy holding an AK-47.

When it became obvious that we really were going to leave as peacefully as we had come, the subgovernor heaved a barely perceptible sigh of relief. He gushingly invited us back for more social visits. Brewster set the date for the next one.

While I realized that for us to show up unannounced was anxiety-producing for Ibrahim Khan, having him know when to expect us was a source of stress for me. I didn't trust him a bit. Of course, he was playing both sides. He couldn't know who was going to win the war, and his life depended on his making the correct estimate. As the tribal leader he couldn't just stay neutral. The Taliban had to be making demands on him. Moreover, in time I would come to recognize that most of his tribe was pro-Taliban. Nothing in war is safe, however, and throughout the deployment Brewster took calculated risks—as was required of him.

When the date of our return arrived, all of us were ready for anything. In spite of my concerns, we arrived safely. Our appearance this time was greeted by a greatly relaxed subgovernor. Even Hajji Mohammed was unarmed—and we were introduced to other subdistrict functionaries. They had been invited by Ibrahim Khan.

It was the beginning of a long series of visits that would enable us to wrap our minds around the substrata of the valley we were trying to calm. For Lieutenant Slocum and me, it also became the first step in the creation of tribal maps and personality flow charts that would show the interconnectedness of the key players in the AO. In short, Slocum and I would get busy working together as investigators.

The most important introduction, for Slocum and me, was to one of the assistants to the subgovernor, "Hamid Khan." He was a man well versed in both the law of Afghanistan and the demographics of the Golestan valley. We would spend countless hours together, the three of us, in hot, stuffy rooms or in the shade of hot, stuffy alcoves, working through an interpreter. In the end, we possessed an excellent map of every single rural community in the huge valley, with the name of the village written in both Pashto and English. In addition, the tribe to which each village belonged was color-coded.

More importantly, after countless visits, often by silently listening, we were able to identify the two principal Taliban leaders and their "civilian" associates. We prepared a typical law-enforcement flowchart that demonstrated at a glance their relationships to one another. All of that came much later. But it began with this visit.

If traveling to the subgovernor's compound was stressful, leaving it was worse. To claim plausible deniability I realized it would be in his best interest if we were attacked after the visit, not on the way. My "street radar" convinced me that he was under intense pressure from the Taliban, and I felt there was at least a fifty-fifty chance that we would be attacked during the return trip.

But the lieutenant was no fool. We carefully made our way back to the FOB by an entirely different route than the one on which we came. An ambush would have been impossible. And we stayed off roads nearly all the time. It made for a long, jarring, bone-banging ride, but none of our vehicles struck an IED.

As was the case traveling to and from the subgovernor's compound, Bravo squad didn't always patrol on foot. Often we ranged far from the FOB, searching for signs of the enemy. To exist in the desert, one has to know where the water is. Whether it will come from one of the widely dispersed settlements with wells or from a hidden spring, no one travels very far from water. Especially the Taliban, who walked on foot over the burning mountain ranges. If we could find the hidden springs, we might be able to surprise the enemy.

Like the cavalry in the old Southwest, we were hampered by our means of travel. You can't drive up a donkey track. And like the Apache, I knew the Taliban would spot our dust cloud from miles off. Since no lookout could just sit on sizzling hot rocks and live for long, I reasoned they must have a place of shade as their lookout posts.

One day Sergeant Holter was acting on a tip about the location of a spring along a hidden Taliban-traveled path. We searched a number of areas by vehicle and on foot. We came upon a remarkable patch of green grass hidden from ordinary view. There was no water in sight, but there had to be water somewhere—there was no other explanation for green anything in that arid environment.

Looking up, I spied a cave. It was halfway up a rusty brown burnt rock mountain, and from it I knew one could see for miles in the direction of our FOB. It would afford shade to a lookout. Between the green spot and the cave I felt we were onto something. I just had to climb up there.

It was a steep climb over loose rocks hot to the touch. I would need to lighten my load even more than I already had if I were going to make it. So I left everything behind except for my war belt with pistol and a couple of spare magazines for my rifle. Our squad corpsman, Mike "Doc" Foley, watched the stuff. Wearing only my soft cover for shade and carrying only my rifle, I stuffed a couple more M16 magazines in my cargo pockets as an afterthought. Better too much ammo than not enough.

Then I started the ascent. The squad had fanned out along the base of the mountain looking for any sign of the enemy. In the distance our vehicles were spread out, with only the drivers and turret gunners. The latter would provide covering fire if any of us needed it. It took some doing, but I managed to climb to an elevation equal to the cave opening. I was behind it; if anyone was inside, they could not have seen me. That was good because I was blinded by the fierce sun, and trying to look into the darkness within would have been futile. I had to know.

I slung my rifle over my shoulder and drew my pistol. If anybody with an AK was waiting, I'd have maybe an instant to get off a couple of quick shots provided I rushed into the cave with no sound of my approach. The rifle would have gotten in the way. At the last moment the gravel rock gave way beneath my feet and started a mini-landslide down the rock face. I knew I was in for it if anyone was home, but I had to know. So I threw myself into the cave anyway.

It was empty.

It was also a shady place with a perfect vantage point for a lookout. I could see even farther than I had thought I would be able to when I had been on the level plain below. I could also see a natural cut in the mountain that could be used as a path upward and over the top. I had no radio, yelling would have been foolish, and climbing all the way back down to tell Sergeant Holter what I was doing just didn't seem like the thing to do. It had been a knuckle-scraping, hot-rock-blistering climb. I didn't want to do it twice.

So I did what I always do—I just went. I figured if the enemy was watching, the odds were still in my favor. Up to that point I hadn't seen much from the Taliban that resembled marksmanship. They seemed to prefer the "spray and pray" method of shooting. So I kept one eye out for the nearest cover—large boulders in most cases—and cautiously made my way up the mountain. It was an intense and exhilarating experience. I was alone in Apache country.

I must have been crazy. I liked it.

I felt certain an enemy would miss with an opening volley unless God willed it otherwise, and I'd be behind cover before they could get off a second shot. I was coiled up inside myself like a spring. I noted a covered and concealed way to get back down the mountain with every step I took. It all took quite a period of time while I was watching, listening, and *feeling* for the presence of the enemy. As I neared the top of the mountain, I had to decide whether to continue on over. As badly as I wanted a look at the other side, my sixth sense was talking to me—loudly. I felt that I was being watched. Maybe it was just my imagination—I knew that at the time—but I have learned over time to trust my instincts.

Being shot dead was not the worst thing that could have happened. Being taken alive was. I was mentally prepared to save my last pistol shot for myself if it came to that. As a prisoner I would have had zero chance of survival. Therefore, I reasoned, it would not really be suicide. If I were wrong, I'd have to hope that God was as loving and understanding as I believe He is.

I kept going. I had long since gone out of sight of any Marines below, including the turret gunners. I was really on my own.

Finally the radar pings inside my head were insistent. My way up the mountain had taken so long that if there had been Taliban anywhere near, they would have been able to predict where I would crest the peak. There might not be any time for me to do anything as I went over. As curious as I am by nature, and as desperately as I wanted to know if the long-searched-for trail was on the other side, I did an abrupt ninety-degree turn and scrambled up an adjoining finger of rock outcrop.

There may not have been an enemy within a hundred miles of me. I'll never know this side of heaven. But as crazy as I sometimes think I am, I don't believe I'm stupid. It would have been stupid to continue alone.

The tension was as thick as London fog. It's like that in a war zone. Even when nothing happens, it's tense.

Figuring that if I had been under observation the Taliban would have been setting up for a live capture at the point of logical cresting, I also felt reasonably at ease working my way along that mountainous finger. All in all, I did a large inverted "U" and scouted the many draws and fingers that opened themselves to my view from the new vantage point. I realized I had been gone a very long time. And I decided I ought to head back. As I started making my way back down the mountain, a far piece from where I had originally gone up, I thought I could hear Sergeant Holter calling my name.

He was.

Good old Lance. He was calm and collected when I got back. He would have been well within his rights to chew me out good for going off like that, or to have reported me to Lieutenant Brewster as an idiot. But I always knew he trusted my judgment—as I trusted his. He took my absence in stride. I told him what I found, and what I didn't. Then we mounted up and returned to the FOB. It was nearing sunset.

Nothing had happened. But it may have been the most exciting day I spent in the 'Stan.

The last few members of the Army left the FOB, leaving only Lieutenant Slocum in their place. He and I still shared the same space. With the other soldiers gone, the "room" across the "hall" was vacant. I briefly considered treating myself to private quarters when a new arrival took up residence there.

Scott Brown had spent time in the Army and then worked as a cop for ten years in San Antonio. As such he fit right in with Slocum and me. All three of us were way above the FOB average in age and had police street experience. We saw eye to eye on many things. About five foot ten or so and powerfully built, Scott had fiery red hair with a full, flaming beard to match. He reminded me of a Viking. I could envision him carrying a battle-ax.

Scott was a heck of a nice guy, and it didn't take long before he was immensely popular with the young Marines. He was employed by a civilian corporation, different from my own, whose mission was solely to train the ANP. He had been sent to us because ANCOP had pulled out and the ANP had returned. They were to be his primary responsibility. He brought a lot of specific experience about working with them and he had no illusions regarding their capabilities—or lack thereof. Slocum and I were relieved that we wouldn't be saddled with the ANP burden by default.

Brown was incredibly savvy in battle tactics and patrolling. I often wondered if he had been a member of one of the Army's elite units. I never asked him and he never said. As fearless as he was ferocious-looking, he and I would often go on patrol together in the weeks to come.

It was great having another pair of street cop eyes outside the wire. When it came to the "human terrain," we both could read between the lines.

When Brown, Slocum, and I put our heads together, weighed the facts, and formed a unanimous opinion as to what was going on, it was a safe bet that we were correct. Lieutenant Brewster may have been the only platoon commander in the Marine Corps with his own personal intelligence section.

One day Lieutenant Brewster went somewhere without me—that wasn't usually the case. He liked having me in the background, watching, listening. I think I was probably on foot patrol with Bravo Squad when he left the FOB. Charlie squad went with him.

Anyway, on the way back his vehicle struck an IED. Fortunately, only the engine was destroyed. The charge had been placed expecting a vehicle from the other direction and had detonated prematurely. All the same, the occupants of the vehicle were thrown about pretty badly. Brewster had a massive purple contusion on his thigh when I saw him next. He walked with a severe limp for days and had to have been in a lot of pain, but he never complained.

I seriously doubt he was ever awarded the Purple Heart—for wounds received in action—even though he unquestionably earned it after that encounter with the IED.

When Bravo squad went out on mounted patrol, I always rode in the same vehicle with Sergeant Holter. He and I had long since forged a rifle partner relationship. And he always led from the front. While all the patrol commanders were as careful as they could be about staying off roads or stopping to check on foot for IEDs at any choke points, what had happened to Brewster's vehicle—and too many others throughout the battalion—could happen to any vehicle at any time.

Holter was meticulous in choosing the route. Sometimes, though, we were forced by the lay of the land to cross some terrain feature at a place we would have preferred to avoid. When we came upon such a spot, Holter would stop the convoy and dismount by himself. Well, not exactly by himself; where he went, I went.

Together we would walk the dangerous ground, eyeing it intently for any sign that the earth had been disturbed. Typically, he and I would split up. He would take one side of the road and I'd take the other. If there was gravel on the path, we'd brush it aside with our hands or boots until we were satisfied the ground below was concrete hard. From time to time, I would get down on my knees and poke with my bayonet—listening for the hollow sound it would make if it struck the wood that invariably surrounded the kind of IEDs we encountered in the AO. That would have been insufficient pressure to connect the copper plating and set off the charge.

I was silently gratified that he trusted me with the enormous responsibility of discovering an IED before one of his vehicles carrying his Marines would strike it. Most of the time, he and I were certain the ground we checked was safe and we would get back in the lead vehicle and continue on. If we had been wrong, we—and unfortunately the driver and turret gunner—would pay for our error.

Every once in a while, however, there was still some slight, lingering doubt. Whichever side of the road the suspicious spot was—his or mine—the last thing either of us would do was step on it. The weight of a man would have been enough to cause it to blow. It wasn't a suicidal impulse. It was being ready to "take one for the team." It was our responsibility to find the IEDs, and our young Marines ought not to suffer if we were wrong. Many times I recall holding my breath, then letting it go with a sigh of relief.

What was probably strange about our routine—to anyone but another Marine—was that both of us would stand there. Really, there was no need for two of us to take the chance; one of us should have moved away. But we didn't. We were brothers in arms, and we were in it together. We'd lock eyes; then whichever of us had just checked the spot would step forward.

It was life as usual in Golestan.

On one return trip from the subgovernor's residence, we were traveling up a very wide dried riverbed that comprised the largest river in the region. Almost everyone used it as a road, and it would have been difficult for the enemy to decide where—on that wide expanse—one of our vehicles might wind up. Off in the distance ahead of us, Sergeant Holter spied one individual—in the middle of the riverbed.

He was digging with a shovel.

Normally calm, cool, and collected, Holter was electrified by the sight. Our driver had only recently come to the platoon as a reinforcement of sorts. Colonel Hall had shaken the battalion CP tree and sent us any rear-echelon Marines who fell out. Our driver was inexperienced. Holter gave a firm command: "After him!"

The driver didn't quite know how to maneuver the vehicle up and down the deep ruts and over or around the huge boulders that made up the riverbed. The individual who had been digging looked up—saw us—and started to run.

Holter shouted, "HEAD HIM OFF!" The driver did his best. It wasn't working.

The runner was heading for a village on the opposite side of the riverbank. Once he got there, he could have disappeared. Without a moment's warning, Holter was out of the vehicle and running after the man on foot. Alone. The rest of the patrol was strung out way behind us, and ours was—as usual—the lead vehicle.

I was mortified. "Holy shit! Let me outta here!"

The doors of an up-armored Humvee are strongly locked with levers—to keep angry crowds from opening them. They also weigh a ton because of the armor, particularly if the vehicle is canted due to the nature of the ground, as it was in the riverbed. I struggled to get the rear door of the vehicle open. I had to push it with my leg. It took too much time. I ran just as fast as I could to catch Holter, but he was about to run smack into that village—all by himself. Hell, it could have been the headquarters of the 5th Taliban Horde, for all I knew.

It was bloody hot. I was running with boots, rifle, ammo, water, and other gear in soft, yielding riverbed sand. Not easy for a fifty-eight-year-old guy. Fortunately my body didn't realize how old it was. Holter got there first, but I kept coming on. Whatever was going to happen, we were in it together.

As soon as the lieutenant—probably in the second or third vehicle—caught sight of what was going on, he issued the appropriate orders. The column swung into action. They came up fast and formed a protective 180-degree semicircle around us, then quickly dismounted.

All the same, it took time. The first man I saw covering us was Scott Brown. He had been in the second vehicle. Scott positioned himself, alone, off to the left, behind cover and watching. Calmly and carefully watching—everything. Now there were three of us.

As I've written before, sometimes even when nothing happens, it's pretty nerve-racking. This was one of those times.

Our suspect was a frightened young boy, probably only about twelve or thirteen years old. He had been out playing in the dirt when he looked up and saw us. Worried about what we might think, he dropped his shovel and ran for home. We had to wait for one of our terps to come up and translate for us, but some kinds of communication are universal. It was clear that the man with the boy was his father. Several old gray-haired elders arrived as well. Their expressions were of concern but without fear.

The boy's father bore the look of fathers everywhere—his son was terrified and crying. He wrapped his arms around the boy in a protective gesture. His countenance remained calm and serene. The lad was only playing—that was clear. His posture and expression told me that he was not worried. The boy was too young to have been planting IEDs by himself.

Although a sergeant outranks a corporal, Sergeant Holter is a prime example of what has been described as "the strategic corporal"—that is, the "lowly" NCO who wins or loses insurgency wars where they are fought, down in the dirt. Holter took it all in, arrived at the appropriate conclusion, and conveyed through the universal language of facial expression and body English that all was well. It was a simple misunderstanding. The arrival of the interpreter just put the finishing touches on the piece.

I had learned as a young rookie cop that things aren't always the way they seem. But a trigger-happy soldier or Marine might have shot the boy while honestly believing he was a "fleeing felon." Instead Holter chose to put himself at risk—by rushing off alone into an Afghan village—rather than "shoot first and ask questions later."

I'd cover his six o'clock any day.

Soon after, recalling the movie *Tombstone*, about Wyatt Earp and his friend Doc Holliday, I began to call Sergeant Holter "Wyatt." I was his Doc Holliday and would remain so for as long as I was in Golestan. Some friendships can only be understood in context. And wartime friendships can only be understood by those who have been there and formed them.

Not long after, a civilian bus, traveling down the same dry riverbed, struck an IED. Several civilians were killed, including the bus driver, and others were injured—some seriously. The injured were treated by our corpsmen, led by Hospitalman First Class William "Doc Z" Zorrer. It was the first time there had been a fatal IED attack in our platoon area of responsibility. Slocum, Brown, and I put our heads together.

The head of the ANP—occupying the same mud FOB that the ANCOP had left—was a man we didn't trust. "Abdullah" wore a perpetual "felony look" on his face. Nothing about him inspired confidence. We three believed he had connections with the Taliban, and we believed he knew about the IED. It was meant for us, of course. Not happy about the deaths and injuries of innocent civilians and frustrated at the subgovernor's lack of governance, Lieutenant Brewster made a trip to "Ibrahim Khan's" compound. I accompanied him along with others.

I could see that the lieutenant was getting pretty frustrated with the subgovernor. The man served tea and conversation under the shade of his "backyard" bower, but nothing ever changed. Brewster couldn't seem to get the man to actually *do* anything. This time—possibly still in pain from his own IED encounter—Brewster was pretty pointed in conversation. He wanted to know what Ibrahim Khan knew about the IED that had nailed the bus.

Abdullah was present. Both adamantly denied any knowledge whatsoever. I just sat and listened. The subgovernor mumbled that IEDs were one of the reasons he stayed home even though his job required him to be in Golestan.

As soon as we stood up to leave, while everyone was putting on their gear and grabbing helmets, Ibrahim Khan and Abdullah looked positively relieved. Their change in expression told me they had been holding something back. I knew from experience that a moment like that was pregnant with opportunity. Their guards had been up, but now they felt safe. They had just let down their defenses. Looking straight at the subgovernor, I spoke for the first time during the meeting.

"I just have one question." Everyone stopped and looked at me.

"Why didn't you tell the *bus driver* where the IED was?"

Before he could stop himself, Ibrahim Khan gestured toward Abdullah and said, "Well, I told *him!*"

Brewster looked like he had been slapped. Ibrahim Khan immediately realized he had just screwed up. Brewster was livid. He fairly shouted, "YOU KNEW! YOU KNEW AND YOU JUST SAT HERE AND LIED! YOU KNEW AND YOU DIDN'T TELL US!"

Ibrahim Khan and Abdullah started passing the buck back and forth between themselves.

"I told *him*"—gesturing toward Abdullah—"that it was the brother of—"

"Well, I was conducting an investigation," stammered Abdullah, as their self-serving back-and-forth continued.

I didn't say another word.

Crucial events were beginning to stack up one atop the other.

From that point on, Brown joined Slocum and me as we began to piece together a flowchart of who was in cahoots with whom in the Golestan area. Before we were done, we had connected two local tribal chieftains—one of whom was the subgovernor—with two separate Taliban warlords—the chief of police (Abdullah)—and many other key people in the area. It was standard police work. Like in small-town America, the cops figured out what was going on. Naturally, the chart was given to Lieutenant Brewster. But I made sure the intelligence section at battalion also had it after I left Golestan; they were ecstatic. It was the kind of intangible work LEPs were supposed to produce.

For his part, Abdullah seemed concerned that he might be turned over to some heavy-handed special operations types. He began to fall over backward trying to convince us that he was really our ally. Soon after, at another meeting held adjacent to the FOB, his cell phone rang. He excused himself and walked outside. When he returned, the soul of innocence, he blurted out:

"That was (a *'Taliban warlord'*) who wanted to know what Marines were presently doing in the town he was hiding out in." Brewster was flabbergasted. Charlie Squad was on patrol in that town.

I smiled to myself. The Taliban clearly regarded Abdullah as their informant. And he was trying to convince us of his loyalty by telling us about the call. To an experienced investigator, used to interpersonal machinations, it was beautiful. I had some ideas about how to use him. Unfortunately, that would have been "outside my lane." The issue passed out of my hands and into the hands of those who were tasked with such matters. The details are classified.

All the same, Slocum, Brown, and I quipped privately, "Nice. The Taliban have Abdullah on speed dial!" Cops have a matchless sense of humor.

Trying to lighten his own mood, Brewster asked Abdullah jokingly, "When was the last time you heard from a 'different Taliban war lord'?" Not the sharpest tool in the shed, Abdullah replied, "Oh, I haven't heard from him in over a month."

The lieutenant hadn't expected that answer; he was just kidding. Taking it all in, I just smiled. We really had this guy's number.

15

The Trap

About a dozen new cops fresh from ANP training in another province showed up at Golestan. One was a fifteen-year-old boy. He looked about twelve. I couldn't believe anyone would put a uniform on someone so young. His uniform was about ten sizes too large for him and it made his small frame seem even smaller. In a country where men generally wore beards, his smooth face really stood out. The kid looked innocent and homesick. He was in over his head. I think he missed his mother. He and two men from the same village asked to go home on leave. Abdullah granted their request.

On July 29, while on foot patrol in the hot, dusty streets of "downtown" Golestan, Scott Brown and I listened intently to Sergeant Holter's radio. We could hear a conversation between the lieutenant and the chief of police. Abdullah had just notified Lieutenant Brewster that all three—including the "fifteen-going-on-twelve-year-old"—had been beaten to death by the Taliban. Their bodies were lying in the dirt in the center of the town where they had lived and gone on leave. I could only imagine the grief of the poor boy's family. Abdullah wanted Brewster to get them.

Scott Brown and I looked at each other. "NO WAY!" we both said to each other. "It's a trap!" Abdullah was trying to play both sides, but he was a Taliban informant, no question. Scott and I were relieved when Brewster told Abdullah to go get them himself—that the dead were *his* men.

Upon returning to the FOB, I was even more relieved to hear that the lieutenant planned a mounted patrol to a distant village. By this time I had been out on enough patrols around the platoon AO to develop a pretty good street cop feel for where the bad guys were—and where they weren't. I expected no trouble where Brewster was going. I believed the trip would be uneventful and my presence would not be needed.

The day was a scorcher—as always. And coming off foot patrol I was wrung out—as always. Scott and I decided we had earned a nap. Somehow he had liberated a chocolate cake. He pulled it out from under his cot and we both had a delightful snack—chocolate cake and warm water—yummy. Then it was off with our boots and sleep.

We awoke to the distressing news that the lieutenant had changed his mind. He was going after the bodies after all. Abdullah—for all his insistence—declined to go at the last minute. He wasn't feeling well, he said. He sent along a number of his men. Scott recognized the names from his intimate work with the ANP. They were people Abdullah didn't like.

We were thunderstruck. Slocum concurred. When Slocum, Brown, and I were in unanimous agreement, I cannot recall a single instance in which we had been wrong. It was going to be a bad day.

Gunny Mendoza was still at the FOB. Brown, Slocum, and I let him know we were sure the bodies were cheese in a mousetrap. Most likely the trap was set for Brewster. But it was possible that what the enemy really wanted was to weaken the FOB by siphoning off manpower so they could accomplish what they had failed to do a few weeks prior: overrun the place. Brewster and the other survivors would be thirteen hours behind enemy lines with no ammo resupply, no water, and no gasoline. They'd have been in serious trouble.

The gunny ordered all Marines to stand to. Scott had squirreled away a couple of ANP machine guns—RPKs—and these he set up in tactically sound places around the FOB. We didn't have enough men to man them, but at least they were ready if needed. The gunny ordered some mop sticks to be sawed down and painted black. They were placed at intervals around the FOB. From a short distance away it would look like the FOB was bristling with machine guns.

Slocum and I manned the armored vehicle atop the heavy metal storage box that the Army had used when the FOB was attacked on July 2. Two green rear-echelon Marines who had been sent from battalion by Lieutenant Colonel Hall were posted in the "shithouse bunker." Scott built a little sandbagged position on top of the box where Slocum and I were. He had one of his RPKs there and was ready to use it. We were all facing the most vulnerable side of the FOB—the stonewalled clinic and the wood line. Then we waited. Slocum, Brown, and I knew what was going to happen. We just couldn't be sure where.

Several hours into darkness Gunny Mendoza sent us word that all hell had broken loose where the lieutenant was. So now we knew where.

Anxiously we waited, still standing to. It was possible the Taliban would still attack the FOB. I feared the worst for Brewster and those Marines with him. The lieutenant had taken Bravo squad with him. Although Sergeant Holter had heard what Brown and I said while listening to Abdullah earlier that afternoon, he was a Marine. He would not challenge the lieutenant. But they were my guys. If I had had the slightest idea they were going, I would have gone with them—*if* I couldn't have talked the lieutenant out of going in the first place.

The gunny kept us middle-aged cops in the information loop. The ambush had been sprung, some people were wounded. No more details were available. The radio chatter was typical of a unit under intense fire. We continued to wait. Finally we noticed tracers arcing up at about a forty-five-degree angle from the direction the patrol would have to come. I thought they must be ricochets. Then we could hear gunfire. The returning patrol was running a gauntlet. They had been ambushed twice more.

The two lame ducks in the shithouse bunker were more interested in the fireworks in the sky than watching the still dangerous avenue of approach to the west. Slocum, an Army lieutenant, told them to turn around and pay attention. One of them wise-assed something in response—and I went from zero to ninety, straight into Marine officer mode. I dressed them down with near ferocity. I was in no mood for insubordination. They turned around and paid attention.

When Brewster and all got back, there was plenty of commotion at the corpsmen's post. The wounded turned out to be ANP. Miraculously, no Marines had been killed and none wounded badly. But several of the ANP were seriously wounded. Doc Z and his guys did their best. No one died, so their best was good enough. An emergency medevac helicopter landed just outside the FOB and took the wounded to the hospital at Bastion. It was about a forty-five-minute flight.

The fifteen-year-old ANP kid was unrecognizable. All three had been literally beaten to a pulp. The Taliban are savages. They are religious Nazis. What they do to their own people is inexcusable even in war. It sickens me that they do it in the name of God.

The boys from Bravo Squad filled me in. It had been quite a show. The enemy had used the bodies as bait, all right. The bodies were where the majority of the incoming fire was aimed at. Fortunately the Taliban don't have night-vision goggles, or things would have been worse.

Sergeant Holter was everywhere at once. His normally calm and quiet demeanor was gone; in its place was a Marine NCO caught up in the passion of war. Lance Corporal Bryan "Davey" Davidson had to scramble for a rifle—another Marine snatched his by mistake when the firestorm broke. Corporal "Grandpa" Joe Billington—so named because he was an old man in his late twenties—outdid himself. He was a hero among heroes at all times, using his 60mm mortar in the handheld mode with deadly effect—but he outdid even himself this night.

The ambush began shortly after dark from about three hundred meters away. The enemy opened up with RPGs and PKMs (a different type of machine gun). There were twenty-two ANP with Brewster and Bravo Squad, and they were caught out in the open. Billington did his best to organize the ill-trained ANP to return fire, but with little success.

Scott Brown and I would later describe trying to organize and control ANP under fire as "herding cats." The term caught on around the FOB.

Lieutenant Brewster ordered the ANP bodies recovered before pulling back. Billington backed his Humvee into the kill zone, where machine-gun fire was raking the area. The rest of the Marines returned fire with fury in an attempt to gain fire superiority. Billington's turret gunner blasted away at the unseen enemy as Billington—with no regard for his own safety—made multiple trips over fifty meters of fire-swept ground with some ANP to recover the bodies. He was grazed by a machine-gun bullet in the right arm but ignored the wound. When Brewster learned that Billington had been hit, he radioed his concern.

The corporal's reply to Lieutenant Brewster was at once classic Marine and typical Billington, "Sir, I don't have time to bleed."

As the patrol headed back to the FOB they were again ambushed. RPG and PKM fire from multiple positions inside houses swept the column. One ANP truck—they only had Ford Rangers, not armored vehicles—was struck by an RPG. Four ANP were seriously wounded. Once again Corporal Billington positioned his vehicle within the kill zone and loaded the wounded ANP into a trailer he was pulling.

Lieutenant Brewster put Billington up for the Bronze Star with combat "V." It's the fourth-highest medal for bravery.

When the enemy opened up on the column for the final time—inside Golestan itself—Brewster ordered his automatic weapons to fire above the houses; that was the cause of the tracers Slocum and I saw. The lieutenant didn't want to cause innocent casualties by firing back at an enemy hiding among the people. He hoped the muzzle flashes and the sounds of automatic weapons would help to suppress the ambush.

All in all, we had been lucky.

Within the next day or so, a roving detachment of MARSOC—Marines Special Operations Capable—unexpectedly arrived. Commanded by a major, they were a handpicked group. They were part of the Marine Corps' contribution to the Special Operations Command, along with Army Special Forces and Navy SEALs. To a man, they wore uncharacteristically long hair, and all were sporting full beards. That was the easiest way to tell a MARSOC Marine from any other. It wasn't just for show—they operated behind the lines in out-of-the-way places. They needed to be able to blend in on foot from time to time.

This group—like all the MARSOC groups about which I was aware—came and went like clouds before the moon. What they did and where they went were none of my business. It was definitely above my pay grade. They had arrived out of nowhere and planned on staying a few days to rest and perform preventive maintenance on their vehicles. The rugged Afghanistan desert could really tear up one's means of transportation. Most of ours were out of service for repairs.

Individually the MARSOC Marines were older, bigger, and stronger and of higher rank than the average Marine. They were also friendly to a man. There was no putting on airs or a holier-than-thou attitude in a single one of them. They reminded me of British Royal Marines that I had had the pleasure of meeting back at Bastion.

Our war was ratcheting up in intensity. In less than a month the platoon had been in two major battles with the Taliban. The rest of 2/7 was slugging it out as well. Bill Osborne continued to keep me up to date on the news from the "outside"—including my own battalion. The casualties of 2/7 were up. Way up.

One of the news articles he sent referenced someone from the Marine hierarchy saying "This is no training mission."

Whoever said that was a master of understatement. But at least higher command had finally figured it out.

During the evening of August 1, 2008, I sent an email to Lieutenant Colonel Jack McMahon, USMCR (Ret.). He saved it. He just sent it back to me. It read,

Jack:

Well, its 2100 [9:00 p.m.] here and no white light—even this computer screen is dimmed. I just watched—from inside my mud-walled hooch—the movie *We Were Soldiers* with Mel Gibson. When it came out in the theaters in 2002, I had to walk out a few minutes into the movie. I never did watch it. I realize now that it was guilt I was feeling. I could have made it to 'Nam just before they pulled out. I became a cop instead. I guess I always felt guilty about that.

Well, now I can watch it. I balanced the computer on my chest as I lay on my cot inside my mud hooch. A few meters away was the bunker I helped defend for three hours about a month ago. There's still empty shell casings just lying around on the ground. Everywhere. There's incoming shrapnel tears in the cammo netting where a lot of my empty brass got ejected when I came out from cover for a better shot at the enemy on the hill to our north that night.

And a few meters away from where I lay is the wall they might have come over, and might tonight. Or tomorrow. I'm sitting at the corpsman's computer in dim light, no white light after dark, in my OD green shorts, T-shirt, flip-flops, and M16. It's right by my side. Just in case. Right under the bunker is the shithouse. There's about two feet between the back of it and the mud wall. That's where I cried on 19 June when my two buddies got killed.

Recently the platoon commander very politely said, "Terry, next time we go out and expect to get into a firefight, please wear your

Kevlar [helmet]." He didn't know I had already taken the SAPI plates out of my carrier. Too damn heavy for quick movement. And Bravo squad sergeant always picks me to ride in his vehicle when we go on mounted patrol. He and I are the lead vehicle and IED catchers. I get out with him and walk in front to check for IEDs. We scratch around in the dirt together, and I poke things with my bayonet, listening and feeling for the tip to hit a hollow-sounding piece of wood . . . then we look at each other, and step right on the spot. One last check before we let the vehicles come on. Taking one for the team, so to speak.

Not bragging. You know me better than that. And not suicidal. It's just the way things are. Got a job to do. Finally doing it. Finally. After all these years.

So now I can watch *We Were Soldiers*. I guess I finally earned the right.

McG.

16

The Battle at Feyz al Bad

The next day—the morning of August 2—was exactly one month after our first combat with the Taliban. It was hot, but not as hot as the day would get. I was enjoying a little casual time. Wearing only desert camouflage Marine trousers, a regulation olive drab T-shirt, and a pair of flip-flops, I had declined to go out with Bravo Squad earlier.

I was relaxing in the shade of the staff NCO tent, chatting with Staff Sergeant Justin "Obnoxious" Wells and Hospitalman First Class "Doc Z" Zorrer. After the soul-searching email I had written the night before, I felt like taking a day off. The squad was somewhere near a town called Feyz al Bad.

The staff NCO tent is adjacent to the command post. Suddenly the lieutenant emerged from within. What he had to say shocked me as probably nothing in Afghanistan had—before or after. Bravo Squad was under attack; there were two casualties. We didn't yet know how badly the wounded were hurt. We also didn't know who they were. But they were in trouble, and we were going to get them. I felt extreme anxiety for the injured.

I am Irish by ancestry. In my family there seems to be a touch of what the Irish call the "Sight." To an American that means extrasensory perception. I spoke of it as my "sixth sense" when I climbed the mountain alone. Just the evening before, as I passed Lance Corporal Jeremy Boucher's cot, with him on it, the Sight kicked in. I had the strong feeling that he wasn't going to be with us much longer. I wasn't sure if that meant KIA or WIA, and my rational mind dismissed the notion out of hand. The lieutenant's announcement brought it screaming back into consciousness.

Boucher—pronounced "Boo shay"—was known to one and all as "Butcher," which is how they read his name tape, or affectionately as "Badass Bobby Butcher." Just nineteen years old and freckle-faced, he didn't look the part, but he really was a badass. He came to Afghanistan with no prior Iraq experience and had already proven himself in two major engagements, not to mention numerous patrols.

I knew in my soul that he was one of the casualties. I was forty years old when he was born. To me he was just a kid. And losing kids was not what I had come to Afghanistan for. I had to get up there. Hell, I shouldn't have taken the day off. I should have gone with them. I felt intensely that I should have been under fire with them at that very moment.

Most of our vehicles were down. We didn't have enough transport to make it to Bravo Squad. General Patton once said that he had one motto, "Audacity, audacity, always audacity!" Lieutenant Brewster was the soul of audacity and knew what had to be done. We would march across the dry riverbed and take the ANP trucks. Although they were merely Ford Rangers, with no extra armor, they could seat five inside and more in the bed of the truck.

If one of them struck an IED, everyone on board would be killed. Brewster was putting himself at serious risk if anyone had wanted to second-guess him. But there was no time to waste on niceties—such as getting permission from higher up. He would worry about repercussions later. Silently I approved. It was so—well—Brewster. And it was Marine leadership as I had always known it.

Then he lowered the boom. Knowing how I felt about the squad, he took me aside.

He said, "Terry, I'm sorry. There's just not enough room in the vehicles. You'll have to stay behind."

I would have followed on foot.

I immediately grabbed Scott Brown—our ANP trainer—and asked him if he was going with the ANP. Of course he was. "Got room for me?" I asked. He said yes.

I rushed back to Brewster and told him. With a slight smile, he approved.

That was good, because I really would have walked.

We were major-league lucky that MARSOC was there. We needed the extra help. The Taliban were numerous and pressing Bravo Squad hard. Although a major outranks a second lieutenant considerably, the MARSOC major volunteered to follow Brewster's battle plan.

I ran back to my cot to get my gear—and my boots. This time I would fight with boots on. In my haste, I forgot my night-vision goggles. "What the hell?" I thought. "It's only morning. It's broad daylight and will be for many hours yet."

Before the day was done, I would miss them sorely.

We crossed the riverbed on foot and marched boldly into the ANP compound. Abdullah didn't have time to bow out—not that we would have cared if he did. Personally I felt it would be poetic justice if he were killed by one of the Taliban. The lieutenant commandeered as many vehicles as he needed and set off with the main Marine force. Scott Brown and I followed with the ANP.

Scott is as cool and unflappable a warrior as can be found anywhere. A native Texan, he and I started the trip in the bed of a truck with one ANP and a swivel-mounted machine gun. It was rough going—off-road and at speed. We were getting bounced around pretty hard. The ANP gunner was young and inexperienced. He tried to sit on the edge of the truck bed. He nearly got bounced clean out several times. Although we didn't have an interpreter, it was uncanny how Scott could make himself understood with gestures and facial expressions. He got the young guy to sit down.

Then Scott turned to me and said, "Hey, what could be better? We're off-roading and going hunting! All we need now is beer and country music!" Despite the seriousness of the situation, I laughed. I was glad he was my partner. I was also glad to be riding. I really didn't want to have to walk.

After being bounced around unmercifully for a while, Scott decided that we had had enough of being cargo. Still without benefit of an interpreter, he managed to get the vehicle stopped, and the passengers into the bed of the truck. We took their places inside the cab. The driver didn't speak English and Scott didn't speak Pashto, but hey—details. He managed to make himself understood. I still don't know how he did it, but he kept the driver going where Scott wanted him to go.

Just us two Americans, surrounded by ANP, without an interpreter, we gave new meaning to the term "herding cats" that day.

While we were racing to their aid, Sergeant Holter managed to get his badly shot-up vehicles, with wounded, extricated from the ambush. There wasn't a tire with air in it, nor a vehicle that hadn't been riddled with enemy bullets. Fortunately, the up-armored Humvees could withstand small-arms fire. They had met up with Brewster and the lead elements of the relief column just south of town. There, helicopters extracted the wounded. I would learn the particulars of what had happened when we were all back at the FOB. For the present, I still had no idea what was going on with them.

The Taliban were holding a fishhook-shaped steep-sloped ridgeline south and west of the village of Feyz al Bad. Brewster's plan was to assault up the nearest ridge, at the bend in the hook, taking it by fire and movement—then work his way down the ridgeline, clearing it as he went. Some of the MARSOC vehicles, along with Scott, myself, and the ANP, were designated the left flank. On the way to our position, Scott and I started taking incoming small-arms fire.

We both kicked open our doors to return fire. Unfortunately, neither of us could tell where it was coming from, so we fired back at wherever we thought the enemy might be holed up. A rock ledge here, a depression in the ground there—at least we were doing something besides catching lead.

When we got to the farthest part of the fishhook, Scott and I and the ANP dismounted and took cover in a dry riverbed up against the bank. It was about three and a half feet or so high and provided cover of a kind. We were still taking incoming, and we still didn't know where from. So we continued to return fire wherever we thought an enemy might be hiding. A couple of MARSOC vehicles—two or three, as I recall—were down on the left flank with us but behind us on higher ground farther from the base of the ridgeline we faced—it was the tactically sound place to be. Scott, I, and the ANP were the *extreme* left of the left flank.

Scott was about as lighthearted as a man could be. The enemy fire wasn't terribly accurate—they hadn't hit any of us—and I found myself laughing at his jokes. One of the ANP carried an RPG launcher. Unfortunately for his buddy, he really didn't know how to use it. Nor did he have the sense to tell anybody that he was about to fire the damn thing. They make quite a racket when going off. He managed to hit the mountain, I'll give him that much, but not where it would have done any good. And he blew out the eardrum of his buddy. The man had clear fluid tinged with pink blood flowing out of his ear.

All the while dirt was kicking up sporadically and inaccurately around us. Somehow Scott and I found it all highly comical. We were surely insane. We still didn't have an interpreter, but somehow we managed to communicate with those guys. We tried to tell the guy with the ruptured eardrum to come to our FOB for medical assistance when we got back. He needed it.

Scott and I finally gave up shooting at rocks and just let the enemy drop rounds on us. I always went on the "big world, little bullet" theory anyway. I figured there was a greater chance of being struck by lightning during a storm than getting hit that day, and I began to size up the position we were in. The fishhook-shaped ridgeline was about eight hundred meters high and ended suddenly and steeply to our left front. It ran roughly north to south. About two hundred meters north of us, on our left, a smaller, sugarloaf-shaped ridge ran east to west.

Right about then, straight to our front and on the summit of the eight-hundred-meter fishhook ridge, a Taliban with an RPG leaped to his feet and fired off a rocket at us. He missed by a mile. Then he jumped up, waving his arms and yelling something. If he was trying to entertain us, he succeeded. Scott and I thought it was hilarious. He kept it up, alternating between waving his arms and shooting an occasional rocket. We tried to time his movements. One of us would aim carefully and say, "I wonder if he'll jump up . . . NOW!" BANG. "Nope. I wonder if he'll jump up . . . NOW!" BANG.

I began to wonder what was going on in this crazy fool's mind. Suddenly it dawned on me that he might actually be trying to hold us in position. His antics might be designed to keep us where we were. The Taliban are known to turn flanks and maneuver into the rear. I mentioned it to Scott, who optimistically quipped, "Well, at least we have cover."

I responded with "COVER! COVER! WHAT COVER? I'M *YOUR* COVER. THERE'S NOTHING TO *MY* LEFT!" It was all said with a degree of hilarity. We really were having way too much fun for guys getting shot at.

The sporadic fire seemed to slack off, and I couldn't help but wonder why the turret gunner in the nearest MARSOC vehicle didn't try to take the guy out. So I decided to take a walk and chat with them. A corporal in the rear seat told me later of their impression when they saw me walking toward them.

"We looked out and saw you coming and said, 'What the hell?! Who is this old guy? Does he think he's out for a walk in the park? Doesn't he see the bullets kicking up dirt around him?'"

Truth is there wasn't that much incoming and I just didn't have a lot of confidence in Taliban marksmanship. I figured if they hit me it would be an act of God or an accident. Provided they were aiming at me, of course. My concern up against the dry riverbank was that they'd aim at Scott and hit me by mistake.

So they opened the rear hatch and said, "Yeesss?"—with a tone of incredulity. I said, "Hey, do you guys realize there's an RPG position on the topographical crest of that mountain there?"—pointing at it. They replied "Yeesss," whereupon I said, "Oh, okay," and turned to walk back to Scott.

I didn't ask them why they weren't shooting at it, and they didn't say.

I hadn't gone very far when that damn RPG gunner popped up and fired one off right at me. I could see the smoke trail clearly and hear the WHOOOSSHH as it went over my head. It exploded, if that corporal is to be believed, about fifteen meters from me. If so, I was really in luck (or God still had plans for me), because that's inside the casualty-producing radius of one of those things.

Well, I admit it *did* take me by surprise, and my reflexive response amazed even me.

I flipped the guy "the bird" and yelled at the top of my lungs, "FUCK YOU! FUCK YOU! FUCK YOU! YOU CAN'T HIT SHIT!"

. . . and just kept walking back to Scott. I'd be damned if I'd give the enemy the satisfaction of seeing me run. An old guy has his dignity to preserve.

I will admit, however, that I was straining to look out of the corner of my eye at that mountaintop. If that guy had popped up again, I figured he'd be able to adjust his aim. I was fully prepared to take off like a jet—blue flame out my butt and all!

In an email exchange between Scott and me last summer he wrote:

Best memory ever—you walking through a dry riverbed, RPG rounds
landing only meters away from you, and you're calmly walking and
shooting the finger back. Good times.

I replied,

I wasn't as calm after the RPG as I appeared—I was looking out my
ear if that fuker [sic] had popped up again I'd have run like hell!!!

Scott wrote back,

Well then, you fooled me! I thought I was seeing a reincarnation of
Stonewall Jackson himself, or you possibly practicing for another Civil
War battle reenactment!!

That RPG gunner really had pissed me off, though. I gave serious consideration to working my way up the mountain and taking him by surprise—that is, until I realized there wasn't so much as a baseball-size stone to take cover behind if he popped up and saw me before I got there. I'd have been a sitting duck. I'm crazy sometimes, but not stupid.

As we stayed crouched up against that riverbank, time passing slowly, I began to consider that we just might be there all night. I sorely missed my night-vision goggles, and I wished I had brought even more ammo than the 330-plus rounds I had started out with.

Fortunately, Brewster was fighting his way along the ridge by then and the enemy was forced to abandon their position. The MARSOC major appeared at our location and informed us of the master plan—it was time for us to make an end run. In addition to not having an interpreter to help us "herd cats," neither Scott nor I had a radio. We had been just playing everything by ear. It's amazing what one can tell about the dispositions of fighting forces and progress just by listening to the sound of gunfire.

Anyway, the major, a MARSOC gunny, Scott, I, and our "herd of cats" started out around to the left of the fishhook. The major repositioned a couple of his vehicles north of the worrisome sugarloaf ridge, and that protected our flank. We began the climb up, toward the RPG position. Along the way we found corroboration of the enemy's presence: discarded water jugs, some ammunition, and other evidence of a fighting force.

When we crested the ridge, stretched out below us was the rather large village of Feyz al Bad. Between us and it was a mud-walled compound. It was typical of all the Afghan compounds, an adobe house surrounded by walls. We approached it from the elevated side of the mountain.

The MARSOC gunny, whom I had become pretty tight with back at the FOB, assumed de facto command. He positioned me with the ANP along the wall in a covering position. Then he, the major, and Scott scaled the wall to secure the house. The ANP were their usual selves. It was time for a smoke break and some cheerful banter. They weren't covering anybody.

Just before hooking around to the front of the house, the gunny looked up at me. His eye contact told me I was where he wanted me to be, doing what he wanted me to be doing—watching—ready to provide covering fire.

Then they disappeared from sight.

As soon as they were out of sight, three Taliban, farther down the slope inside the outskirts of the village, AK-47s in hand, darted from cover and ran into some leafy trees. I lit the place up firing where I figured they would have gotten at the last course and speed that I had seen them. I have no idea if I hit them.

The ANP decided they wanted to join in the fun and started shooting up an irrigated cornfield a couple of hundred meters to our right front. I had no idea where Brewster was, or what his plan was—for all I knew his Marines could be moving through that high corn, clearing it of the enemy. Therefore I couldn't allow them to continue shooting. I had a devil of a time getting the ANP to stop.

About then the assault team reappeared with a solitary old man—the occupant of the house. The old man was freed and allowed to return to his home. I told the gunny and the others what I had seen and where I had last seen them. We held where we were, and Scott took over working with "the cats." There was a lot of activity in the village below us and beyond. Clearly Marines were pressing the Taliban from the south. Several MARSOC vehicles were repositioned behind us, with their turret gunners ready to provide overhead fire.

Right then I spotted a Taliban with an AK-47 running from north to south. Since he was running in the direction of Brewster's main force, I knew he was still in the fight. Unless he suddenly had a change of heart, he was a threat to Marines. I said to the MARSOC gunny, "Look there." He said, "Where?"

I said, "Way over there, the opposite side of the valley, about eight hundred meters." The gunny still couldn't see.

I said, "Watch for my dust" and squeezed off a single shot. Although I had been elevating my weapon, the round still felt short. But the gunny now saw the enemy.

I took more careful aim, adjusting for greater elevation, and led the man, as I had learned to do while hunting running deer. I squeezed off a shot. Although an M16 has very little recoil, it does have some. Just enough so that at the instant the round leaves the barrel the target is obscured by the rifle.

The gunny said, "I think you got him."

I said, "I don't know. He's still running."

The man had jumped into a narrow, dry wash. I never did ask the gunny why he thought I had shot a man who was still running. Maybe he saw the guy lurch or something that I couldn't see in that moment.

It was a pretty long shot, and the round was probably near the end of its terminal velocity—meaning it was getting pretty weak. The Taliban might've said "Oww" when it hit and run faster.

The lieutenant saw me shoot from atop the ridge, and later he told me it was about a thousand-meter shot. I was glad I had chosen the long-range M16A4 back in the States. Even so, it took a lot of "seat of the pants" shooting experience. I was aiming at a small cloud.

A moment later, an M40 (a 40mm grenade "machine gun") from one of the MARSOC vehicles filled that wash with bursting grenades. A cockroach couldn't have gotten out of there alive. Some of the MARSOC Marines said a total of five Taliban had taken cover in that wash.

To our right and higher up the ridgeline where the RPG position had been was a solitary body. Knowing my law enforcement background, the MARSOC gunny asked me if I wanted to check it out with him. It wasn't morbid curiosity; we needed to check the body for any intelligence information he might have on him. We left the cover of the adobe wall and walked over. As we drew nearer, I thought I was looking at a mannequin instead of a corpse. The complexion was all wrong and the skin had the appearance of wax.

Closer examination revealed the gruesome wounds that had taken this man's life. He had bled completely out, hence his color. A pocket search revealed he was a Pakistani. He had come for jihad. I hope he came to die in jihad, because that's the only glory he got. He wasn't going back to Pakistan with tales of heroic deeds done—ever.

Since the Taliban never leave dead or wounded behind for us to find, the body's presence was telling. The Marines had forced the enemy to retreat in great haste. Marines nicknamed the corpse "Bernie"—after the hit movie *Weekend at Bernie's*, where one of the actors was supposed to be dead.

After a time we linked up with Lieutenant Brewster and the main force. Together we entered the outskirts of the village, securing it compound by compound in an ever-widening perimeter. It was movement to contact in an urban environment. If the Taliban had chosen to contest our advance, it could have gotten ugly. Even reinforced by MARSOC, we were still pretty shorthanded.

We probably secured about a quarter of the village when the lieutenant ordered a halt. He was co-coordinating MARSOC, his Marines, and the ANP—plus we finally had air on station. Without a radio I don't know who was flying the jets, but they were overhead. Scott and the ANP stayed back—as per the lieutenant's orders—and took care of the civilians we encountered. The women were allowed to stay in their homes, but the men were watched. I stayed with Brewster. I decided at that point that I ought to cover his six o'clock.

The sharp, loud CRACK of a single .50-caliber round breaking the sound barrier over our heads was heard periodically. There was a MARSOC sniper with a .50-caliber rifle on the ridge Brewster had cleared. He was providing overhead cover for us below.

We were stopped at an arrow-shaped intersection of sorts near a wall that encircled some kind of irrigated—and hence green—park. The arrow pointed straight at our middle. Whenever I can't see what's going on, I get nervous. So I peered over the wall to be certain the Taliban weren't trying to get close to us. They weren't.

The lieutenant, probably even more concerned for my safety than I was for his, very politely said, "Terry, please get down."

I was starting to love that guy.

The lieutenant, with his radio, was privy to all the intelligence information about the enemy's movements—as could be gleaned from aircraft, the MARSOC sniper, and every Marine unit involved. He decided it was time to pull back. The enemies were numerous and were massing in the center of the town for a counterattack. Aircraft couldn't engage because of civilians in the area, and where we were was definitely not suited for defense.

Besides, the lieutenant had stripped the FOB of every available man—Gunny Mendoza and Lieutenant Slocum had to be holding their breath—and Brewster was concerned it might be attacked while we were away.

The civilians the ANP had been holding were released to return to their homes. We began to disengage. The Marines to the south of us were still fighting, and the jets screamed overhead. When I got back to the compound near the crest of the ridge whence we came, I could watch the jets in action. Numerous Taliban were spotted running inside a compound outside the village on the east side—a good distance away. It was isolated, believed to be unoccupied by anyone but the Taliban, and I watched a jet score a direct hit with a five-hundred-pound bomb.

Think big boom. Really big boom.

From what I could gather by sights and sounds, we had overlapped the fishhook-shaped ridge that partially surrounded Feyz al Bad. Marines engaged the enemy to the south, some held the high ground to the west, and Brewster and the rest of us entered the village from the north. The enemy was squeezed into the center of town.

Pulling back from north around to the west, ultimately to link up with the forces in the south, was a complicated maneuver. It had to be done fast, before the enemy could realize what we were doing. A retrograde movement is inherently dangerous. We moved out quickly but efficiently. Scott and I herded the cats while the Marines, who were all combat veterans, performed with their expected excellence. It was rapidly approaching dark as we linked up with all our forces south of the fishhook.

In the rush to get moving, I wound up in the same ANP truck as Abdullah. I was the only American. Scott was in another vehicle. It's just the way things played out. Scott asked me if I was all right with the arrangement—we both knew Abdullah was a rat—but he gave me a radio so I could call for help if needed. So I said, "Sure."

I sat in the rear seat right behind Abdullah, who drove. We were driving in pitch dark. I missed my NVGs badly. If Abdullah thought he was going to hand me over to the Taliban, he was badly mistaken. Quite possibly he could have left the column and nobody would have noticed. But I had a plan. I was watching him closely. His body movements, the tone in his voice, although unintelligible, everything about him and the ANP sitting next to him in the front seat. At the first sign of his driving off on his own, I would have put my pistol to the back of his head. If he didn't immediately understand 9mm, I'd have pulled the trigger without hesitation.

It really was that simple.

We returned to the FOB, to the immense relief of the gunny and Slocum. They had broken out the black-painted mop handles again, but they were holding down the fort with even fewer men than the last time.

Back at the FOB, that night and the next day, I learned from Bravo Squad what had happened. As the patrol moved up a wash system, it was ambushed by a much larger Taliban force from the surrounding hills to the east and south. Long-range machine guns firing from two directions—located several hundred meters away—began raking the vehicles with automatic fire. An RPG team about fifty meters to the south stood up and began engaging the Marine vehicles. Their rounds missed but were way too close for comfort.

When all hell broke loose, Lance Corporal Jonathan Zequeida, a fire team leader, made a split-second decision that nearly cost him his life. He got out of the armored vehicle. A machine-gun bullet struck him in the upper part of his leg, breaking the femur. A broken femur is extremely painful. Worse, with the hatch of the Humvee open, another machine-gun bullet entered and struck Lance Corporal Jeremy "Badass Bobby Butcher" Boucher in the leg. The kid was manning his machine gun in the turret. He ignored the wound and kept firing.

In an email to Bill Osborne and the home front sent shortly after I had left 1st Platoon for the battalion command post, I wrote,

Jeremy (is his real first name but everybody called him "Bobby" for reasons known only to God) is a lance corporal. I don't have any contact with him. I never got his email address before he was suddenly removed from us, and he's one of the few in his generation that don't have Myspace.

I just had coffee with the battalion commander (I have "pushed back" to the Brit base at Bastion). We were marveling at the young Marines and their courage and commitment to each other. Jeremy is a case in point. Even with a bullet through his leg he wouldn't leave his machine gun. The squad was in a very tight spot. And he refused medical treatment until his more badly wounded buddy was taken care of. Then he allowed himself to be treated WHILE STILL MANNING HIS GUN and didn't leave it until the medevac chopper arrived to take him and the other casualty off.

Extraordinary courage was ordinary for Lance Corporal Daniel Hickey as well. Hickey got out of his vehicle and rushed to Zequeida's aid. Zequeida was writhing on the ground in pain, and Taliban machine-gun rounds were spraying all around him. Ignoring the incoming fire, Hickey scooped Zequeida up like a doll and stuffed him back inside his armored vehicle—slamming the hatch shut. Then he did something truly noteworthy.

He aimed his handheld squad automatic weapon (SAW) machine gun at a Taliban machine gunner only fifty meters away and went toe-to-toe. It was a modern-day gunfight at the OK Corral—right down to the dry southwestern climate. And it was man-to-man. Instead of Colt .45 Peacemakers at high noon, the duel was fought with machine guns. Hickey won. The Taliban gunner was cut down.

Meanwhile, as "Doc" Michael J. Foley, the squad's Navy corpsman, tried to treat Boucher—still blasting away with his machine gun—an incoming round just missed Foley's head and rattled around inside the Humvee. Boucher refused treatment, indicating that Foley should work on Zequeida instead. After the doc had done what he could for Zequeida, Boucher allowed Foley to work on him. The freckle-faced kid with boyish good looks manned his gun until the medevac chopper arrived to take him and Zequeida to a hospital. The round took a nasty hunk out of Boucher's leg.

"Michael J."—as I always called Foley—got the Navy-Marine Corps Achievement Medal with combat "V" for his work that day. "Badass Bobby"— in addition to the Purple Heart—was awarded the Bronze Star with combat "V." And Daniel Flynn Hickey—I always called him by his full name—well, he got the Silver Star. That's the nation's third-highest award for bravery, and rarely given out—in the Marine Corps, at least.

Corporal Billington was his usual self. He had his handheld 60mm mortar with him—which he used to great effect. Once contact had been broken, Sergeant Holter called for medevac choppers for Boucher and Zequeida. But the Taliban weren't done with the squad yet. Like mountain Apache, they started maneuvering along a high ridgeline, seeking a new firing position. Billington employed his mortar to drive them off.

When Brewster arrived, Billington linked up with him and used his mortar as directed. In recommending him for the Bronze Star, the platoon commander wrote, it was "reported by four local nationals held hostage inside the compound, that Corporal Billington's fires destroyed six enemy fighters, and displaced many more. They visually confirmed that one round impacted an enemy fighter directly on the head."

I learned that the jets were American F-18s, and they were guided on target by Staff Sergeant Justin Wells. He was responsible for blasting the enemy out of their strongholds.

As mentioned earlier, I used to write to the folks back home—the West Side Soldiers' Aid Society—and tell them about the platoon they were supporting. It helped them to feel connected. Sitting in the shade of the staff NCO tent, still broiling from the desert summer heat, I had returned to the T-shirt and flip-flops—casual wear—that I had so hurriedly shed when Bravo Squad was ambushed only the day before. I was back on email. It was August 3, and I had just received a list of the goodies we could expect—including the beloved pancake mix—from Bill Osborne.

I sent them this:

OUTSTANDING! And on 2 August we went after the Taliban. They had ambushed one of our squads. Nice op. We got off lucky. No KIAs, 2 WIAs [wounded in action]. Not critically. One was a Wisconsin young Marine (whose name I can't release in order to give the family time to be notified) [*Boucher*]. But you will be pleased and proud to know that after taking a bullet through the leg he crawled back into the turret of his vehicle and continued to fire his machine gun until medevaced. A process that takes some time being out as far as we were. The other guy [Zequeida] will be medevaced back to the States, where his firstborn daughter is due to be born later this month. With any luck, he'll be there for the occasion.

Modern marvels—I had a reply the very next day. Bill Osborne wrote,

Thank you so much for the updated report. You all are in our prayers for safety and success. Tell the Marines they are truly appreciated and supported 150%. It is an honor and a privilege to be able to help in any way. We just got back from the Civil War Shoot in Boscobel WI, and have enough to fill at least twelve more boxes. Tell the Gunny I got him two camping griddles made of aluminum and Teflon coated. A set of cheap plastic cooking utensils. Gotta have something to flip the pancakes. I was just asked by Terry Arliskas if you need frying pans?

MARSOC, having arrived in the nick of time like the proverbial cavalry, disappeared again like a wisp of smoke. Life returned to normal at the FOB. Well, as normal as it could with two of our favorite personalities abruptly snatched from us—Zequeida and Boucher. It was strange watching the guys pack up their personal items to be shipped back—toothbrushes, shaving razors, and whatnot. Any Marine gear that the other guys wanted was divided up. There was a long-standing joke among Marines that whoever dies first, the others split his gear.

It took a while to realize that we weren't going to see them every day—and not for a long time at that. On patrol and sitting around passing the time, their faces, their voices, their individual senses of humor, were part of the tapestry of the squad and part of what made life on the edge of nowhere bearable. Not having them around took a lot of getting used to. I was thankful that they were alive, at least. Lieutenant Brewster kept us apprised of their condition. They were healing well. That was a relief. Zequeida was shipped back home pretty much immediately, and Boucher followed him after a while.

17

From the Alamo to Fort Apache

About this time my "roommate," National Guard lieutenant Kyle Slocum, got rotated out to some other godforsaken FOB far from Golestan. I have to admit I missed him. The good news is that he was replaced by another "civilian" from the same company that signed Scott's checks. I put "civilian" in quotation marks because this guy, Dennis Francis, was one more former Marine who had it in his head that he was *still* a Marine and always would be.

A former North Carolina state trooper, he was the perfect replacement for Slocum. We still had three street cops on hand, and when all three of us were in agreement, we were never wrong. Even better—in a brown, dry, hot, austere land, Dennis had an incredible sense of humor. Forget *The Tonight Show with Jay Leno*; if the producers of the show had spent ten minutes with Dennis, Leno would have happily left the show—laughing. For my part, Dennis touched my funny bone in a way that left me begging for him to stop—I couldn't breathe. And he would start laughing at my laughing. We three old guys—Scott, Dennis, and I—were surely insane.

The powers that be never intended that 1st Platoon, Golf Company, should be stuck in a place so like the Alamo—they just weren't able to pull together the heavy equipment we needed to construct a typical Hesco FOB—and get it up to us. That changed about this time, and construction began in earnest. When the new place was completed, I dubbed it "Fort Apache." I couldn't quite shake the notion that we were fighting Apache in the old Southwest.

Looking back, the analogy still seems right.

Things were beginning to change for the better. While still back in the States I had commented to Lieutenant Colonel Hall that the reason there were no "incidents" in the area we were heading to was because there were no Americans there yet. He just looked at me with the same perceptive smile I learned was his trademark "I know" facial expression.

But the folks from up the chain of command had it in their heads that 2/7 was on a mission to train Afghan police. As a result, we didn't arrive in country with everything Marines usually take to war—such as our own air assets. Happily, the informative emails from Bill Osborne kept coming. He told me that Marine helicopters were en route to us from Iraq. Once they arrived, what had been a torturous thirteen-hour-plus trip would then take about fifty minutes.

Bill also gave me some incredible information: the commandant of the Marine Corps (CMC), General James T. Conway, was coming to visit 2/7. Moreover, word had it that the CMC would visit FOB Gole-stan. If the appearance of a lieutenant general at FOB Delaram was news, the coming of the CMC to Golestan was regarded as earthshak-ing. In the Marine Corps the commandant is considered to be just below St. Peter in rank. He is to Marines what the pope is to Catholics.

The CMC's arrival was preceded by a deafening near-ground-level buzzing by a Marine helicopter gunship—a Cobra. It was the first such helicopter I had seen in Afghanistan. The pilot—flying at extreme low level—was looking to draw fire. He circled the entire FOB swiftly at very low altitude. His wingman—another gunship—remained aloft, ready to swoop down and light up any enemy forces that might have been foolish enough to engage the first chopper. Only when no ground fire was received did the commandant's transport helicopter appear and land right outside the FOB.

The Stars and Stripes along with my Marine Corps flag were proudly displayed on the south wall of the mud hut that Bravo Squad and I called home. Camouflage netting was set up to provide shade from the August sun. I could hardly believe my eyes when the number one Marine in the whole Corps, packing a pistol, strolled into our mud-walled, partially enclosed FOB. The man was a giant—he had to be six-foot-six at least, possibly taller. Of course with his status he could have been a midget and I'd have been impressed.

Dennis Francis and I, two old guys who still believed that "once a Marine" meant "always a Marine," were proud as hell. The commandant is a four-star general who sits with the Joint Chiefs of Staff. He routinely confers with the president and other Washington, D.C., movers and shakers. But he wasn't afraid to come and see his Marines at the "tip of the spear."

Only slightly removed in reverence is the number one enlisted Marine in the Corps, the sergeant major of the Marine Corps. Sergeant Major Carlton W. Kent arrived with the commandant.

Scott Brown, Dennis Francis, and I watched from the back of the pack as many Marines sat on the ground to hear what the two had to say. My old pal Lieutenant Pat Caffrey had arrived with the CMC's party. Pat had been promoted to first lieutenant, and the general did the honors.

I had broken out my old tricolored Marine eight-point cover to mark the occasion. Lieutenant Brewster made it a point to introduce me. The CMC took one look at my old cover and said, "Former Marine! Who were you with?" I told him my unit, and we exchanged pleasantries for a brief time. I have a picture shaking hands with him. I'm only five-foot-eight, and next to him I looked like a Hobbit.

Soon after the CMC's departure the new Hesco-walled FOB was ready for us to move into. The new FOB was as huge as the old one had been tiny. It was quite a change. We had no sooner moved out of the old "Alamo" when the people of Golestan began ransacking the place. They ripped mirrors off the "shithouse" bunker's walls and grabbed anything that wasn't nailed down.

Like looters everywhere, they destroyed what they didn't take. Their actions were both disgraceful and a testament to how close to the poverty line these people had been living. As was noted when I arrived at Delaram, the uncountable billions in foreign aid that had been spent on Afghanistan over the years did not trickle down to the ordinary people— at least as far as I could see.

It was equally obvious to me that they didn't regard us with dread— as they had the Soviets. From stories told by old mujahideen, the Soviets would have shot them all.

Not wanting the place to be used as a staging ground for an attack on the new FOB, Lieutenant Brewster ordered it demolished. The heavy machinery the platoon had received ground our old fortress to dust. Nothing remained but the outline of the perimeter. I was almost sorry to see it go. By now the "Alamo" seemed like home to me, and I was quite comfortably ensconced in my mud quarters.

Although located only a couple of hundred yards away, in the devilish summer heat I dreaded moving gear to the new FOB—"Fort Apache." I sat on the "back porch" as long as I could. Finally I joined Scott and Dennis under a blue tarp up against the giant sandbag walls. We weren't far from the lieutenant's new command post.

The tarp dipped down at an angle running from the Hesco wall to a point about three or three and a half feet above the ground. It was put up that way to minimize our exposure to the hellish sun. I had to duck every time I went in or out of our crude, homemade hooch. I fastened my Marine Corps flag to the lip of the tarp so it would provide all the shade I could get on my cot. We no longer had a flagpole.

A couple of portable chairs materialized from somewhere, and that made things almost downright homey. In deference to our age, I posted a sign that read, "SHADY ACRES REST HOME." Probably since he was also old—in his late twenties—"Grandpa" Billington set up his cot nearby. Pretty much every morning when I'd get up Billington would say, "You're not dead yet?"

I'd respond with, "Nope. Who's got tomorrow in the pool?" It was a tongue-in-cheek reference to an imaginary bet as to when I'd kick off from old age.

Moving severed our Internet connection for quite a while. The good news was Scott had a portable satellite dish provided by his "check signers." The bad news—it was cantankerous as hell. He carefully placed the dish atop the Hesco ramparts directly over our heads and did his best to aim it at the correct place in the nearly featureless sky. It took some doing. Then, when it wasn't too hot, or too windy, the damn thing might work. Sometimes we went for days with no connection while it did whatever it had to do to reset itself. It was maddening, but it was still something. It allowed me to keep up correspondence with the home front—albeit sporadically.

Before we left the old mud building, I used to watch a movie at night—whenever circumstances allowed—on my laptop computer. Thanks to Lieutenant Slocum, I had quite a collection of good flicks to choose from. Naturally, any Marine who wanted to watch would just cram in and find a place from which to see the relatively small screen. We needed Lance Corporal "the Steve" Jorgensen's help rigging up some kind of extra speakers. The laptop alone wasn't loud enough for the back row.

The Steve was a former 1st Platoon Marine who had gotten siphoned off to provide part of the company commander's personal security detail (PSD). About midway through the deployment he managed to get back to us at Golestan. Steve and I buddied up while I was still rolling with the CO, and it was good to see him again.

It wasn't long before I realized that even as I watched Sergeant Holter's back, the Steve was watching mine. There were no more Lone Ranger moves for me after that. Whenever I turned around, the Steve and his light machine gun (Squad Automatic Weapon or SAW) were right there. After watching the movie *Appaloosa*, about a pair of badass lawmen in a southwestern town, I began to refer to Steve and myself as "Cole" and "Hitch"—the names of the fictitious marshals in the film. Now I was "Doc Holliday" with "Wyatt" Holter and "Cole" with "the Steve."

I just couldn't shake the notion that we were in the old Southwest.

I continued the movie tradition at the new FOB. I called it the "base theater" and passed the word at chow what "tonight's feature presentation" was to be. The show would start right after dark, when the screen could be seen without blinding glare from the sun—and when the temperature would drop from hellish to something almost "Earth-like." It was the high point of my day. There wasn't an awful lot else going on.

During this period—mid-August to early September—it became obvious to the three former lawmen—Scott, Dennis, and me—that the Taliban had had enough of 1st Platoon. Information we received indicated they had pulled far up the Golestan valley in an effort to be out of our reach.

That wasn't good news for Dennis, as he was itching for a fight. So much so that when it was time to escort new ANP recruits all the way back to Delaram, he volunteered to go. Almost no convoy got through a particular pass in the mountains without taking some kind of small-arms fire, so it seemed a sure bet that Dennis would get some trigger time. I went too. There really wasn't much else to do, and it meant a visit to Delaram and the Marines I had left behind there.

The only seat left in the convoy was in one huge seven-ton truck that would haul many ANP in the back. It was only the driver and I in the cab, and it was *much* more comfortable than riding in the back of a Humvee. I unscrewed a circular hatch in the roof of the cab so in the event of an ambush I would be able to stand up and shoot back. The windows were bulletproof and didn't roll down. However, no ambush—down or back—materialized. As a former Marine, Dennis was disappointed.

It was symptomatic of the change that had overtaken the Golestan valley. There would be no more fighting for the remainder of the deployment. One thirty-day period—from July 2 to August 2—had seen it all.

The first objective in combating an insurgency is to provide security for the population. That had been accomplished in the Golestan valley. The second objective is to get the local government up and running. The subgovernor, while still sequestered in his well-protected compound, was at least talking about coming to Golestan to conduct business. That was progress.

Flash back to a conversation with the battalion commander many months prior—police without courts aren't police, they're a militia. At about this time a fistfight between two pairs of Afghan brothers escalated into a knife fight. No one was seriously hurt, but what was amazing is that the ANP actually did what police are supposed to do. They conducted an investigation, made arrests, and turned the defendants over to the local prosecutor. The prosecutor hadn't prosecuted anything in years.

It's not my purpose here to expound on Afghan law as I learned it through study of the Afghan Constitution; suffice it to say it would be as unrecognizable to an American as our system of jurisprudence would be to them. What was truly remarkable in my eyes, and equally noteworthy, is that the civilian system had been revived. The prosecutor invited me to witness the proceedings. With Bravo Squad as my escort, I sat at a long outdoor table in the shade of the ANP barracks and watched the law of Afghanistan in operation.

It was a turning point in the war against the Taliban in the Golestan valley. Justice was done—the Afghan way. The fathers of both pairs of brothers were fined for allowing their sons to disturb the peace. The trial had taken two days.

Brewster's counterinsurgency plan was succeeding.

One of the planned improvements to the new living arrangements was the installation of a trailer-like privy/shower building. With water pumped out of a newly drilled well, using power from new, more powerful generators, it was a little bit of heaven while it lasted—which wasn't long.

The interior of the immense new FOB was ground to talcum-like powder by the heavy machinery and Humvees. It was "moon dust," as I had experienced it at Delaram. The pump kept getting fouled with dirt, and the water wouldn't stop running. The waste storage tank had to be pumped out nearly constantly. As a result, it was soon closed for use.

The showers had been heaven. Moon dust got into everything.

I regarded boredom as my greatest enemy, so I set to work on PowerPoints for the battalion's intelligence section and for 3rd Battalion, 8th Marines (3/8), who would replace us. In so doing, I incorporated all the work that Slocum, Brown, and I had done. Then I set to work on an English-language version of the Afghan Constitution. I called that one "Afghan Law for Dummies."

On August 10 I emailed "Uncle Frank,"

> Things are pretty quiet here now. I think I've "worked myself out of a job" again. Looking around for some way to be value added. I plan on being home before Turkey Day to keep a promise I made to my now 84 year old mother. I promised I'd take her to see my brother and the grandkids and I plan on doing it. I don't think she's got much longer left.
>
> Meanwhile, if things don't pick up here (remember boredom is my enemy) I think I will start to make my way back to Bastion after September 1st. And if there's nothing for me to do there, head home. Have to see what plays out in the next couple of weeks.

I get along great with every soul on this FOB, thank God. The
[other contractors] are great—there's two of them here and we kid
around and cooperate with each other like you and I did. Lieutenant
Brewster of 1st Platoon is a pleasure to work with/for.

So what's new with you? Where are you and when are you going
home? Maybe I'll link up with you or something.

Terry

When I couldn't think of anything else to do I sought out Lieutenant Brewster to see if I could help him with anything. He was buried
in paperwork. He had to finish after-action reports, write up recommendations for medals for Marines, and perform a myriad of other
duties frustrating to all officers. Fortunately I had been a Marine officer
and knew what to do to help.

My birthday rolled around on August 20, and I turned fifty-nine.
My brother referred to me as a "mutant" for being as old as I was in
Afghanistan. I think "idiot savant" might have been more appropriate,
but I accepted his judgment. Lieutenant Brewster, Gunny Mendoza,
and others held a small celebration for me. I was given two birthday
presents: a little rock to remind me of the hellish place, and a small
piece of shrapnel from a five-hundred-pound bomb that had been
dropped on the Taliban at Feyz al Bad. I still have them somewhere.
They're the best presents I ever got.

Visits to the subgovernor's compound continued routinely. Although
the battalion had received confirmation that the usual seven-month
deployment had been extended to eight months, we could see the end
of the tour approaching. Ever the statesman, Lieutenant Brewster
assured the subgovernor that there would be a follow-on Marine battalion that would continue to keep the Taliban at bay.

For all the intrigue surrounding the subgovernor and his entourage,
I enjoyed our visits to his place. His shady, green, irrigated garden with

its fresh scent was a welcome change from the smell of burned dirt that usually greeted my nose. Realizing that our time with him was nearing its conclusion, and coinciding with the harvest, he invited us to a traditional Afghan feast.

When the day came, the lieutenant and I—along with Abdullah and a smattering of other local dignitaries—were seated on the ground instead of the usual table and chairs. Under the shade of his bower of grapevines, Ibrahim Khan had spread ornate Afghan rugs and cushions. Prior to the arrival of the meal, many diplomatic pleasantries were exchanged—all through an interpreter, of course. We pretended not to know that Ibrahim Khan and his party were playing both sides, and they pretended that they would miss us when we were gone. Breaking with my usual routine of saying little, I did my part to enhance the charade.

Since everyone was in a very good mood, we were asked questions that had probably long been on the minds of our hosts, such as, "How many tribes are there in America?" Brewster and I smiled at one another. There was no way a stratified tribal society, so isolated from the rest of the world, could understand America. We tried to explain, but I'm sure they didn't get it. Taking a cue from Marines in Iraq, where the sheiks of Al Anbar Province finally decided that Marines were the strongest tribe—and decided to forge an alliance—we portrayed ourselves as the Marine Tribe. They could wrap their minds around that.

They still could not grasp that young Lieutenant Brewster was actually the man in charge. Finally, Hajji Mohammed "figured it all out." He took me aside and said, "My brother-in-law needs a job" (working for a salary on the new FOB). I replied, "Why tell me? Tell Lieutenant Brewster." He just winked and with a knowing look repeated his request to me.

I knew what had transpired. They had "figured out" that Brewster was a front man for me. I was obviously the man in charge—with my gray hair—and I used Brewster to run interference so I wouldn't have to be bothered with the little things. Brewster and I both got a good laugh out of it. They really couldn't conceive of a society like ours.

242

The main part of the meal was a sheep on a huge bed of rice. The sheep's eyes were still in its attached head. They were considered a delicacy and were offered to us first. We declined gracefully. Sheep eyeball is still not on my "bucket list." Each of us—surrounding the spread—would rip or cut off portions of meat and grab handfuls of seasoned rice. It was all done with hands alone. There wasn't much that needed washing afterward. The meal was delicious. I ate until I felt I would burst.

I reflected on the journey that had taken me—via Colonel Thompson—from America to the world. It had been quite a ride.

18

Struck Down by the Plague

Unfortunately, I got horribly sick—probably from eating that food. The symptoms were nonstop dysentery. I couldn't keep anything inside me. Even though the portable latrine was closed, I still used it. It had a real porcelain bowl to sit on and—more importantly—it was very near "Shady Acres." Just the same, I barely had enough time to get to it. I would grab up bottled water to flush with, then sit for what seemed like hours. I couldn't leave the place. When I did leave, it was to grab some more bottled water, then dash back. I couldn't make it through a single night without repeated trips.

My stomach wouldn't tolerate anything more substantial than saltines and sips of water without ulcer-like discomfort. I was a mess. "Doc Z," our head corpsman, did what he could, but it wasn't enough. I lingered on for the remaining days of August and into September, miserably hoping the next day I'd be over it. I kept getting weaker instead. It got to the point where I barely had it in me to walk the short distance to the latrine. I finally had to accept that I needed a doctor's attention.

Gunny Mendoza arranged for me to fly back to battalion on one of the newly arrived choppers. I was damn glad I didn't have to try to make it through thirteen hours overland. I don't think I would have left the FOB if that had been the case. They could have just buried me there. One can't keep stopping in open desert swarming with unseen enemies to do what I would have needed to do—and spend the time waiting for me to do it. I thanked God for those choppers from Iraq!

I didn't expect to return to Golestan. We were originally scheduled to return home in October. Before I knew that the battalion would be extended an extra month, I had promised my eighty-four-year-old widowed mother that I would take her to see my brother and her grandkids for Thanksgiving. It was September and I thought I might as well just keep pushing to the rear—all the way back to the States. It seemed that all I could possibly do at Golestan had been done, and I didn't believe the enemy would come back for another go at it.

I was weak from illness and really feeling poorly—so I didn't have the strength to say good-bye to hardly anyone. I felt bad about that but I just wanted to drag myself onto the helicopter when it arrived and get to a doctor. It wasn't the way I had hoped to leave the FOB. I was taught growing up to remain stoic in the face of illness or injury. The Marine Corps reinforced that mentality. "Suck it up and keep marching" was a common catchphrase. Therefore, I doubt that those around me had an inkling as to how sick I really felt.

When the day of departure came I could barely carry my gear onto the chopper.

I left the FOB on September 9. As I was leaving, Lieutenant Brewster gave me a three-page handwritten letter of thanks. With all he still had to do, and all he was responsible for, his thoughtfulness amazed me. I was blown away by what he wrote. There is no doubt in my mind that he will shake his head when he reads this, but I have it framed. It's hanging on my wall:

Terry,

I want to take a moment as you depart Gullistan [sic] to say thank you. From the moment you arrived I was not sure what to think, and I'm not sure you did either. Our first meeting shall be remembered by me always and I am thankful we were able to see eye to eye by the end of that talk. From there all else grew.

You have been a tremendous help throughout your time here. Your service to me as my sixth sense was invaluable. The countless hours you have spent debriefing, questioning, and compiling info has saved me a ton of leg work, and supported the platoon's operations. The initiative you displayed towards learning Afghan law has helped tremendously.

I have appreciated your wise counsel, and listening ear. You have walked a very fine line well, and you have my gratitude. Between you and Lt. Slocum I felt overwhelmed at times, but you both reassured me of your intentions and good will. When you told me I did well after the attack on the outpost that meant the world to me.

You have been in contact with [under fire with] my Marines twice and I'm sure that you have all the old man stories you could want. You performed well on both occasions, and I'm sure learned some things about yourself. I have two moments that shall forever be seared into my mind. One is of you in flack and no shirt atop the post on the morning of the attack with a smile ear to ear. The other is of continually looking down into the wash in Faydz Abad [sic] and seeing you "herding cats" as the enemy's fire was falling everywhere.

Thank you for the power points [sic] you have compiled. It will benefit the follow on unit very much.

For everything, I appreciate your hard work and personal initiative. You have been a vital piece of [our] platoon, and you will be missed.

Benjamin Brewster

———

That same day, I arrived back at the British base at Bastion. The choppers made one heck of a difference. Fortunately, there was a vehicle waiting and I didn't have to walk. I'm not sure I could have. I was a lot sicker than I let on. I had held out for as long as I could at Golestan, hoping to get well on my own.

I was assigned a bunk with a real mattress inside a large tent with Captain Van Osborne, Bill Osborne's son, and other officers I already knew. It would be days before I'd actually see Van—he was always at the front somewhere in the thick of things. I didn't want Bill to worry, so I didn't tell him that at the time. If Bill thought Van was safely tucked away behind a desk, so much the better. It was my first taste of air-conditioning since leaving Bastion many months before. I was glad I still had my British army sleeping bag. Without it I would have frozen to death inside that tent.

I checked in with one of the battalion doctors almost immediately, and it was arranged for me to be seen at the British hospital. I had to wait a couple of days for an appointment, and I still couldn't eat much. But Bastion had a small PX, and they sold Ritz crackers and real milk! After living on saltines and water, this was a step up. It was also the first time I drank real milk in months. I bought it by the liter and drank it all in one sitting.

The PX was about a quarter mile away, and I had to drag myself to get there. I was still very weak. Along the way I stopped at every latrine and Porta-John that I passed. It was the only way I could go anywhere. Often I would spy a Porta-John up ahead and quicken my pace so I could make it in time. During my middle-of-the-night trips I didn't always make it. Fortunately, the PX sold underwear in human sizes.

Next door to the PX was a small gourmet coffee shop and reading room combined. It had books sent by caring British citizens for their soldiers to read, and there were enough good titles to keep me happy.

It also had deep-cushioned leather chairs to sit in. Each day I would savor the crackers and milk, then—never too far from a number of Porta-Johns—settle into a comfortable chair and read.

The base Internet trailers were very near there as well. Feeling too ill to do much of anything else, I passed a good bit of time on a computer. Fast, reliable Internet was a huge treat. On September 10 I sent another "human interest" story to the home front:

His name is Daniel Flynn Hickey. He has red hair and stands about 6'1". He's lean, not overly muscular, but I wouldn't want to pick a fight with him. He's obviously got Irish roots with his name and hair, but he doesn't talk about them, so he's probably not too aware. He's a quiet, soft spoken all around nice guy, who I'd be calling a "nice kid" under other circumstances. He's probably about 21 plus or minus a year. He has an infectious smile and soft spoken manner. The "nice guy next door" type.

He's the Marine who left the relative "safety" of his armored vehicle to pull Lance Corporal Zequeida from the machine gun swept mountainside where he had gotten shot through his femur. A broken femur is a painful injury. Very painful. And it's perilously close to the femoral artery. Too much thrashing about on the ground and the jagged bone edge could have severed the artery that the bullet, thank God, missed. A severed femoral artery will kill a man in a VERY short time. And, of course, Zequeida, whose wife was imminently expecting their first child, would most probably have been shot again and again, had he remained where he was.

I like to "tease" Hickey a bit by always calling him by his full name, DANIEL FLYNN HICKEY, whenever we meet in passing. He just smiles from ear to ear. I asked him if "Flynn" was his mother's maiden name. He said, "no" it was from his father's side. Last time I saw him, he was covered in dirt—desert dirt called "moon dust" by Marines. It's got the texture of talcum powder. Daniel Flynn Hickey was just about to take a well-earned shower. Unfortunately there was no water. I broke the news to him. He just grinned and said "OH NO!" I said, "Oh yeah." And he went on his way without a murmur of complaint.

But I digress, on that same day, 2 August; he didn't get back into his armored vehicle. He took his light machine gun, between the Zequeida vehicle (where Boucher was also hit and still shooting) and opened up on Taliban PKM (medium machine gun) positions an estimated 50 meters away. 50 meters is up close and personal. It's probably about 55 footsteps away. Daniel Flynn Hickey "suppressed" the enemy fire (which is Marine-Speak for "either I've already killed you, or if you pick your head up I'll blow it off for ya"). The other Marines were in a tight spot but Daniel Flynn Hickey came through.

He just continues to do his job, standing post, going on patrol, filling sandbags, whatever. And is as quiet and unassuming as ever he was. He's a Marine. He just did what Marines do. If anybody called him a hero, his face would turn as red as his hair. Well there's another little bit of 1st Platoon, Golf Company, 2nd Battalion, 7th Marines for y'all. I have a picture of him but I'm on the base computers at Bastion and can't attach it. Maybe some other time.

McG.

Neither the battalion doctors nor the British doctors at the base hospital could find anything wrong with me. At about this time the unstoppable dysentery finally abated and I could handle real food—nothing fancy. But my stomach was killing me. Mindful of my age and all the things that might have gone wrong with me, the Navy doctor at battalion decided to play it safe and send me back to Kandahar Air Field (KAF) for more tests. The hospital at Bastion was too small to have the facilities necessary.

On September 15 I wrote to the home front:

I've been sick with God knows what. Had it for weeks. They're flying
me to Kandahar hospital tonight for tests. They're checking for 1)
hepatitis, 2) gall bladder disease, 3) gallstones. Personally I think its
4) an ulcer brought on by eating local food, subsisting for months on
heavily over spiced crappy rations, and the stomach flu that went
through the entire FOB. But we'll see.

Still weak, I turned my weapons in at the Marine armory. I didn't
think I'd need them anymore. Bastion was vast, and its defenses seemed
more than adequate. Besides, I didn't think I'd be pushing forward
again. Before I left, I wrote to my brother:

I caught a chopper out of Ft. Apache and am now back to the Brit
base called Bastion. Might be able to Google it if so inclined. When I
first got here it was the most austere place I'd been to up to that point.
Right now it feels like heaven. It's a friggin RESORT! I had been living
under a blue tarp up against a giant sandbag wall. Ahhhh. I just ate
real mashed potatoes for the first time in three months!!!! Will
definitely be home for Turkey Day and maybe as early as next month.

Comfort is relative. It dawned on me that I had gotten used to the
heat. It no longer bothered me. In fact, I barely noticed it.

Slowly my strength was starting to return. My stomach was still in
an uproar but I was able to eat a bit more. I got a ride to the helicopter
terminal and checked in with the Brits who ran the place. Then I waited
for the chopper to arrive. As had been the case in Iraq, all unnecessary
flights were made at night. Having endured so many bone-jarring,
teeth-rattling, cramped, endless hours in the back of Humvees, I was
truly starting to like flying. We landed at KAF at 1:00 a.m. It had taken
two long days overland to get from KAF to Bastion. It took about
forty-five minutes to fly back.

I left Bastion with instructions that I was to be billeted in the Marine "transient quarters"—a couple of air-conditioned tents on the south—or main—side of the airfield. I had been told that there were a handful of 2/7 Marines still at the huge base and that transportation would be waiting for me. It wasn't.

I remembered the layout of the base and had a pretty good idea how to get to where I was going. So after leaving the plywood building that passed for an airport terminal, I hitched up my pack and started walking. It took about an hour, but I found the place. The tent was tan instead of the usual olive drab green. Unlike those that housed permanent personnel, it was not ringed with four-foot-high sandbags around its perimeter. The sandbags were meant to protect against indirect fire (IDF).

I wasn't worried about that. I still felt that being hit by IDF at KAF was somewhere below a shark attack in the ocean or a lightning strike on land in terms of probability.

There were only a handful of sleeping Marines present when I walked in. Most of the racks were ordinary cots, but all the way at the end was a bed with a mattress. It even had a folding partition between it and the rest of the tent. It seemed like the closest thing to a private room, so I tossed my pack on it. Then, not wanting to be awakened in the middle of the night by a pissed-off Marine—who may have had a prior claim to it—I woke Sergeant Greg Lunsford, who was sleeping nearby, and asked him if anyone else was using it. He told me it was up for grabs.

I had shed my uniform back at Bastion and was happily wearing sneakers, tan cargo pocket pants, and a tan civilian shirt over my olive drab issue T-shirt. It was "contractor casual" attire. Greg asked me no questions, and I just crashed. Once again I was glad I had my British army sleeping bag—it was air-conditioned cold inside. I had gotten used to the heat, but not to air-conditioned cold.

The next day—setting my own schedule and answering to no one— I strolled over to the base hospital. It was about an hour's walk, but I didn't mind. I was well used to walking by this time. I didn't need to rush off to the latrine during the night, so I slept well. Blood was drawn, tests were run, but I was already beginning to feel better. Not 100 percent, but improved.

Within a couple of days, the doctors at the hospital informed me that they had found nothing that concerned them and concluded that I most probably had gotten sick from the bad food. That, in turn, caused such distress to my stomach that it would take time to heal completely. After getting antibiotics, antacids, and other stomach-soothing medications, I was told to be patient and wait it out.

I determined to wait it out at KAF.

19

Disney World

As had been the case at Bastion, I now regarded KAF as pure paradise. What I had considered austere in the extreme only six months prior was now a veritable Disney World. I regarded my sojourn there as "R&R"—rest and recreation—time. My contract with my "check signers" specified that I was entitled to an expense-paid two-week vacation at the destination of my choice sometime during the deployment. I had no intention of leaving my guys, so I just didn't take it. In my mind, I was taking it at KAF. KAF still had free popcorn to go with free movies, and it still had the Dutch recreation center and the Boardwalk. I enjoyed every charming moment of it.

There is a custom among Marines that if one had been in a firefight, one was entitled to wear a bracelet made out of braided olive drab green paracord. Paracord is a nylon "shoelace" that is almost as universally useful as duct tape. If one had been hit by an IED it would be black. If one had been through both, the bracelet was woven both olive drab and black. One of the guys had made an olive drab one for me right after the July 2 attack on the FOB, and I have worn mine ever since. Everybody in 1st Platoon rated it, so it was no big deal.

I made friends with Sergeant Greg Lunsford and the handful of other Marines languishing at KAF—the "far rear." It was clear that, civilian attire notwithstanding, I was a fellow Marine to them.

Greg had the entire *Grey's Anatomy* TV series stored on his laptop. He and I and one or two other Marines gathered around at the same time each evening to watch a couple of episodes. It's amazing how the little things in life can bring such joy when you are deprived of them for so long. It became the highlight of my day. My condition continued to improve, and I was able to enjoy KAF more and more.

In time I took renewed notice of the dining halls. They had seemed cafeteria-like and second-rate when I was last at KAF. The air-conditioning had felt inadequate, and I recall sweating a lot while eating. Like the entire battalion I also had to balance my rifle with my food tray and keep it from banging and crashing around when I sat down to eat. That was all new to me then. Now, sans rifle, in comfortable clothes, totally inured to the heat, the food tasted gourmet great.

Life at KAF was sweet.

Marines have a name for rear-echelon troops—they are disdainfully called "pogues." A pogue today is what a REMF ("rear-echelon motherfucker") or "Remington raider" (so named after the Remington typewriters they pounded) was during prior conflicts. Since "Hobbits" have become well-known as a result of the popularity of the *Lord of the Rings* trilogy, "pogues" were also known as "Fobbits"—in reference to those who always stayed far behind the wire at the various large, sprawling FOBs.

One evening at chow, I hadn't been able to locate any of my new Marine buddies in the heavily populated eating facility. There must have been hundreds of people packed in there. So I sat down next to two civilians with heavy Scottish accents and enjoyed my food. Eavesdropping was out of the question—I couldn't understand a word they said. Suddenly the IDF sirens sounded. To my utter astonishment, everybody in the place dove under the tables!

Everybody, that is, except my Marine pals. They, and I, were still sitting and eating.

I thought, "Oh, there they are! Great!" I picked up my tray and joined them at their table. We couldn't get used to the pogue mentality at KAF.

In short order civilian dining hall workers ordered everyone to vacate the facility and take shelter in the bunkers. It was more than an overreaction, I thought—I wondered if a flight of German bombers was on the way. It seemed more in place with London during the Blitz than at KAF. Acting rather too nervously, I believed, people quickly filed out of the building. Not the handful of Marines; they kept eating. When personally asked to leave by a nice civilian woman, they complied. I was enjoying my newfound freedom too much and opted to accept the "risk" of eating dinner. I volunteered to keep the flies off their food until they could return.

Unfortunately—being the only person left in the large dining hall— I was rather conspicuous. Nothing quite unnerves a pogue like someone who doesn't share their fear. It makes it all seem so unnecessary, I supposed. When personally asked to leave, I did. I apologized to my buddies for being unable to keep their chow "fly free." I walked outside with a fried chicken leg in my hand. Damn, the food was good!

The same kind of overreacting silliness infected the base during the daytime. I was at my old "office"—the Dutch recreation center—when the sirens went off again. The nice people behind the counter anxiously told me I'd have to leave, as they were closing down and taking shelter. I couldn't help but wonder how many times the sirens had gone off in the months since I first arrived at KAF. The only time I had even heard a round hit vacant ground was immediately upon arrival—and if anyone had been injured the news would surely have reached me. It would have been a big deal. I just couldn't understand what everybody was worried about. "Oh, well," I thought, sighing.

I began the long stroll in what used to be oppressive heat—now just a pleasant, sunny day—back to the Marine transient quarters and the Marines I expected to find there. Every one of the amusing places around the boardwalk was shut down tight. All along the route, every bunker was full of edgy civilians and pogues. They all looked at me as I passed with disbelief on their faces. I found it all highly entertaining. I decided they were waiting for me to be struck by lightning.

When I got back to our quarters, Greg and another Marine were sitting on the ground outside in the shade the tent provided. All along the tent row were reinforced concrete bunkers where uneasy pogues were waiting for the all-clear to sound. One civilian actually had his Kevlar helmet on. We found that extremely funny. We imagined the stories he would tell the folks back home about his "dangerous time in Afghanistan." Greg decided to put it all on video. He conducted a make-believe interview about the "devastating attack" that had just taken place. I pretended I was a reporter for CNN. I think it's still on YouTube.

Then we decided to make a PowerPoint. We named it "A Fobbit's Guide to Life at KAF."

Some of the slides we made up read:

- REMEMBER: ALWAYS TAKE COVER WHEN THE IDF SIRENS SOUND!
  - Even though they NEVER sound until AFTER the IDF is over . . .

- YOU WILL FEEL KEWL! You can make believe you really WERE in danger!
  - And try to elicit sympathy from the folks back home who don't know any better!

- A simulated phone conversation:
  - "Gosh Honey, I had a CLOSE one today . . ."

- You can wear with PRIDE any of the following [T-shirts]:

  - I am a Taliban Hill fighter

  - Operation Enduring Freedom, Because Freedom Isn't Free

  - Professional Taliban Hunter, Afghanistan

  - And many, many others!

- Send the pictures home!

  - Those lovable old veterans who stormed ashore at Normandy and Iwo Jima will be dying to buy you a beer!

And next to a picture of a tired, dusty combat Marine from Golestan with his .50-caliber machine gun the last slide read:

- Just crop this guy's face out of the picture and paste yours in!
- Those guys at the VFW will be THROWING beers at you!
- Chicks will DIG you!
- You'll go home a real KAF WARRIOR!

But it wasn't all fun and games at KAF. Several 2/7 Marines were killed while I was enjoying myself. One was a man whose body was then due to be shipped home via KAF. A sergeant had been killed in action by an IED. Once at KAF, his body lay in state—in a flag-draped closed coffin inside the post's nondenominational chapel. The memorial service was held the next day. It was packed. Marines, American, British, and Canadian soldiers—all were fully represented. Not everyone could get inside the chapel. Almost no one—myself included—knew him personally.

A 2/7 Marine gunnery sergeant asked me if I wanted to be part of the Marine's escort during the Ramp Ceremony that night. That is, if I wanted to be one of the Marines who escorted his body from the vehicle that brought it from the chapel to the airfield and then onto the

C-130 that would take it home. He probably asked because I was from the same battalion as the dead Marine. I declined. I wasn't in uniform. My fellow Marines felt it didn't matter. But it mattered to me.

So instead I stood silently in the background and marveled at the Marines and soldiers—Americans, Canadians, and Brits who turned out in the middle of the night to pay their last respects to a Marine who was undoubtedly a total stranger to them all. A Canadian sergeant wearing a kilt played "Amazing Grace" on the bagpipes. What I beheld is called "The Ramp Ceremony."

———

One day a new arrival took up residence in our tent. Fresh from the hospital at Bagram Air Base outside Kabul, I met Lance Corporal Jamie Nielsen from Echo Company. He was returning to the company by way of KAF. Blond-haired and with a midwestern accent, he took the cot on the other side of my "private room" partition. I noticed his black and green paracord bracelet right away.

Being older, I had listened to a lot of Marines in the eight months I had been with 2/7. I suppose in a way I was a sort of father figure to many of them. It was just as well; I regarded them all as "sons" and "younger brothers" anyway. Jamie had a story to tell, and I had an ear to listen.

IEDs had been especially problematic in Echo Company. So Jamie was out of his vehicle on August 15 doing what Sergeant Holter and I had done together many times—peering anxiously at the ground, searching for any sign of a disturbance. The baked-hard dirt road couldn't have held a hidden IED—so Jamie thought. He walked on. The ground exploded beneath him. He had stepped right on one.

It hurled him quite a distance from the blast site. After he woke up, he couldn't see. He was blind. He felt someone touching him, and he said that "freaked him out." He began feeling around for his rifle but couldn't find it. Finally, he got a little of his vision back and realized it was one of his guys. The guy said, "You're okay. You've got all your parts."

Meanwhile, the corpsman dragged him two hundred meters from where he had landed. All the while Nielsen kept saying, "I'm fine. I'm fine. I'm doing okay."

In the interim—about forty-five minutes after Jamie got nailed—another lance corporal was seriously wounded by a different IED. They were flown together by chopper from Echo Company's command post at Sanguin to the British hospital at Bastion. There they cut off all Jamie's clothes. He reminisced that it felt "funny in a hospital gown." It was embarrassing to him. He begged for a pair of cammies. Then he walked to a C-130 that took him to Bagram. The other lance corporal was on the same plane, only he was carried aboard on a stretcher. They both talked and joked the whole way.

Jamie remembered walking off the plane and into the hospital. There they "threw him on a gurney and cut his clothes off again." He kept telling them, "NO! I'll take them off." They said "no" and cut them off. He recalled that he had "tons of IVs in him" and that he had multiple surgeries performed on him.

Finally, he was healed well enough to be allowed to walk around Bagram, but not sufficiently to return to our battalion. At one point he was walking around, still suffering from a concussion and groggy from painkillers. He got lost. He had dark glasses on. He guessed that he must have walked past an Army officer. He could barely see and barely hear. What vision he had was blurred. Not recognizing that the man was an officer, Jamie didn't salute.

Apparently the officer called to him, but Jamie didn't hear him. That probably pissed the officer off because he grabbed Jamie "forcefully and spun him around." The officer said, "HEY DEVIL!"

Recounting it all to me, he was still upset.

Jamie finally realized what was going on. So he said, "Pardon, I didn't hear you. Did you just say 'Hey devil'? Are you a Marine?"

That—in my former line of work—would have been known as a clue.

The officer replied, "No. I'm Army. But how about 'sir'?"

Jamie said, "I apologize, sir"—and took off his dark glasses and cover. His face was "all screwed up." He had bad bruises, gauze patches on one eye—it was black-and-blue all over. He was a real mess to behold.

Jamie continued, "I still can't see or hear too well, sir."

The officer—speechless—turned and walked away.

Hearing that, I was certain the man in question was a second lieutenant and probably not from a combat unit. Mistakes will happen. Things aren't always the way they seem at first. Hell, I had been a second lieutenant at one time myself. But a decent officer would have made things right with an explanation and an offer to help.

I don't know if Jamie realized I was a former officer. But I believed that it would help him if I explained things a bit. In the eyes of that officer, Jamie was being deliberately insubordinate. Too many Army officers allowed that kind of behavior in my day, and the Army was the worse for it.

I didn't try to excuse the man—inside, I was livid—but I think seeing things from the officer's perspective helped Jamie somewhat—particularly the whole "devil" item. Jamie was really upset about being called "devil." I guessed I would have been too if I had just had the same close brush with death that he had.

"Devil" is short for "devil dog," and devil dog is the English equivalent of something the World War I Germans had dubbed Marines: *Tufelhunden.* I explained to Jamie that the officer probably picked up on what Marines call each other and didn't mean for it to sound the way it did.

I think that helped him. That was my purpose—but deep inside, I was still furious.

At Bagram, Jamie was self-conscious for a long time about his vision and hearing loss. He didn't want to be a "fifth wheel," and he no longer felt like everybody else. But he hung out with Marines who were stationed there, and their genuine friendliness finally got through to him. It put him at his ease. The Marines stationed at Bagram took good care of him until it was time for him to leave. As a former Marine officer I was particularly relieved when Jamie told me that a Marine major had told Jamie that he was proud of him—that Jamie had done a good job.

That was more like it. That major made Jamie feel a lot better.

We talked about the IED and how it was that he remained among the living. When he told me that the road he had been on was only a short distance from the cut-out bank of a dry riverbed, I reasoned it out. The force of an explosion will follow the path of least resistance. When the powder in a rifle cartridge is set off, for example, the result is a small explosion. The path of least resistance is out the barrel. The projectile is forced along on the mini–shock wave, and that—in simple terms—is how a bullet is fired.

The Taliban had obviously tunneled under the road from the cut in the riverbank. That explains why a veteran like Jamie didn't see any signs of digging. There weren't any—on the road, at least. And the path of least resistance for the explosion was back out through the tunnel that had been dug. Even if it had been filled back in, the earth had to be looser and more giving than the concrete-hard, sunbaked road surface. Most of the force of the explosion had gone away from Jamie. Enough force remained to pick him up and toss him as it had. It's the only explanation for his being alive.

It must have been quite a blast—he told me it had been determined that the charge for the IED was not one, but two 155mm artillery rounds. That's significant. Clearly the enemy had intended on destroying an armored vehicle.

When I got back to Bastion I sent another "human interest" story to the folks back home. It read,

Well as you probably know I was "in the rear" getting my health issues straightened out. I'm back at battalion now, and am seriously considering requesting to return to 1st Platoon. The "tug" is like gravity, it pulls me back.

Anyway, while at the battalion's transient tent, I met young Lance Corporal Jamie Nielsen from outside Indianapolis. He was just making his way back to the battalion, and Echo Company, from the hospital at Kabul. It seems that on August 15th, near Sanguin, in Helmund province, he was on foot when an IED went off and nearly sent him to the next life.

A quiet, soft spoken, blonde haired young guy, he is very friendly and very much *wanted* to talk about what happened. He was not in the least boastful, or fearful. He just wanted a quiet talk. The green and black 550 cord "bracelet" he wore around his wrist told me, visually, that he had been in at least one firefight (probably more) and had been hit by at least one IED. I don't know if that's a universal tradition, a Marine Corps tradition, or simply a battalion tradition, but that's what the "bracelets" mean.

Jamie is lucky. That's a massive understatement. The IED was comprised of two 155mm artillery shells wired together. That's a lot of boom. Fortunately, in an effort to defeat his purpose of spotting disturbed earth, the enemy had tunneled under the road from a nearby dry river wash. My analysis is that the path of least resistance for the explosion was back out towards the river, not up through the concrete hard sun baked roadway where he was standing. And the blast seems to have pushed him away, carrying him on the shock wave, rather than turning his insides into jelly. It launched him quite a distance but he's still alive. Had he been inside a Humvee, he, and the others, would have likely absorbed enough of that massive blast to kill them all.

He was partially blind and nearly deaf afterwards. Today he has all of his vision and 40% of his hearing back. He's optimistic of regaining the rest of his hearing. He has only a small several inch scar on his face to show for the incident.

Thanks be to God.

We held the memorial service for Sergeant _____ today. He was a mechanic in H & S Company. He was 29 years old, married, and the father of 3. An IED killed him a couple of days ago. Three others were wounded in the same blast.

This is no police training mission.

Terry

———

Shortly after the Ramp Ceremony I decided R&R was over. I had been so damn sick for so long—but now I felt good. So good, in fact, that I wanted to get back to my guys at Golestan. I was starting to worry about them. I think the Ramp Ceremony had something to do with that.

20

Return to Golestan

It had taken several weeks of healing time to finally feel 100 percent. My stomach had been savaged by whatever had gotten to it. I caught a rare daytime flight back to Bastion. There waiting for the aircraft's arrival was Zach Wolfe. He had been promoted to corporal and was reassigned to the battalion command post. He was the driver. It was good to see him again—I hadn't seen him since I left Bala Baluk in what seemed to be almost a lifetime ago.

On September 23 I wrote to one of my cousins,

Well they ruled out all the horrific stuff that they were testing for, like HEPATITIS, GALL BLADDER DISEASE, and GALL STONES! It's a torn up stomach from the wicked stomach flu that swept the FOB (thank the friggin flies, the National Bird of Afghanistan) which I believe was followed by a bacterial infection in the stomach. After antibiotics and now taking all the friggin ulcer med stuff I feel fine again. They said it would heal up in one to two months. Meanwhile the meds keep me OK.

As much as I want to get back [home], and I can go in about a week if I want, I'm really feeling a tug to stay. It's the bond that developed. My guys might be going back out into the fight again and if they do, I want to go with them. I don't know if I can get back there or not, I figure it's in God's Hands. If He wants me there, I'll get there, and if not, I won't.

I had been prepping Lieutenant Colonel Hall that I might decide to return to the States early, so when I checked back in with him and asked to return to Golestan, he seemed surprised. Pleased, but surprised. He was going to fly up in a couple of days, and I asked to join him on the chopper.

Bright and early I sent the following email to the West Side Soldiers' Aid Society folks:

For those who might not have gotten the word, excuse me I've been up half the night and am groggy. I got the OK from the Battalion Commander to return to 1st Platoon. Should be there in two to six days. Just can't leave 'em.

The attached photo is of two 19 year old professionals. Alex "Sean" Allman, Indiana, left, and Devin Benz, Seattle, right.

God I'm getting old. I was 40 when they were born.

After receiving a request for more information on Allman and Benz I wrote back,

Alex Allman is "Little Red" who was blown off his perch by an RPG near miss the night they attacked the FOB. He's been chomping at the bit to get back to the platoon ever since (he has). Devin Benz has been in at least 3 nasty firefights. He was with the squad that got ambushed when Zequeida and Boucher got it. They're both only 19. Now that's amazing.

Except . . . they're Marines.

And Hickey and Boucher and Nielsen and countless others.
These guys just do the amazing and it's routine and ordinary to them.
Admiral Nimitz had it right when, after Iwo Jima, he said,
"Extraordinary valor is a common virtue." That's still true today. I
thank God for the opportunity to be with these guys.

Thanks again to all of you for supporting these young MEN.

Respectfully,
Terry

Then I emailed "the Steve" at FOB Golestan,

I'm COMING back! Got the aminus dominus [Marine slang for
"blessing"] from the Big Guy this morning. I PREFER to roll with
Bravo [Squad]!!! (Somebody needs to cover Sgt. Holter's six . . . that's
MY job). I will be there in no more than 6 days, maybe sooner. I finally
feel good again.

Oooh rah!

McG.

I drew my rifle from the armory, but my pistol was no longer available. It hadn't lasted long—it had been issued out almost as soon as I had returned it. I climbed back into uniform and flew with the colonel. By this time the ambient temperature was downright pleasant during the day, and was getting a bit chilly at night. Inside "Fort Apache" a team of Marine combat engineers was constructing plywood buildings to house those who would be spending the winter. Not 2/7 Marines, of course, but those who would take over.

Shady Acres had been torn down, and in its place stood a nice, wood-floored, wooden-roofed plywood "rest home." I greeted Dennis and Scott and moved back in. Lieutenant Brewster was surprised to see me, as were the other Marines.

Bravo Squad was billeted inside its own plywood barracks—surrounded by high Hesco barriers against IDFs. I spent many hours playing 500 Rummy with the guys I had been with for months and the new guys who had been sent as replacements. The platoon had been reinforced and after a few additional days of patrolling I became more convinced than ever that the Taliban would continue to avoid us.

During this period Lieutenant Brewster left a guard on the FOB and tactically deployed about seventy Marines to the top of "Russian Hill." We all took group photos. The view during daylight from that old fortified position was extraordinary. Scott Brown and I rode up and back in an ANP pickup truck. It was a long, steep climb, and we opted for an old man's perk.

At about this time I had a remarkable conversation with one of the local merchants—through an interpreter, of course. He was one of the principal shopkeepers on the main dirt street in Golestan, and we had spoken with him many times throughout the deployment. On this day he seemed uncharacteristically happy. I remarked, "You're pretty chipper today. What's up?"

I will never forget his reply. "Because you guys are here, I could shave today."

The Taliban, religious Nazis that they are, would have beaten him if he didn't let his beard grow to the prescribed length. I thought, "The freedom to shave . . . it doesn't get any more fundamental than that."

The boys' school was still open. The girls' school was still open. School supplies were coming in from folks back in the States. Men were shaving. People were glad to see us and to stop and talk when we went on patrol. Kids with big smiles swarmed us everywhere. The Taliban had pulled back out of reach.

Brewster's counterinsurgency plan had succeeded.

I hung around the FOB for a while, maybe ten days or two weeks, before finally realizing that there really was no good reason for me to remain any longer. My job there was done. I believe Lieutenant Brewster wanted another crack at the Taliban, but my street investigator instincts, honed by the time I had spent at the FOB, convinced me that 1st Platoon's war was over. I felt "my guys" were safe. It was okay to leave them.

The battalion commander had only stayed for a couple of days, so I arranged to fly back when the next helicopter brought still more reinforcements. It was already October, and I intended to keep my Thanksgiving promise to my mother. I needed to turn my thoughts to home.

This time I said good-bye properly.

21

Going Home

Back at Bastion once again, and feeling well this time, I searched for a way to be "value added" one last time. Aside from making sure the intelligence section had everything I could give them, it was a stretch. My work was done. Happily, "Uncle Frank" showed up. He had grown a full beard and sported a deep tan. He looked just like an Afghan interpreter. From a distance that's what I thought he was when I first saw him. We still enjoyed each other's sense of humor and got caught up on what stories we each had to tell.

I fell into a routine of working the night shift. It fit in well with the rest of my tentmates' schedules. Typically I'd be up all night, and then sleep most of the day—warmly ensconced inside my sleeping bag with the hood secured around my head. All the tents were super air-conditioned. Outside, the temperature was still very hot. Dinner was breakfast. And dinner—now that I could eat—was marvelous. The British dining hall was large and outstanding. I started to gain some weight back. The prolonged illness had taken its toll.

The lines out the door were typically long but worth the wait. One evening incoming IDF landed only about a hundred meters away—an unbelievably long shot. It hit right on the path I and others took walking to the chow hall. Fortunately, it was a dud. I would have taken a picture of it, but moon dust had long since killed my camera. Luck or Divine Providence—it should have killed several people.

As a result, though, the Brits had to "stand to." And that cleared out the overwhelming number of men eating or waiting to eat dinner. American Marines were overjoyed. The prodigious lines shrank to nothing, and we feasted while our British cousins kept us safe.

I resumed my habit of hanging out near the PX, reading in the cushioned comfort of the coffee shop and surfing the Internet. I had noticed that outside the PX/coffee shop area, little cliques of British soldiers—each from the same regiment, as evidenced by their shoulder patches—would stand around chatting. I recall as I passed these small groups that I couldn't understand a word anyone was saying. We—Americans and Brits—are two peoples divided by a common language.

Their officers were the exception to the rule. I had no trouble conversing with them. Particularly given the difference in slang, I decided that American was a dialect of English. I also noticed an absence of commingling of American Marines and British soldiers. I didn't sense any hostility in the air, but Americans stayed with Americans, and Brits stayed with Brits.

Finally a contingent of British Royal Marines arrived to replace an outgoing regiment, and all that changed. Once the Royal Marines arrived, all I would see were numerous small groups of American and British Marines chatting with each other. Everybody was curious about life in the "sister service" and life at their respective homes. It was heartwarming. There is a noticeable comradeship between Marines, whether British or American.

Uncle Frank and I had come over to Afghanistan with the battalion executive officer as part of the ADVON—advance party—and we received word that we'd be going back the same way. Preparations to pull out got under way. During this period I had a long talk with Colonel Hall. I made sure he had every piece of intelligence I had gleaned, all the PowerPoints I had compiled—some strictly humorous—and every photograph I had. I still couldn't bring myself to drop the dime on the Golf Company commander, but I was sure the colonel knew something wasn't quite right with the man.

Of course he did—he fired the CO not long after.

At any rate, realizing that Lieutenant Brewster had not had the benefit of guidance from his captain and being certain that the company CO would not do Brewster justice—by way of recommendations for decorations—I requested permission to recommend the lieutenant for the Bronze Star with combat "V." Colonel Hall smiled wryly and said, "Well . . . title it 'Witness Statement' as opposed to 'Recommendation.'"

I grinned. I wasn't the company commander and I was technically a civilian. I really didn't have the right to formally "recommend" anybody for anything. But I cranked five pages of reasons I believed Brewster should be decorated. Before I left the country I gave it all to Major Helton.

What I wrote is reproduced in the appendix.

The ADVON left for home two weeks later. Major Helton had led it into Afghanistan, and he also led it going home. We had arrived in Afghanistan on March 28, and we left it on October 28. Seven months had felt like seven years. I was glad to be going home. And although I hadn't yet realized it, I had changed a great deal.

After a ridiculously scrupulous examination by an Army MP, wherein every single piece of clothing and gear had to be laid out for inspection, we packed it all back up again. He was acting on behalf of the U.S. Customs Service, so I guess I shouldn't be too hard on him. He did his duty efficiently, and if I had been his commanding officer I would have been pleased. Past wars saw all manner of contraband smuggled back to the States by returning GIs. This middle-aged sergeant—probably a National Guard soldier and cop in the "real world"—was taking no chances. I guess I was getting a tad anxious to get home.

Once inspected, our seabags, flight bags, and anything else we were bringing were taken from us to be loaded onto aircraft. We wouldn't see any of it again until we were back in the States. I was back to my one lone pack. I was okay with that. I had lived out of that one pack for weeks at a time. All my material possessions of any worth fit inside it. I still use it. We carried our rifles, as they had to be handed in individually back in the States.

Unlike previous generations of returning veterans, we were not allowed to bring back any war souvenirs. I mean *nothing*. Not even a spent cartridge from a firefight—I was greatly disappointed about that. I thought they would make great presents for my brother's kids. Fortunately, and unbeknownst to me at the time, a single spent cartridge from the repulse of the Taliban on July 2 had somehow wound its way into one of the crevices inside my pack. I hadn't been the one who fired it, but it would do.

We climbed aboard a C-130 and flew from Bastion straight to the Manas Air Base at Kyrgyzstan. I hadn't expected the direct flight out of Afghanistan, since coming into the country we had entered by way of KAF. Kyrgyzstan was as wonderful as Uncle Frank and I had remembered it. It had been the opening days of spring when we last saw that small country, and it was the beginning of fall when we returned. We all piled into the same marvelous big bright yellow canvas tent with its metal skeleton and endless bunk beds with mattresses. Rifles were staged under guard, and we were free of them. Frank and I retraced the pleasant steps we had taken months before and drank gourmet coffee at the same shop. It was grand.

That evening all the Marines were actually allowed into the Air Force Club. We were restricted to two beers each, rigorously enforced by the Air Force, but at least they let us in the door. Marines have a fearsome reputation and are particularly feared when alcohol is involved. But everyone, officer and enlisted, was in great spirits. I tried my everloving best to acquire more than my allotted two beers. I even offered a ridiculous price to buy one of the beers one of the other Marines was allowed, but to my dismay there were no takers. It had been a long seven months. I had forgotten what a beer tasted like.

A third beer really wasn't necessary. I was half pickled on two. I bumped into the Golf Company gunny at the club. I hadn't seen him since Baqua. He had a strange and serious expression on his face. I remembered him as being thoroughly professional, but upbeat. I thought he was mad at me or something, so I asked him about it. He seemed genuinely surprised by my question and he answered, "I'm not mad at *anybody*. Why?" It was the look on his face. I decided he had lost too many fine young Marines. If he wasn't angry—and the man wasn't shy— he would have told me. He was feeling intense at leaving without them.

Our stay at Manas was extremely brief. We'd all have loved to have stayed longer—especially because we were going home instead of into a war zone—but we flew out the next day. A large white commercial jetliner leased from some unheard-of airline whisked us up and away. This time Uncle Frank joined me in first-class seating.

Our next stop was the tiny nation of Azerbaijan. Like Kyrgyzstan, I had never heard of the place before landing in it. I thought that Azerbaijan was a place where bad wizards were sent to keep them away from Harry Potter. Located on the shores of the Caspian Sea, it was one of the Soviet "republics" prior to the dissolution of the Communist empire. This time, however, we never got off the plane. We refueled and took off again. The trip home would not take nearly as long as the trip over.

I slept like a baby in the spacious, leather-upholstered first-class seating. The next thing I knew, we were touching down at Shannon Airport, in Ireland. I hadn't been to Ireland in decades, and I loved the very idea that we were there. I still have family in Ireland—distant cousins—although I would not get to see them on this trip.

Happily, though, the entire plane—except for the rifle guards— debarked. The bad news is that virtually every soul lined up at the airport bar. It took nearly the whole time we were on the ground just to get served once. I think I ordered two pints of Guinness just for myself.

Having studied some Irish Gaelic—known in Ireland as "Irish"—I reveled at the prospect of ordering my drinks in that language. Alas, Ireland is a member of the European Union, and the barmaid had no idea what I was saying. She was from somewhere in Eastern Europe.

After that, I slept pretty much all the way across the Atlantic. We landed after dark, but not after closing time, at an airport in Maine. The Marines were forbidden to drink at that airport by Major Helton. I imagine it was his realization that the drinking age across the United States is twenty-one and most of our contingent was underage.

I pulled my customary Lone Ranger routine and discovered a connection between the airport and a hotel. Since I was wearing "contractor casual" attire, I didn't stand out, as I might otherwise have. I reveled in the company of American civilians at the hotel bar until I grew concerned that I might miss the plane. I got back just in time. I slept again until we touched down in California. It was not quite sunup, local time.

I was feeling jet-lagged as we entered the same terminal we had left seven months earlier. As we stepped off the runway, we were met by an amazing assortment of people, young and old, who greeted each and every Marine as a hero. Some of them were relatives of returning Marines, most were ordinary citizens.

Personally I felt embarrassed by the attention. I felt unworthy. I didn't know what to say when people would reach for my hand and greet me with, "Thank you for your service." I don't know why I felt as I did, but I'm still not comfortable dealing with it.

After a sleepy bus trip back to Marine Corps Base (MCB) Twenty-nine Palms, my thoughts turned to finding a place to stay. I knew I could crash in the barracks with any one of a hundred Marines—a lot had changed since I first arrived at 2/7; these guys were my buddies now. But I was hoping I could get a room at the Holiday Inn. Uncle Frank lived in California and was heading back to his wife. He offered to put me up, but I declined, of course—he was heading back to his wife after a very long absence.

The sky was just beginning to lighten as our seabags were unloaded off trucks. As soon as I got my gear, Frank was going to give me a ride to the Holiday Inn. My car was parked in the driveway of a battalion staff lieutenant who was still deployed.

Suddenly, I saw Boucher! I hadn't seen him since the evening of August 1. He had been wounded the next day and shipped out. Yet here he was, unloading seabags! It was like spotting a long-lost brother. We made arrangements to go out for dinner and drinks—on me—as soon as possible.

Frank and I turned in our rifles. He introduced me to his wife, and they dropped me off at the Holiday Inn as planned. I was optimistically counting on finding an available room. Actually, the place was pretty much full, but upon learning that I had only *just* returned from Afghanistan, the folks there were kind enough to squeeze me in. It dawned on me, as I sat on the edge of the bed, that this was the first time I had been ready to sleep under a *roof* in seven months. It was also the first time I had been *alone* in seven months—not counting my trip up the mountain. I relished the feelings. Then I slept.

Although I was closer to some of those Marines than I was to my own family, I kept to myself a lot in the ensuing days. I cherished "alone" time. I just enjoyed being by myself. I ran the hills and mountains behind the inn, as I had done before shipping out. Only this time, my conscious mind had to override my feelings. Except for a little bit more vegetation than I was used to seeing, the landscape reminded me ominously of the desert of western Afghanistan. I had to consciously tell myself that there were no Taliban in those hills before I could force myself to go there. Gazing out on the sun-scorched brown mountains, I sorely missed my rifle.

Prior to deploying, my eyes searched everywhere for rattlesnakes. I remembered all too vividly the two Marines who had died after being bitten back in 1977. This time I was watching intently for more than just snakes. I couldn't stop myself from peering everywhere, looking for any sign of the enemy as I ran. My awareness had definitely heightened. And emotionally it was very uncomfortable running without my rifle.

For the longest time, back home, I would find I couldn't get comfortable at night unless I was on the couch with my hand on a gun. I didn't really sleep. I just lay there with my eyes closed—listening. Once the sun came up, I would go to bed and sleep soundly. It was a reaction to the 1:00 a.m. attack, I suppose. Sometimes I still awaken in the middle of the night and find myself listening. The gun is no longer necessary, however.

A steak dinner with drinks was high on my list of priorities. I rounded up Jeremy Boucher and Devin Bentz—both Bravo Squad guys—and Dave Demanske, who had been the driver into Baqua. Little Red Allman was sick and couldn't make it. It was agreed that nobody would be driving back to base after drinks, so we all ate a great meal, then crashed at my room at the inn. The next day I took them back.

Soon after, I flew home and kept my Thanksgiving promise to Mom.

At about this time I received an email from a well-meaning person regarding civilian contractors with the military. It was a joke, the gist of which was that contractors are overpaid and can get away with anything. Reading it really pissed me off. I know the sender—a wonderful person and a terrific American—so I never let on as to what my reaction was. But I forwarded it to a couple of personal friends with the following rebuttal:

> I am a US MARINE Contractor. Once a Marine, ALWAYS a Marine is my code. I am a contractor because the dim bulbs inside the beltway believe I'm too old to do what I do for chump change and MRE's and told me I couldn't come back. But I'm not too old to do what I do for big bucks. I look out for ALL my Marines. I get out of the vehicles and check for IED's on foot with my rifle partner.
>
> I check caves half way up a mountain by myself. I man a post like every other Marine when under attack. I jump in the back of a pickup truck to get to where my buddies are being ambushed. I give and take

fire. I cry behind the shithouse when one of my buddies gets killed. I worry when they get wounded.

I don't even know how much money I'm making. I try and get outside the wire as often as I can, eat the same fly covered crappy food as everybody else. Although my contract states I'm entitled to a cost free vacation home, during the deployment, I don't take it because I wouldn't think of leaving my guys.

When I get sick from eating local food and get sent to the rear to get well, I return to my unit as soon as I can. When we get back, I fly cross country for the memorial service. I'm going back on my own dime for the belated Marine Corps Ball. I love every one of those guys like brothers. I would've done it for free because I AM STILL A MARINE.

But if the morons inside the beltway want to pay me big bucks I'm happy to take it. It kept my mother out of a nursing home when she ran out of money. It's still keeping her out of a nursing home. I can't think of a single luxury I've spent the money on for myself. I can't afford a boat. I'm keeping mom out of a nursing home.

I turned 59 in a shithole. The guys gave me a rock for a birthday present. I loved it. I could have stayed in the rear with the gear and made the same money, slept in an air conditioned tent with mattress, ate great chow and had access to internet, a PX and a coffee shop, but I went forward to an under strength platoon because the intel said they were going to be overrun. I'm not entitled to so much as a fire watch ribbon or any VA benefits because I am a "civilian." But that's ok because:

I am a US MARINE Contractor.

Many contractors are just like the below [in the offensive email]. But damn sure not all. I served with two other guys who were just like me.

22

A Terrible Beauty Is Born

After Thanksgiving I returned to Twenty-nine Palms. The remainder of the battalion was back by then, and in early December a memorial service was held for those killed in action (KIA). The sky was gloomy and overcast. A chill wind blew, kicking up dust and hurling it in our faces.

The weather fit my mood. I was told the battalion had taken 20 percent casualties. That's about two hundred Marines. I don't think I had realized the magnitude of 2/7's war until I heard the numbers—and knew that each one had a name.

We had twenty KIAs. That number would have been much higher but for the heroism and dedication of men like Fighting Doc Hancock. Even so, many of the surviving wounded bore horrible scars. Amputated limbs, faces burned beyond recognition—it was a sobering sight. There were any number of badly burned Marines who wore pictures of how they used to look around their necks so their friends would recognize them.

It's an image of war that has to be felt to be understood. "There but for the grace of God go I" flashed through my mind.

Death is not the worst thing that can happen to a man in war.

And a funeral for twenty can be a bit overwhelming in and of itself. So can writing about it.

Immediately prior to the service, a relative of one of the dead Marines—to whom I had written while in Afghanistan—sought me out and shook my hand. He and the rest of the family had really been hurting when their Marine was KIA.

I knew the Marine personally, but I'm not going to name him here. I had written to them and comforted them as best I could at the time. I told them what had happened—how their loved one had died—and how much he was missed by his brother Marines. When the relative said, "Thank you for your service," I looked at my shoes and shuffled the dirt.

After he left I confessed to a lieutenant with whom I had been speaking of my extreme discomfort at hearing those words. He smiled a knowing smile and said, "Well, I just say—'thank you for your support.'"

That's what I still say.

I was beginning to realize how much the experience of war had changed me. Gone was the desire to don a uniform with the proud rank insignia of an officer of Marines. I'm sure I could have worn it—the Silver Star ceremony of predeployment days had established the precedent. The battalion executive officer and sergeant major were the same men. The battalion commander was the same man and surely would have given his permission. And it's not that I had any less reverence for the uniform—I still considered myself to be a Marine, as I always will.

I just didn't want to stand out in any way. I wanted to blend in with the other anonymous "civilians" who were there in abundance.

That day wasn't about me. I was still alive. I wonder now if "survivor's guilt" was at work. Why did I live when these fine young men died? I was fifty-nine. I had lived my life. Why them and not me?

I wore a navy blue suit and stood off to the side of the bleachers by myself, watching as the ceremony unfolded. Watching and trying not to let the tears show, trying to set a good example for my young brothers as the closest friends of the fallen paid their respects to guys who had become closer to them than their own kin.

It was a deeply moving ceremony. Twenty pairs of boots, twenty rifles with fixed bayonets planted upside down into the ground. Twenty helmets placed with the reverence of a crown atop the butt of each rifle. Twenty photographs of the dead. Twenty sets of dog tags hung from each rifle.

And all of the above accomplished with the reverent formality that has long been a hallmark of the United States Marine Corps—by handpicked Marines who had some deep personal attachment to each and every one of the honored dead.

I used to think that humility was a lack of self-esteem or something. It sounds an awful lot like "humiliated," after all. I never really understood what humility—the virtue—was. I began to learn its meaning in Afghanistan.

What I have learned of it came from watching, firsthand, the sacrifices made by eighteen-year-old to early-twentysomething Marines. It was the realization that—like their civilian contemporaries who did not serve—I could not have done what they did at their age.

It was watching them do the impossible—endure the unendurable—routinely, without self-pity or complaint that planted the seeds of understanding.

It was uplifting. It was life-changing. It was humbling.

Humility came like the dawn. Slowly the darkness turned into gray light as the unknown became known. It crested the horizon of consciousness with the realization that at any moment any one of a thousand Marines might have to give up his young, promising life. It shone directly into my eyes like the fierce desert sun the instant that bright orb topped the eastern mountains.

I knew on that bleak December day when I saw the excruciating sense of loss in the eyes of their brave friends that fate had left behind. I knew I had turned a corner. I was not the same man I had been before.

I began to see. This was all another piece in the puzzle of life. As each piece fits into place the picture—the *meaning* of life—begins to be revealed.

The sun of knowledge climbed higher into the morning sky as I realized that countless other—similarly young—Marines had done as much and more house-to-house in Fallujah, in the jungles of Vietnam, in the frozen wastelands of North Korea, in the sulfuric ash of Iwo Jima, or on the killing fields that was France in 1917–18.

Humility—for me—came with the realization that every Marine anywhere, at any time in history, paid with blood for the reputation of the Corps. And I was granted the undeserved honor of calling myself one of them.

Like grace, the honor was unearned. To truly earn it, one had to have made the ultimate sacrifice. I finally realized, in that moment, that I was a Marine by the grace of countless thousands of fine young men who had died on thousands of battlefields.

The title is a gift.

My long journey into the Corps and into war was finally over.

Epilogue

GOLESTAN

Lieutenant Ben Brewster's understrength platoon was replaced by a full company from 3rd Battalion, 8th Marines (that means three rifle platoons each with three rifle squads, and a weapons platoon). For as long as Marines were in that valley, the Taliban stayed away. Then all Marines were pulled out of western Afghanistan and sent south to Helmand Province to reinforce the "surge."

The tiny nation of Georgia garrisoned Golestan. The Taliban returned.

The subgovernor, "Ibrahim Khan," resigned in an attempt to keep his life.

His comrade from the Soviet war "Hajji Mohammed" was shot dead by the Taliban as he walked the streets of Golestan.

The girls' school was forced to close under threat of murder.

An elderly science teacher from the boys' school was murdered, presumably because he taught science.

A young, enterprising subcontractor who arranged with us to hire dirt-poor laborers to work on the new FOB was murdered.

I presume the purge didn't stop there. The "powers that be" lost the counterinsurgency war in the Golestan valley that a young second lieu-tenant had won.

THE MEN

I have remained in touch, even if only slightly, with pretty much every-one I've written about. It's a marvel of the modern age that I'm able to do so. The Internet is a wondrous thing to someone who was born before the Korean War and remembers fuzzy black-and-white TV.

Ordinarily I would have written a nice, informative piece about those mentioned in the book, where they live, what they do for a living, the names of their wives and kids—all the good stuff that brings closure to a book about war and those who fought it. In this day and age, however, I will keep such detailed information to a bare-bones minimum. The wondrousness of the Internet comes with a price tag—it's too easy to find people who may not want to be found.

In the order in which they appear in the story:

Zach Wolfe—went back to his home area, where he met and mar-ried his wife. They have a precocious daughter. They just had their second child, a baby boy. He is named in part for "Whit"—his middle name is Whitacre.

Alex Allman—is an avid mixed martial arts enthusiast. He and his lady recently had their first child. He regularly drops out of sight, only to reemerge when he's ready.

Joe France—left the Marine Corps and became a security contrac-tor in Afghanistan. After a full tour of duty he returned to the States. Currently he is back overseas doing what he does best—working with a gun in his hands.

Mike Michalak—has been a police officer for the past two years. He's married and has one child.

John J. "Jack" McMahon—retired as a lieutenant colonel from the Marine Corps Reserves. He also retired from the state attorney's office in Rhode Island, where he was a prosecutor for twenty-five years. He is currently working as a contractor-prosecutor on Okinawa.

"Colonel Thompson"—when he's not gallivanting around the world, which he is doing at the present moment, he happily resides with his wife in England. They have two grown children.

Major Lee Helton—was tragically killed in a motorcycle accident shortly after the memorial service. He leaves a wife and children.

Colonel Richard D. Hall, USMC—was promoted to full colonel and given command of the 4th Marine Regiment stationed on Okinawa.

"Uncle Frank" Canson—is alive and well, living with his wife and doing security work inside the United States. Frank did two additional tours in Afghanistan as an LEP.

James McKendree—is the owner and operator of an independent business.

Captain Van Osborne—is an active-duty Marine. He was promoted to major and lives with his wife, a Navy officer who recently gave birth to their first child.

Bill Osborne—is still very much involved with the West Side Soldiers' Aid Society, along with his wife, Becky. They live in a wonderful house in a peaceful part of the country, where they enjoy visits from their many friends and family.

Kyle Howell—returned to his home area, where he met and married his wife. They have an infant daughter.

Matt Arguello—resumed civilian life. After a period of time adventuring around South America, Matt returned to the Rocky Mountains of the United States, where he continues the life of a born explorer.

Lieutenant Ben Brewster—was promoted to captain. He redeployed to Afghanistan and came home again. He is currently living with his wife and their four children near his present duty station inside the United States.

Sergeant Lance Holter—remains on active duty. He recently became engaged.

Dave Blizzard—is a firefighter in his hometown.

"Chaps" Russ Hale—continues to serve as a Navy chaplain. He and his wife are enjoying life with their children at an overseas post.

"Doc" Adrian Miclea—left the Navy and works as a doctor inside the United States.

Pat Caffrey—returned to Afghanistan, where he had several encounters with IEDs. Pat was promoted to captain, left the Marine Corps, and works to help veterans who have suffered traumatic brain damage due to IEDs. At the moment Pat is living the life of a modern-day Hemingway in Southeast Asia.

Nick Harris—went back home. He worked for a time at a local gun shop. He is currently attending a specialty school. I expect wedding bells in the not-too-distant future.

Stacey McKinnon—the last time I saw her she was living in Milwaukee and staying active in veterans' affairs.

Cory Becker—returned to his home area, where he married his fiancée. He is a police officer for the U.S. Air Force. He and his wife have three children.

"Doc" Kody Watkins—is an active-duty Navy corpsman. He and his wife have two children. They were just transferred from Italy to the opposite side of the world.

Gunnery Sergeant Manny Mendoza—was promoted to first sergeant prior to retiring. He lives with his wife and children.

Staff Sergeant Justin Wells—stayed in the Marine Corps. He recently returned from another tour of duty in Afghanistan. He and his wife have been married for ten years. They have three children.

Dave Demanske—returned to his home area, where he met and married his wife. They have one child.

Justin Durham—is an active-duty Marine. Shortly after returning from Afghanistan he and his wife married. They have one child.

Brady Christiansen—went back to his home area. When he isn't working, he's at the gym.

Mike Trujillo—recently left the Marine Corps. He is a devoted father to his young son.

Tim Perkins—resumed civilian life, where he enjoys life as only Tim can—which is to say immensely. He's attending college and recently became engaged.

Steve Jorgensen—stayed in the Marine Corps and was promoted to sergeant. He married while still on active duty. Recently he returned to civilian life and to his home area. He and his wife have three children.

Bryan Stuart—left the Marine Corps and returned to his home area, where he is attending school.

"Staff Sergeant Striker"—continues to serve in the Marine Corps. He has deployed several more times to Afghanistan and is currently stationed in the United States with his wife of many years and their children.

Curt Bartz—remained in the Marine Corps. He was recently promoted to staff sergeant. He and his wife have several children.

Steve Paine—went back to his home area and began college. Steve is his usual zany self.

Bobby Harless—left the Marine Corps and married. He and his wife have lived in several parts of the United States.

Cody Peterson—is still in the Marine Corps. He remains with 2nd Battalion, 7th Marines.

Brett Miquelon—relocated after leaving the Marines. He graduated from college and married. He and his wife have one young son. Brett is a police officer.

Dustin Housley—returned home, where he met and married his wife. They just had their first child.

Kyle Slocum—retired from his local police force as a lieutenant. He is the owner-operator of a small business. He lives with his wife and children.

Jonathan Zequeida—made it back in time for the birth of his daughter. He is currently a police officer and a very devoted father.

Jeremy Boucher—returned to his home area, where he regularly participates in "tough mudder" events despite the hole in his leg. He is a police officer.

Bryan Davidson—resumed the life of an avid outdoorsman.

Rory Compton—rejoined the civilian world, where he is an avid physical fitness buff and devoted father.

Justin Gauthier—went back home, where he lives life to the fullest and volunteers at a local fire department.

"Fighting Doc" Jim Hancock—remained a Navy doctor. He was promoted to captain shortly after Afghanistan. He lives with his wife and their children.

The West Side Soldiers' Aid Society, Milwaukee, Wisconsin—and particularly Bill and Becky Osborne, Patrick and Patricia Lynch, Terry and Tom Arliskas, and Laura Rinaldi, are still active in Civil War living history events—and helping veterans at the Milwaukee Veterans Administration Medical Center.

Bill "Doc Z" Zorrer left the Navy and returned to his home area, where his friends know him as a passionate sports enthusiast.

Terry "Cookie" Huggins—left the Marine Corps and returned to his home area. He is enjoying life.

Scott Brown—spent several more years in Afghanistan. He was seriously wounded when an IED took out the vehicle in which he was a passenger. He has made a full recovery and lives with his wife on their ranch in the western part of the United States.

Michael J. Foley—left the Navy and resumed civilian life. His father owns a local tavern, and Michael J. helps him run it.

"Grandpa" Joe Billington—left the Marine Corps and went back home. He met and married his wife and is now a proud papa.

Daniel Flynn Hickey—was awarded the Silver Star for gallantry at Marine Corps Base Twenty-nine Palms approximately two years after returning home. It's the nation's third-highest award for bravery. He is currently married with a couple of kids. They live peacefully on a farm.

Dennis Francis—is still an overseas security contractor. He is in fine health, great spirits, and fighting the good fight even though he is older than dirt. He couldn't tell me where he is currently located or he'd have had to kill me.

Greg Lunsford—left the Marine Corps. He is married and has a child.

Jamie Nielsen—left the Marine Corps and resumed the life of a civilian. He is attending college.

Devin Bentz—left the Marine Corps and returned to his home area. He's learning how to be a helicopter pilot.

My mom—lived to the ripe old age of eighty-eight. She got to see her old son come home from Afghanistan. I kept my promise and took her to visit her younger son and grandchildren for Thanksgiving and Christmas. After 2008 she was too frail to travel. She then lived happily in a lovely home in Florida for the remainder of her days. She died peacefully shortly after Thanksgiving 2012.

Each year as the anniversary of the death of cherished comrades rolls around, the Internet is full of photos and sentiments from Marine buddies. They may be gone, but they will never be forgotten.

Sadly, we keep losing 2/7 Marines to suicide. It's been seven years since the war. Our home front dead now outnumber our KIAs.

Those magnificent youngsters who made up 2nd Battalion, 7th Marines in 2008 are in their middle twenties or early thirties now. Whether they remain on active duty or not, they still regard themselves as Marines.

Afterword

What you have just read is not a history. A good history is checked and cross-checked for accuracy as to dates, times, and places. This account is subject to the limitations of my perception and memory. However, it is true and accurate to the best of my knowledge and belief.

A lot happened in the more than eleven months I was privileged to be with 2nd Battalion, 7th Marines in both the United States and Afghanistan. I made friends with a lot of Marines, shared their hardships, and bore witness to their stoic fidelity to duty as they performed deeds both great and small. It's not all in this book. Their names are not all here. The story has to flow. It was necessary to leave out a great deal. My apologies to one and all—you are all great Marines, worthy inheritors of a proud legacy. Take comfort in the knowledge that when I wrote about the battalion—or any part of the battalion—I was writing about you. Especially Bravo Squad, 1st Platoon, Golf Company—when I wrote of Bravo Squad I wrote about you, whether or not your name appears in print.

Some individuals were described only by nicknames. This is because either there is lingering concern for their safety—or that of their families—during this ongoing global war on terror (GWOT) or because I have lost touch with them and couldn't get permission to use their names. I declined to name anyone who hadn't personally given me the okay.

With one exception: in the book I took to task a certain key individual. The reader will understand the reasons for this by now. I declined to use his name so as not to cause him or his family embarrassment. My opinions as to his actions and omissions are my own and just that— opinions. Others may have perceived him in a different light.

I owe a debt to many people that I can never repay. I am particularly grateful to Bill Osborne and the members of the West Side Soldiers' Aid Society of Milwaukee, Wisconsin, for reasons outlined in this book. Amy LaViolette, who although not mentioned in this story sent aid packages and emails of encouragement to me and many others overseas. Lieutenant Colonel John J. "Jack" McMahon, USMCR (Ret.), who kept me going when I hit a writer's "wall"—and first edited the book.

I am especially grateful to Colonel Richard D. Hall, USMC, who believed in me enough to let me find my own place in the battalion's area of operations (AO). He could have kept me on a short leash; he didn't.

To all Marines: past and present, particularly our honored dead— *semper fidelis.*

Appendix

[*I don't recall when Lieutenant Brewster was promoted to first lieutenant; obviously it was prior to the date of this statement.]

The writer, an honorably discharged Captain of Marines, was attached to 1st Platoon, Golf Company, 2nd Battalion, 7th Marines at Forward Operating Base (FOB) Golestan from 17 June 2008 to 9 September 2008, and from 1 October 2008 to 10 October, 2008. Lieutenant Benjamin Brewster commanded. The Platoon was minus one rifle squad, reinforced by one 81mm mortar squad. Only one 60mm mortar tube was available. No reinforcements were available within less than six to eight hours by vehicle. During most of this period, helicopters were available for medevacs only. The approximate time for air on station was over 45 minutes.

1st Platoon occupied the strongest position then available, an Afghan-built mud-walled compound with only two mud buildings and a concrete shower building within. The walls did not completely enclose the FOB. Approximately sixty meters to the west of the platoon, a concrete clinic surrounded by a two-foot-thick stone wall provided a potential enemy force with a covered and concealed means to approach, a covered assembly area, and excellent firing positions.

Adjacent to the platoon, to the south, a concrete boys' school hindered observation and obscures a draw which began at a dirt road in a natural defilade position. It runs west to a dry river bed. To the southeast, a hill elevated approximately 800 to 1000 meters above the platoon, contains mud wall ruins which afford an enemy an excellent covered observation or indirect fire position. The ruins are reinforced with large rock walls constructed during the Russian invasion. Some positions are impervious to indirect fire other than a direct hit.

To the immediate east, a road, frequented by local pedestrian and vehicular traffic, ran parallel to the platoon. To the northwest, a wooded area obscured any movement from the north down a dry riverbed. Adjacent to the wooded area, a ridgeline provided excellent enemy firing positions for direct and indirect weapons.

The terrain in the Platoon's area of operations (AO) consists of open desert, rugged mountains and numerous dry river washes. Contained within the AO are many villages inhabited by local nationals from several different tribes, various sub-tribes and numerous clans. The District Center is comprised of four distinct villages from two tribes. Three villages are Sunni Muslim and one is Shia.

Intelligence reports commencing prior to the writer's arrival and continuing until approximately mid-August, indicated the enemy planned an attack on the platoon with a force of between one hundred and one hundred fifty combatants.

Lieutenant Brewster organized firing positions, bunker strongpoints, and pre-planned fires. The Lieutenant ordered the reinforcement of all external walls with layers of sandbags and utilized razor wire to the fullest extent possible. Claymore mines were placed inside the razor wire. The Lieutenant ordered a bunker constructed on the roof of the school. Due to the extreme distances between the platoon and the company and battalion headquarters, Lieutenant Brewster was often unable to obtain the guidance from higher which would normally have been available to an officer of his rank. Lieutenant Brewster epitomized the Marine tradition of "adapt, improvise and overcome." The Lieutenant strengthened the platoon's position to the maximum degree achievable.

Enemy forces attacked the platoon, commencing at 0100 2 July 2008, with indirect fire, rocket propelled grenades, machine guns and small arms fire. A rocket propelled grenade passed through the combat operations center wall early in the attack narrowly missing the Lieutenant. Another Rocket Propelled Grenade passed through the walls near the combat operations center. It splintered upon impact and a piece of shrapnel struck the Platoon Sergeant's Kevlar helmet. The Platoon Sergeant was knocked senseless at a critical point in the engagement. Undaunted, Lieutenant Brewster remained calm and in control of the entire platoon.

Other Rocket Propelled Grenades struck the walls of the FOB knocking another Marine unconscious. A fragment of a Rocket Propelled Grenade passed directly through the 81mm mortar position. It destroyed a metal chair and embedded the leg of the chair in the opposite FOB wall. Incoming machine gun tracer rounds and bits of shrapnel filled the air, tearing holes in tents, a flag and camouflage netting. Through it all, the Lieutenant remained calm, cool, collected and in command. Lieutenant Brewster's demeanor inspired confidence in his Marines.

As the attack continued, Lieutenant Brewster ordered mortar fire on enemy positions. When muzzle flashes indicated the enemy had moved into the northwest tree line, Lieutenant Brewster shifted Marine forces to that portion of the FOB where suppression fire could most effectively be brought to bear.

In response to reports of enemy forces moving southward toward the concealed draw south of the FOB, Lieutenant Brewster ordered Marines in vehicles to a position where they could effectively block an enemy attack from that direction. When additional reports of enemy movement to the south came in, Lieutenant Brewster ordered mortar fire on that location. Although air did arrive on station, it could not be utilized due to the relative position of the enemy to friendly forces, and difficulty the pilots had in making positive identification of the FOB.

The stone-wall-enclosed concrete clinic to the west of the FOB remained a position of critical vulnerability. During a temporary cessation of enemy fire, Lieutenant Brewster ordered a rifle squad to clear the clinic grounds. The Lieutenant ordered other Marines to repair damage done to the FOB's defenses. Before the enemy could renew the attack, Lieutenant Brewster ordered the Marines back inside the FOB.

As enemy fire appeared to dwindle, the Lieutenant sent a mounted squad out to assess and, if possible, to flank and attack the enemy. As enemy forces broke contact, Lieutenant Brewster ordered the mounted patrol to attempt to pursue. The attack lasted for approximately three hours and ended just prior to dawn. Lieutenant Brewster ordered mounted and dismounted patrols sent out.

On another occasion, Lieutenant Brewster's vehicle struck an improvised explosive device (IED). The vehicle was destroyed and the Lieutenant and several other Marines were injured. Despite a large, noticeable bruise on his leg, and obvious pain, the Lieutenant remained with the platoon and continued to command. His uncomplaining dedication to duty served as an inspiration to all the Marines of the platoon.

On or about 29 July 2008, enemy forces cruelly tortured and murdered three Afghan National Policemen (ANP). The three were at their homes in a village several kilometers north of the FOB. On 29 July 2008, Lieutenant Brewster personally led a squad of Marines with twenty-two ANP to recover the bodies.

As darkness fell, the Lieutenant and the squad were caught in a complex ambush. Enemy forces positioned approximately 300 meters to the north and west of the bodies fired Rocket Propelled Grenades and machine guns. The

Marines and ANP were, due to the necessity of recovering the bodies, caught in the open. The ill-trained ANP were panic stricken and of little use. The presence of frightened ANP added an element of confusion and disorganization to the fire fight. Lieutenant Brewster, with little regard for his own safety, positioned himself, under fire, wherever he could best command and control both the Marines and the ANP.

Lieutenant Brewster ordered the bodies to be recovered before breaking contact. He directed counter fire which suppressed the western ambush position. Effective enemy machine gun fire raked the area around the ANP bodies as Marines attempted to gain fire superiority in the darkness. As the patrol moved out to return to the FOB, it was again ambushed from a draw by Rocket Propelled Grenade and machine gun fire. One ANP truck was struck by a Rocket Propelled Grenade and sustained four urgent casualties. Lieutenant Brewster ordered the truck to be recovered and the casualties collected before continuing back to the FOB.

The patrol was again ambushed. The attackers fired automatic weapons from rooftops of houses inside the District Center. Since positive identification of the enemy could not be made, Lieutenant Brewster ordered his Marines to fire over the heads of the enemy thus ensuring there were no civilian casualties.

On 2 August 2008, a squad-sized mounted patrol was ambushed near Feydz Abad. As the patrol moved up a wash it was attacked by a platoon sized enemy force from the hills to the east and south. Enemy machine gun positions engaged the Marines from both directions at ranges of 200 to 500 meters. A Rocket Propelled Grenade team fired at the Marine vehicles from a distance of 50 meters, narrowly missing the vehicles. Two Marines were wounded by enemy fire. The Squad's vehicles sustained four flat tires between three trucks.

Lieutenant Brewster immediately assembled every available Marine and Afghan National Policeman and went to the squad's aid. Quickly evaluating the tactical situation, the Lieutenant ordered Marines with ANP to clear an *enemy held ridgeline. Other Marines and ANP were ordered into an advantageous position in a parallel wash. Enemy forces could be seen on the ridgeline moving tactically back toward the village. Enemy forces could be seen moving in draws and from a compound 1,000 meters to the south across a river wash. The enemy fought stubbornly and gave ground only when forced to do so.*

Conservative estimates place the number of enemy forces at 50 to 65, divided into 4 to 6 squad sized elements. The enemy held the high ground overlooking the village. Lieutenant Brewster maneuvered Marines on foot, Marines in vehicles and the ANP. He controlled mortar fire and utilized air assets. Lieutenant Brewster commanded a complex combined arms attack which drove the enemy from the ground of the enemy's choosing. The enemy retreated into the village.

Lieutenant Brewster led his dismounted Marines and ANP into the village itself. Compound by compound Marines and ANP made certain no enemy forces were near their position. Lieutenant Brewster, pistol in hand, personally cleared several compounds. Under the Lieutenant's personal direction, Marines and ANP continued to penetrate the enemy held town until the coming of darkness shifted the Lieutenant's concern to the safety of the FOB.

Marines and ANP were withdrawn in an orderly fashion. The Lieutenant ordered strict accountability for all personnel, personally supervising while his orders were carried out. An estimated 20 enemy personnel were killed; the body of one Pakistani was recovered. A machine gun, Rocket Propelled Grenade launcher and 10 Rocket Propelled Grenades were recovered.

Lieutenant Brewster had a decisive impact on the platoon AO. The Lieutenant had to utilize an understrength platoon to fullest advantage, strengthen a seriously vulnerable FOB, control the District Center, and patrol many miles of open and rugged mountainous terrain. His intelligent, audacious leadership inspired his Marines and daunted the enemy. After Feydz Abad, the enemy withdrew far up the river valley, out of reach of the Marines. In so doing, the enemy abandoned a training camp in one village, a headquarters in another village, and a third village which had been strengthened by trenches and other defenses.

Lieutenant Brewster met often with the sub-governor of the district, the district prosecutor, and the Commander of the Afghan National Police (ANP) and encouraged them to become more involved in district affairs. As a result of his efforts, the District Prosecutor conducted a judicial proceeding, the first held in the district in years. The ANP, under the guidance of the District Prosecutor, arrested four individuals and charged them with assault and battery. The individuals were tried without interference from Marines and were convicted and punished in accordance with Afghan civil law.

Lieutenant Brewster tirelessly met with village elders from the District Center and other villages scattered throughout the AO. He demonstrated a degree of statesmanship rarely found in an Officer of his rank. He actively engaged the local nationals in conversation on every possible occasion. Lieutenant Brewster's actions produced a noticeable change for the better toward Marine presence in the AO and resulted in a highly comprehensive tribal mapping of the entire Golestan Valley.

Lieutenant Brewster espoused the cause of education of both boys and girls, giving encouragement to principals and teachers, providing security for the schools in the face of Taliban threats, and distributing what school supplies could be acquired. As a consequence, teachers and students have come to regard Marines as friends.

Lieutenant Brewster utilized civilian subject matter experts to their fullest potential. His demeanor toward the civilians was always that of an Officer and a gentleman. As a result, they seamlessly integrated with the platoon and enhanced the platoon's mission. One effect of this integration was the providing of the ANP with the highest quality training which might reasonably be expected at this point in the ANP's development.

It is this writer's belief that Lieutenant Brewster's impact on the AO is such that the local nationals want the Marines to stay, hope the Marines will defeat the enemy, and are confident that the Marines have come as protectors and not as conquerors. It is this writer's belief, as a former Marine Officer, that Lieutenant Brewster's exemplary leadership, personal courage under fire, skillful handling of troops in combat, and statesmanship in dealing with local nationals should not go unrecognized.

The writer respectfully requests that every consideration be given to awarding Lieutenant Benjamin Brewster the Bronze Star with combat device.

Very respectfully submitted,
Terrance P. McGowan
Law Enforcement Adviser
14 October 2008